# FLOWERS FROM HELL

## Jim Harper

Noir Publishing
10 Spinney Grove
Hereford
HR1 1AY
email:noirpub@dsl.pipex.com
www.noirpublishing.co.uk

# Flowers
# From
# Hell

Flowers From Hell
By Jim Harper
ISBN 9780953656479
© Jim Harper 2008, all rights reserved
First published 2008 by:
Noir Publishing
Copyright © Noir Publishing 2008

Photographs taken from the Noir Publishing Collection & reproduced in the
spirit of publicity - any omissions to be corrected in future editions.
Cover Photo:
Ichi the Killer
Back Photo:
Ichi the Killer

Editor's Acknowledgements:
Sterling work from many an individual has aided the
production of this volume but special mention to
Jim Harper, Metro Tartan Video, The Associates,
Eureka Video, Unearthed Films, Universe,
Constantin Films & NTV.

British Library Cataloguing in Publication Data:
A catalogue record for this book is available
from the British Library

Noir Publishing titles should be available from all good bookstores;please ask your retailer to order from:
UK & EUROPE:
Turnaround Publisher Services, Unit 3, Olympia Trading Estate,
Coburg Road, Wood Green, London. N22 6TZ
Tel: 0208 829 3000  Fax: 0208 8815088   www.turnaround-psl.com
Additional Specialist Distribution for The Last Snake Man:-
USA: Maryland Reptile Farm, 150 Bentz Mill Road, Wellsville, PA 17365  www.mdreptilefarm.com
SOUTH AFRICA
Stephan Phillips (Pty) Ltd, Unit 3, Old Brewery, 6 Beach Road,
Woodstock, 7925, Cape Town   www.stephanphillips.com
Other titles available from Noir Publishing:-
Necronomicon Book Three - Edited by Andy Black   Necronomicon Book Four - Edited by Andy Black
The Dead Walk - By Andy Black   Once Upon A Fiend - By Ratfink & Pete McKenna
Shocking Cinema of the 70's - Edited by Xavier Mendik   The Last Snake Man - By Austin J Stevens

# Flowers From Hell: The Modern Japanese Horror Film

# INTRODUCTION

Although few people would have realised it at the time, 1998 would be a very significant year for Japanese horror. Events were set in motion that saw Japanese horror cinema develop from a modest domestic concern into an influential and lucrative international industry. Before 1998, few modern Japanese horror films received any kind of exposure outside the Far East, but in the years that followed, a great number of such movies were released around the globe, both to cinemas and the home video market; in the UK alone, nearly a million Japanese horror DVDs have been sold in the past seven years. Several have been reworked for foreign audiences, spawning their own franchises, while the leading lights of Japanese horror and cult cinema- including Hideo Nakata, Takashi Shimizu, Norio Tsuruta, Takashi Miike, Ryûhei Kitamura and Masayuki Ochiai-have been hired by American studios to helm their own English-language movies or TV projects. In short, Japanese horror has become a significant player in the global market.

Much of this is due to one film, Hideo Nakata's *Ring* (1998). *Ring* provided modern Japanese horror with its first major commercial breakthrough, a feat that did not go unnoticed by studio executives across the world. However, the precise nature of *Ring*'s achievements has not been always been completely understood. It's still possible to find western critics and commentators recycling the idea that Nakata's film single-handedly revived the domestic horror market, awakening it from the thirty years of slumber that followed the passing of the 'golden age' of Japanese horror, the era that saw the creation of such internationally-renowned masterpieces such as Kenji Mizoguchi's *Ugetsu Monogatori* (1953), Masaki Kobayashi's *Kwaidan* and Kaneto Shindô's *Onibaba* (both 1964). Needless to say, such statements oversimplify the issue greatly. While it is certainly true that Japanese horror in the '70s, '80s and early '90s did not receive the kind of international exposure it had done in the decades before that, it's inaccurate and somewhat pretentious to suggest that it did not exist simply because western critics were unaware of it. British horror did not disappear when the glory days of Hammer, Amicus et al came to an end; likewise, the Japanese horror film has enjoyed varying degrees of popularity over the years, but it still remains too popular to fade away entirely. *Ring* did not spring forth fully-formed from the groundswell of Japanese cinema; it has antecedents stretching back decades, and draws upon genre traditions from many different cultures. Like many other landmark horror films- John Carpenter's *Halloween* (1978), for example-*Ring* did not so much invent new concepts as arrange existing ones in a commercially and artistically successful pattern. This is not to downplay Nakata's achievements- *Ring* is without doubt an exceptional film- but to ignore its origins is akin to preparing a study of *Halloween* that makes no mention of *Psycho* (1960), *Black Christmas* (1974) or any of the other films that preceded and influenced Carpenter's work.

The immediate origins of *Ring*, and the genesis of the modern Japanese horror film as a whole, can be found in the crisis that gripped the Japanese film industry after the collapse of the studio system in the '70s. By the end of the decade the industry's popularity, both domestically and internationally, was at its lowest point since the war.

# Flowers From Hell

Those studios that did manage to keep their heads above water did so by producing films with solid commercial potential, either because of genre- Nikkatsu's soft-core pinku eiga, for example- or because of the presence of reliable box office favourites like Kinji Fukasaku. In such a climate, comparatively marginal genres like horror were pushed aside in favour of more dependable ventures like the jidai-geki or historical drama, the perennial mainstay of Japanese mainstream cinema. It did not disappear completely, but many of the films produced during the period fit into the categories named above. A typical example is Nobuo Nakagawa's *Kaidan: Ikitewiru Koheiji*, released in 1982. One of the more successful horror movies of the time, *Kaidan: Ikitewiru Koheiji* was also Nakagawa's return to filmmaking after a fifteen-year break. In the '50s and '60s he had been Japan's foremost director of horror films, producing a number of movies since hailed as classics, including *Tokaido Yotsuya Kaidan*, his 1959 retelling of the popular Japanese legend. The story has been adapted for the screen many times over the past eighty years- most recently by Kinji Fukasaku, who combined it with another of Japan's most enduring legends, the tale of the loyal 47 ronin, in 1994's *Chûshingura Gaiden: Yotsuya Kaidan*- but Nakagawa's version is widely recognised as the best. The director's return to the big screen after such a lengthy hiatus was an event of some significance, and *Kaidan: Ikitewiru Koheiji* went on to perform well at the box office and win a number of awards. However, despite the quality of the work, it was little different to the films Nakagawa and his contemporaries had been making twenty years before- a period piece, drawn from a traditional Japanese story, and driven by betrayal and vengeance from beyond the grave. In short, Japanese horror was stuck in a creative rut.

At the same time that the Japanese film industry seemed to be on the brink of collapse, the signs of its eventual salvation were beginning to manifest themselves, albeit on a very small scale. A new generation of filmmakers was appearing; unlike their predecessors, these filmmakers had grown up without the protection- and without the limitations- of an established studio system. Many of them cut their teeth on the video market, a medium that allowed a greater degree of experimentalism than the studio-dominated theatre chains. While the studios struggled to make a profit from bloated, creatively redundant blockbusters, away from the spotlight talented but as yet unknown directors like Sôgo Ishii, Kiyoshi Kurosawa and Shinya Tsukamoto were exploring their own artistic visions, whether it was through self-financed 8mm films, pinku eiga, television or experimental street theatre. While some found success relatively quickly, for others the journey towards recognition would be a long and painstaking one, lasting well into the 90s. Even so, their struggles laid the foundations for the creatively and commercially successful film industry that Japan now possesses, paving the way for internationally acclaimed directors like Takashi Miike and Hideo Nakata.

Naturally, some of these new talents inclined towards the horror genre; those that did took their inspiration from both western and Japanese genre traditions, as well as from non-horror sources such as the pinku eiga or the kaiju eiga ('monster movies'). The majority of the new horror films discarded the period trappings and theatrical influences of the classic kaidan ('ghost story') in favour of contemporary settings and stories drawn from manga, anime and popular western movies. Contemporary settings were not unknown

# Introduction

in post-war domestic horror, but for the first time they became the dominant form. It is this 'new wave' of modern Japanese horror, beginning in the mid-1980s and continuing to the present day, that forms the subject of *Flowers From Hell*. There might seem to be little common ground between a film such as Toshiharu Ikeda's *Evil Dead Trap* (1987) and Hideo Nakata's *Ring*, but they are both products of a new breed of domestic horror that blends both the old and the new, the Japanese and the western, into an entirely modern incarnation that continues to thrive more than two decades after it first appeared.

Of course, this does not mean that contemporary Japanese horror is 'American-style' or 'Americanized'; the spaghetti westerns of the '60s and '70s are no less Italian because they show an American influence, for example. Neither is my intention to downplay the role of Japanese tradition. There are still films that draw almost entirely on domestic traditions- such as *Sakuya: The Slayer of Demons* (2000)- and as well as others in which the Hollywood influence dominates, like Kiyoshi Kurosawa's *Sweet Home* (1989). Both western and Japanese influences- and many other factors besides- are equally important to the evolution and development of Japanese horror, and the many different results of this blend of ingredients can only be described as uniquely Japanese.

*Flowers From Hell* is not an encyclopaedia or a movie guide, and I have not attempted to cover in detail every *Ring*-inspired 'vengeful spirit' movie or direct-to-video horror anthology that appeared in the late '90s. The purpose of this work is to track the major themes, films and creative talents that have appeared over the past twenty to twenty-five years, so I have concentrated on films that either typify a certain trend or are in some way significant because of content, cast and crew or general quality. Because it is also important to examine these films in the appropriate context, I have organized the book into chapters based around particular sub-genres or- in the case of Hideo Nakata, Takashi Shimizu and Junji Itô- specific personalities. I have not presented a detailed overview of the development of Japanese horror until the mid-'80s- that is a subject that requires several books of its own- although I have included brief histories where necessary to illuminate the current situation. Doubtless many readers will already be wondering why Nakata and Shimizu are the only two directors to warrant their own chapters- why not Takashi Miike? Why not Kiyoshi Kurosawa? Some directors have been denied their own chapters for reasons of quantity. Miike has only produced a handful of true horror films, and a chapter that attempted to focus on only the horror films- probably less than 5% of the man's output- would be thin indeed. Kurosawa on the other hand has certainly produced enough horror films to warrant his own chapter. However, Kurosawa's auteurist approach makes it difficult to create a credible overview of his work without covering his many non-horror efforts; he simply cannot be assessed effectively from a purely horror perspective. In light of this, I feel it is more appropriate to approach his horror films through the various sub-genres they belong to. As a final note, small sections of *Flowers From Hell* have previously appeared at the *Flipside Movie Emporium*, the *Midnight Eye* website and in *Deranged* magazine, while an extract of chapter 5 was printed in *Necronomicon 5* (Noir Publishing). In all cases these have been amended, revised and rewritten for publication as part of this book.

A word on the conventions used in this book. Films under discussion are referred to by their English title, with the original Japanese title included on the first occasion.

Since this is a British publication, where possible I have used the UK release title. If no official UK title exists, I have used the US one; if no US one exists, I have used the original Japanese title. If a film is only given a Japanese title, it is either because the film is known in English-language territories by its Japanese title (e.g. *Uzumaki* or *Tetsuo*), or because no official English title has been devised (e.g. *Ijintachi Tono Natsu*). If only an English title is used, it is because the film's original title is an English loan-word (e.g. *Battle Royale*). In such cases I have used the English spelling instead of the Japanese one: *Ring* instead of *Ringu*. An index of Japanese and alternate English titles is given at the back of the book, which will tell you what title is used in the main index as well as provide details of other alternate titles. Where possible I have also included well-known bootleg titles, although these are not used in the main text. I have also included English titles that have been used in non-English language territories (e.g. *Red Candy*, the Singapore title of *One Missed Call 2*), and these too are not used in the main text.

**Acknowledgements:**
My eternal gratitude goes to Mike Scrutchin at the *Flipside Movie Emporium* (and all the regulars), Jasper Sharp and Tom Mes at *Midnight Eye*, Alex and Mandi at *Snowblood Apple*, Stephen Biro at *Unearthed Films*, *Ringworld*, Harvey Fenton, Scott Foutz, Alexi Glass, Jason Liu, Tim Seeley and Cassie Hack, Rob Bewick and *Deranged*, Mike at *UpcomingHorrorMovies.com*, Doris Harper, *The Tribe*, *Kerrang!* magazine, *Total Film*, as well as a thank you to the multitude of other people who have helped me to acquire films, amass information and process it all during the creation of this book. As always, my mother, father, brother and sister have provided unfailing support and assistance whenever it was required. Last but not least, thanks to Andy Black and Noir Publishing for believing in the potential of this work.

For me, *Flowers From Hell* has been both enlightening and entertaining. I hope it is for you too.

## GLOSSARY OF TERMS

*Anime:* Usually characterised as Japanese cartoon, anime covers much more ground that its western equivalent, from children's programmes like Pokemon to pornographic material.

*AV* ('adult video'): Video pornography that includes hardcore pornography, as opposed to the pinku eiga, which are classifiable as softcore pornography, usually released theatrically.

*Gaijin*: A Japanese word for foreigners.

*Kaidan* ('ghost story'): A term originally used to describe the traditional Japanese ghost stories drawn from popular legends and kabuki plays, it is now also used to describe modern updates like Ring.

*Kaiju eiga* ('monster movie'): The name given to monster movies like Godzilla and Gamera.

*Manga*: Japanese comic books. Unlike western comics, manga is read by people of all ages and covers an even wider range of subjects than anime, including sports, romance, horror, erotica and melodrama.

*Otaku*: The term used to describe socially inept individuals with an obsessive interest in minority-appeal subjects. Although roughly equivalent to the English word 'nerd', otaku also carries pejorative implications.

*OVA* ('original video animation'): Direct-to-video anime.

*Pinku eiga* ('pink films'): Loosely described as theatrically released softcore pornography, but unlike similar material in the west, pink films can also include graphic violence, political commentary or full developed plots and characters.

*V-cinema*: Direct-to-video releases. Originally used by Toei to describe their direct-to-video output, the term later came to be used for all such releases.

# CHAPTER ONE
## Vengeful Spirits, Part One

Ever since the birth of Japanese cinema in the early 20<sup>th</sup> century the dominant strain of domestic horror film has been the kaidan, or ghost story. The wealth of traditional folk tales- many of them already adapted into kabuki plays- provided a near-limitless supply of material for filmmakers to exploit. Since the 1980s manga, novels and urban legends have replaced folklore and classical literature as the chief source of inspiration, but the 'vengeful spirit' story remains the most popular and numerous incarnation of Japanese horror to this day. Like the Hammer films, the majority of traditional ghost stories were period dramas set in occasionally indistinct historical eras. Typically the Vengeful Spirit is a woman who has suffered abuse at the hands of men, either being murdered, forced to commit suicide, or simply abandoned and left to die. Tied to the place of their demise, the ghost remains on the earthly plane until her desire for vengeance is satisfied. Eventually the villain of the piece receives his supernatural comeuppance and the injured party is finally able to rest. When not 'disguised' as a living person, the Vengeful Spirit is usually clad in white, with long black hair that often obscures part or all of her face. The first segment of *Kwaidan* (1964), for example, is simply called 'long black hair'. Despite the many changes the kaidan has undergone over the years, the physical appearance of the Vengeful Spirit has remained largely the same.

Although the main theme- post-mortem revenge- was a consistent feature of Japanese ghost stories, the details could be surprisingly varied. It was not unusual to find male ghosts in the traditional kaidan (curiously, the post-*Ring* wave of horror films has largely ignored the concept). While women were more likely to be murdered by their husbands and lovers, the typical male victim is a lower-class individual tormented by unscrupulous samurai. One of the more complex renditions of the formula is Enchô San'yûtei's *Shinkei Kasane-ga-fuchi*, originally written in the 1860s. Set over two generations, the story begins when a samurai murders a blind masseur (blind children were often trained as masseurs, the most famous example being Zatoichi, the blind swordsman). The masseur's ghost returns to haunt his killer, eventually causing him to kill his own wife. The samurai then commits suicide, drowning himself in the Kasane swamp. Years later, the samurai's son spurns the affections of a teacher in order to take up with one of her students, unaware that the teacher is the daughter of the masseur that his father murdered. Rejected, the teacher commits suicide, and like her father she returns to the land of the living to torment the man she blames for her death. Unable to escape, the lovers throw themselves into the Kasane swamp. San'yûtei's tale has been filmed a number of times, and by some of Japan's most well-known directors, including Kenji Mizoguchi (1926's *Kyôren no Onna Shishô*), Nobuo Nakagawa (*Kaidan Kasane-ga-fuchi*, 1957) and most recently by Ring director Hideo Nakata as *Kaidan* (2007).

The 'golden age' of the Japanese ghost story had come to an end by the mid-1960s, but the films themselves- often spiced up with added sex and violence- continued to attract audiences throughout the remainder of the decade and well into the '70s.

By the early 1980s the conventions of the kaidan had become stale and over-familiar, and the latest rendition of an already well-known tale held little attraction for viewers when placed alongside the pyrotechnic horrors of Tobe Hooper's *Poltergeist* (1982). Just as western audiences eventually abandoned the period gothic of the Hammer films and Roger Corman's Edgar Allan Poe adaptations in favour of the modern day terrors of *Rosemary's Baby* (1968) and *Night of the Living Dead* (1968), Japanese moviegoers were drifting away from Meiji-era ghost stories and looking to *Friday the 13th* (1980) and *A Nightmare on Elm Street* (1984) for their scares.

One of the first Japanese filmmakers to recognize and exploit the potential of modern western-style horror was Nobuhiko Obayashi, director of *House* (*Ie*, 1977) and *Ijintachi Tono Natsu* (a.k.a. *The Discarnates*, 1988). *House* is a dazzling ghost train ride, filled with pop-culture references and a wealth of camera tricks and special effects. The story itself is heavily reminiscent of a fairy tale, with teenager Oshare (Kimiko Igekami, later in Kazuhiko Hasegawa's *The Man Who Stole the Sun*) wandering off to get away from her new stepmother and ending up at the rickety mansion owned by her equally rickety aunt. Unfortunately the house is also alive, and before long it's attempting to consume Oshare and her friends. Despite persistent accusations that Obayashi's film is all style and no substance, beneath the glossy eye-catching visual sheen lies a complex allegory about an adolescent's fear of growing up and the dangers inherent in failing to do so. More subversive is the film's undercurrent of sexuality; obsessed with her dead mother, Oshare is reluctant to progress towards sexual maturity, as represented by her attractive stepmother. Instead she is drawn closer to the withered asexuality of her aunt, wheelchair-bound and confined within her empty house. The house itself is full of clocks- a reminder perhaps of Oshare's own 'biological clock'- and strange toys that symbolize her attachment to her own childhood and her dead mother. One of the most bizarre haunted house movies ever made, House is unfortunately almost entirely unknown outside Japan, with exposure limited to the occasional appearance in film festival retrospectives.

Based on the award-winning novel by Taichi Yamada[1], *Ijintachi Tono Natsu* finds Obayashi dropping the visual trickery in favour of subtler ways to concentrate on plot and character. The fairy tale elements have not been entirely lost, however, revealing themselves partly through a contemporary update of Alice in Wonderland. Obayashi's Alice is middle-aged scriptwriter Harada (Morio Kazama), who becomes lost in Tokyo's sprawling underground railway system while scouting locations for a television movie. When he does finally find his way above ground, he's in Asakusa, the gaudy former 'entertainment capital' of Tokyo, and also his birthplace. Realising he hasn't been there in years, Harada decides to re-acquaint himself with the area he grew up in, but he finds more than just old memories. At an old vaudeville-style theatre, he catches sight of a man in the audience who looks- and sounds- incredibly familiar; just like Harada's long-dead father, in fact. Not as he would be now, but as he was when he died twenty-eight years ago. When the man invites him back to his house for a beer, Harada is too bemused to resist, but when he discovers that the man's wife (Kumiko Akiyoshi from *Love Ghost*) looks exactly like his mother- who also died in the same accident that killed her husband- he

**Kwaidan** - *a seminal Japanese ghost film*

begins to panic. Despite the logical realisation that these people simply cannot be his parents- as they claim to be- Harada's childhood grief at the loss of his mother and father comes flooding back, and he cannot bring himself to leave. Although he does eventually do so, he returns a few days later, and soon becomes a regular visitor at the couple's house.

At the same time Harada forms a relationship with Kei (Yukô Natori from *The Sleeping Bride*), an attractive young woman who is the only other permanent resident of the office block that he lives in. Although she knows nothing of his visits to see his dead parents, Kei has noticed that over the last few weeks Harada's physical condition has declined considerably: his skin is pale and taut, his eyes are sunken and black-ringed and his teeth are beginning to fall out. Harada himself has seen nothing of this- when he looks in the mirror he sees the same face he saw before. As Kei grows more and more distressed, he does eventually tell her what has been happening, but draws no connection between the two occurrences. She does however, claiming that his dead parents are responsible for his condition; it might be unintentional, but they are draining his lifeforce, bringing him closer and closer to the world of the dead. When he next looks in the mirror he finally sees what she does, and recoils in horror.

It is here, with the sight of Harada's increasingly ghastly visage, that *Ijintachi Tono Natsu* begins to turn from a supernaturally-themed sentimental drama into a horror film, a transformation that is only completed in the final fifteen minutes. Thanks to Obayashi's deft misdirection, only the sharpest viewer- or those well schooled in Japanese folklore- will have noticed that there are in fact two ghost stories here. The second is typically Japanese: Kei has been dead since the second time Harada met her, having committed suicide after he rebuffed her initial attempt at friendship. Obayashi does leave a few breadcrumbs for the smartest to follow, however: Kei only ever appears at night; she wore black when she was alive and only wears white afterwards; the oft-repeated song from Puccini's Madame Butterfly that hints at the tragedy lying beneath the surface. Kei covers up the wounds left by her bloody suicide with a story about a childhood accident that has left her horribly scarred, meaning that they can only make love in the dark and Harada must never ask to see her chest. In Yamada's novel Kei is a Vengeful Spirit, draining Harada's vitality in revenge for his rejection, but in *Ijintachi Tono Natsu* she is perhaps closer to the yuki onna ('snow woman') of *Kwaidan*, a supernatural being in love with a human, whose relationship is over if he ever finds out her secret.

When it arrives, the climax is as extravagant as the rest of the film is restrained. In conversation with the building manager Harada's friend Mamiya finds out about the girl who committed suicide months before. Realising that the new girlfriend is not what she seems, he rushes up to the apartment to find her cradling the withered corpse-like Harada in her arms. Her secret exposed, Kei becomes enraged, and the room fills with dry ice while thunder and lightning clash outside, all set to the sound of Puccini. Kei pulls apart her nightgown to reveal the wounds from her suicide, spraying the room- and Harada- with geysers of blood. Harada begs her to take him with her, but Mamiya holds him back, and Kei eventually fades away entirely, revealing her empty apartment. Her hold over him broken, Harada returns to normal, only slightly the worse for wear from his weeks spent with the dead.

A number of aspects of Obayashi's film- specifically the dead lover and the hero's physical deterioration- appear to be drawn from Kaidan Botandôrô ('ghost story of the peony lanterns'), a tale recorded by Enchô San'yûtei in the Meiji era and based upon a Chinese legend. Like many Japanese ghost stories, it has been filmed a number of times over the years and remains a staple of V-cinema and made-for-TV horror. In recent years it has been presented as a dubious television sequel to *Kwaidan* (1964) directed by Chisui Takigawa (later the director of *Ringu: Kanzenban*) and included in one of the many V-cinema horror anthologies hosted by Junji Inagawa. While most retain the period setting, there have been several other attempts at staging the material in a contemporary setting- most notably 1990: *Botandôrô*, which turns the samurai of the original into a rock star and swaps magical symbols for Tarot cards- although none have been as creatively successful as *The Discarnates*.

Rather than updating traditional Japanese folklore for modern audiences, Kiyoshi Kurosawa's *Sweet Home* (1989) takes its inspiration almost entirely from western sources. The first horror movie from a director who would later be recognized as one of Japan's most original talents, *Sweet Home*'s mixture of big-budget special effects, fast-paced thrills and comedy might seem at odds with Kurosawa's later reputation for creating subtle and introspective horror films, but it fits in well with his early attempts at crafting genre works, such as the slasher movie *The Guard from the Underground* (*Jigoku no Keibiin*, 1992) and *Door III* (1996), a revisionist vampire tale. It also boasts some of the best special effects ever seen in a Japanese film at that point, courtesy of American effects maestro Dick Smith, who had previously worked on *The Exorcist* (1973) and would provide effects for the lacklustre *Poltergeist III* (1989) shortly afterwards.

A television crew- the producer, Kazuo (Ichirô Furotachi), his teenage daughter Emi (Nokko), his assistant Akiko (Nobuko Miyamoto), a cameraman and their snobbish restorer/presenter- enter the sprawling Mamiya mansion to film the restoration of a little-seen fresco painted by the artist who lived there decades before. They discover not one but several frescoes, including one that seems to depict the death of a young child in some kind of furnace. That night, the temperamental presenter, apparently in a trance, wanders out into the grounds of the house and digs up a coffin containing the charred remains of an infant. It soon becomes apparent that the child's mother, although dead herself, has not left the house, and is still angered by her loss. When Emi is swallowed up by the house, Kazuo and Akiko are left to battle the twisted, angry spirit. The climax is driven by the contrast between the ever-grieving, maternal Vengeful Spirit and Akiko, a woman who- despite her obvious affection for Kazuo- has effectively sacrificed her mother's role for the sake of her career, and thus cannot know the grief of a mother who has lost her child. By putting on a dress that belonged to the girl's daughter, Akiko acknowledges that she has become a surrogate mother to Emi, and is able to face the creature on equal terms.

A keen Tobe Hooper fan, Kurosawa's crumbling mansion is haunted by the ghosts of *Poltergeist*: his phantoms are Spielberg's shambling grotesques rather than the resentful shades of Japanese legend, and the climax is driven by the need to retrieve a child from the monster's grasp. Like *Poltergeist*, *Sweet Home* is dominated by the sensibilities of its high-profile writer-producer, Jûzô Itami. Throughout much of the '80s and '90s, Itami was one of Japan's most popular directors, responsible for a string of domestic hits including *The Funeral* (*Osôshiki*, 1984) and the internationally acclaimed *Tampopo* (1985), all of which starred his wife Nobuko Miyamoto. Just as *Poltergeist* was saddled with Steven Spielberg's diluted family-friendly horrors, *Sweet Home* is unable to escape from Itami's preference for comedy. This is usually manifested through the bumbling Kazuo or a baseball-loving old man- played by Itami himself- who fills the main cast in on the house's history, before the plot temporarily grinds to a halt while he sings a nostalgic song. Unsurprisingly the comic touches seem somewhat incongruous next to the harrowing tragedy that lies at the heart of the story. The film eventually became the subject of a legal dispute between Kurosawa and Itami, who re-edited the work and re-shot certain scenes for the television and home video release without the director's knowledge. Since then *Sweet Home* has not received an official release outside of Japan, despite Kurosawa's current status and the deliberately western feel of the film.

Equally uncomfortable with its blend of horror and humour is *World Apartment Horror* (1991), the first live-action film from Katsuhiro Ôtomo, director of the landmark anime favourite *Akira* (1989). Sweet Home's sprawling country mansion has been a staple of cinematic hauntings for decades, but *World Apartment Horror* is probably the first ghost story to be set in a ramshackle two-storey wreck inhabited by squatters. When his bosses decide they need the land for a more lucrative building contract, yakuza foot-soldier Itta (Hiroyuki Tanaka, a.k.a Sabu, director of *Dangan Runner*) is sent in to make sure that the current tenants- all of them immigrants, from several different Asian countries- depart within a week, making way for the demolition crews. The task proves to be less straightforward than it might seem- few of the tenants speak any Japanese and most of them just nod politely and ignore him, an attitude that irritates the young gangster. Frustrated, Itta tries a variety of tricks to drive them out, including threats of violence, drunken revelry, loud rock music and even louder sex. More disturbing is the revelation that the last yakuza assigned to this task went mad, and the suggestion made by some of the tenants that Itta should leave before the same thing happens to him. It might have something to do with the building's ground floor- the tenants all live on the upper floor and will not for any reason venture into the rooms below. While dealing with the lunk-headed gangster and his futile attempts to evict the building's tenants, *World Apartment Horror* is on reasonably safe ground. In the final third Ôtomo attempts to shift the balance towards socially conscious horror, and the cracks begin to show. Part of this is due to problems with the material- the stated explanation for the haunting is clichéd and rather pathetic. Equally damaging are Ôtomo's cast: with the exception of Weng Huarong, all of the immigrants are played by amateur actors. This doesn't represent much of a problem when they're scurrying from room to room or smiling politely at the irate Itta, but in the more serious scenes their lack of experience becomes readily apparent.

One of the most important developments of the 1990s was the rise of horror films intended for younger audiences. Teen horror was not an entirely new concept; manga artists like Kazuo Umezu and later Hideshi Hino had been creating works aimed

**Kwaidan**

squarely at adolescents- primarily shôjo manga or girls' comics- since the early '70s, while Daiei had found some success in the late '60s with a run of family-oriented films like *The Great Monster War* (*Yôkai Daisenso*, 1968), featuring a slew of Japan's favourite folkloric monsters, including the water-demon Kappa and the one-eyed umbrella monster. However, by the 1990s the majority of horror films were intended for mature audiences, featuring adult characters and addressing adult concerns. One of the main franchises aimed at younger viewers was the *Haunted School* (*Gakkô no Kaidan*) series. Initially a series of made-for-TV features produced by Kansai TV, the *Haunted School* series took its inspiration not from Japanese traditions or recent western movies, but from popular urban legends. The source was a series of books by Tôru Tsunemitsu, the first published in 1990, intended to cash in on the then-current media fascination with contemporary folklore. The books provide accounts of the many different urban legends and spooky tales propagated by Japanese schoolchildren, gathered through interviews with children across the country. The series, which eventually ran to eleven volumes, proved to be exceptionally popular, prompting Kansai to prepare a television adaptation in 1994.

The first six-part series was handled by four different directors, including two who were destined for greater things: Kiyoshi Kurosawa, already known to genre fans through *Sweet Home* and *The Guard from the Underground*, and Kazuya Konaka. Although largely unknown outside of his homeland, Konaka has been a consistent feature of the Japanese horror and sci-fi scene since the late '80s. He is also the brother of prolific screenwriter Chiaki J Konaka, who wrote his *Haunted School* episode. Konaka's best works are 1994's sleazy psycho thriller *Lady Poison* and the underrated time-travel fantasy *The Dimension Travelers* (*Nazo no Tenkosei*, 1999). Each episode was based around a different urban legend: Kurosawa's episode deals with the legend of Hanako-san, the ghost of a girl who is believed to have committed suicide at school and now haunts the place where she died, the end cubicle in the girls' toilets. Perhaps Japan's most popular contemporary ghost, Hanako-san has since become the star of several separate movies and an anime series.

After the initial mini-series, the formula was expanded into feature-length anthologies, with segments varying in length from three minutes up to thirty. These made-for-TV features quickly became a showcase for up-and-coming directors, and most of Japan's horror specialists have worked on at least one *Haunted School* feature. Kiyoshi Kurosawa has been a consistent presence throughout the series, working alongside future luminaries such as Hideo Nakata, Takashi Shimizu, Norio Tsuruta and scriptwriter Hiroshi Takahashi. A number of these short segments later achieved an historical significance: for example, Nakata's 'Rei Bideo' ('spirit video'), included in *Haunted School F* (*Gakkô no Kaidan F*, 1997), makes an interesting precursor to *Ring*, while Takashi Shimizu's two segments of *Haunted School G* (*Gakkô no Kaidan G*, 1998) introduce the characters of Kayako and Toshio, the Vengeful Spirits from the later *Juon* films. As the series progressed directors were given a greater degree of creative freedom, although urban legends remained a key source of inspiration. In 2000 an anime series was broadcast, featuring a group of regular characters but largely adhering to the same pattern as the live-action TV productions.

# Vengeful Spirits, Part One

The various incarnations of *Haunted School* were successful enough to spawn a number of rip-offs using the same anthology format and school setting, including *A Frightful School Horror* (*Kyôfu Gakuen*, 2001) and the lengthy *Gakkô no Yûrei* ('school ghosts') series. Official follow-ups also arrived, in the shape of four theatrical features, the first released in 1995. All of them were directed by Hideyuki Hirayama, with the exception of *Haunted School 3* (*Gakkô no Kaidan*, 1997), in which the reins were passed to Shûsuke Kaneko, director of the '90s *Gamera* trilogy and the live-action *Death Note* films. Like the made-for-TV specials, the *Haunted School* movies are based around popular urban legends and intended for younger audiences. All of them follow the same pattern: a group of children break into an abandoned school building, the site of countless playground rumours. Once they are inside, the children find they cannot leave; worse still, they are not the only occupants, for many of the old classrooms are haunted by creatures from popular legends. The first film features some of the most famous, including the terrifying kuchisake onna- the 'split mouth woman' who appears to be a nurse, but removes her facemask to reveal a hideous elongated gash where her mouth should be. Other manifestations are less grotesque, such as the spectral Beethoven conducting his ghostly chamber orchestra, or the pink *Ghostbusters*-inspired phantom, and there's even a friendly young girl named Hanako who (of course) turns out to be a ghost. However, since these films are intended for children, few of these creatures are actually scary, and Hirayama keeps the shocks to a minimum. The resulting harmless rollercoaster ride is perfect for younger audiences, but there's little to interest anyone above the age of twelve.

Hanako-san made her own movie debut in Jôji Matsuoka's *Toire no Hanako-san* (1995), released under the unfortunate English title of *Phantom of the Toilet*. Although aiming at the same audience as the *Haunted School* series, Matsuoka- best known as the director of intelligent 'couple' movies like *Twinkle* (*Kira Kira Hikaru*, 1992)- tackles themes that in the west would be considered grossly inappropriate for a children's film. Yuka Kôno stars as Mizuno, a young girl facing her first day at a new school. Initially things seem to be going well, and everyone is eager to make friends with the smart and pretty tenkosei ('transfer student'). Mizuno's problems start when she is seen leaving the last cubicle in the girls' toilets- the cubicle where Hanako-san is believed to have killed herself. Since none of them would dare use that particular cubicle, her classmates soon spread the rumour that Mizuno is actually Hanako-san herself. The area has been recently plagued by a series of child murders, and since many of the kids already believe that Hanako-san is the one responsible, they assume that Mizuno has come to their school to find new victims. When the real killer turns up and decapitates the school goat, Mizuno again comes under fire since she was the one appointed to feed the animal that day. Their suspicions apparently confirmed, her classmates decide to take matters into their own hands: Mizuno will be locked in 'her' cubicle over night, and if she is still there in the morning, they will know she is not Hanako-san. Unfortunately the killer is also prowling around the school, and the children have unwittingly presented him with an easy victim. The surprising climax sees Mizuno and her only friend facing the killer alone, with the adults nowhere to be found. In a scene that seems inspired by the first *Haunted School* movie, the actually benevolent Hanako-san summons all the children to the school to

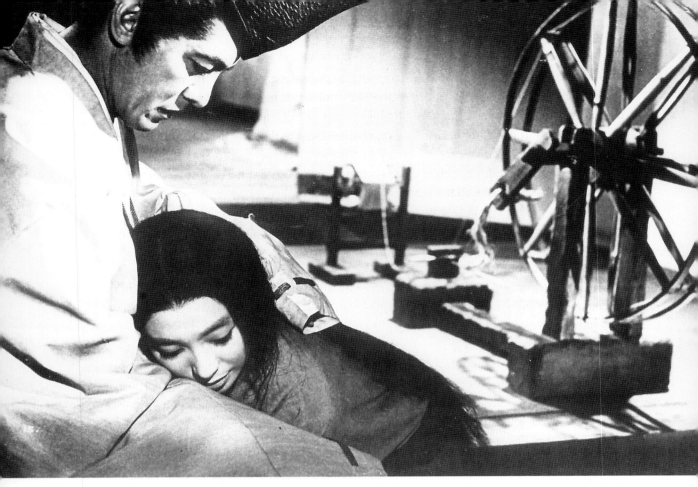

**Kwaidan**

protect their classmates. The children arrive in their hundreds, surrounding the confused killer and imprisoning him until the adults turn up with the police.

The portrayal of children and school life in *Toire no Hanako-san* is refreshingly free of the patronising attitudes and nostalgic sentimentality that so often afflict films aimed at younger audiences. Unlike the *Haunted School* films Matsuoka approaches his subject seriously, and his scares are genuine. Although the supernatural is essential to the story, for the most part he is dealing with realistic events and themes- from bullying and peer pressure to murder- and keeps the fantastic elements off-screen until the final quarter. Hanako-san herself appears only briefly, and aside from a handful of parents and teachers, the film focuses almost entirely on the children; the adults play little or no part in the resolution of the story. Although it's difficult to imagine American or European parents allowing their offspring to watch a film in which young children are terrorized by a serial killer, *Toire no Hanako-san* is easily the best of the Japanese horror movies aimed at pre-teen audiences.

After appearing in a couple of V-cinema films directed by Masato Sasaki, Hanako-san returned to the big screen with 1998's *Shinsei Toire no Hanako-san*, directed by Yukihiko Tsutsumi (*2LDK; Forbidden Siren*) and written by *Ring* scriptwriter Hiroshi Takahashi. This time Hanako-san is a bitter, angry ghost haunting the middle school she attended before

# Vengeful Spirits, Part One

her death. When schoolgirls Ai Maeda (*Gamera 3: Revenge of Iris*) and Maya Hamaoka (*Crossfire*) accidentally summon her, the toilet becomes a gateway to the next world, allowing her to manifest physically. As the Vengeful Spirit begins to take her rage out on students and teachers alike, the girls join forces with Hanako-san's old homeroom teacher to try and push her back to the other side. Despite the typically Japanese story, *Hanako-san*'s manifestations are informed by western ghost stories- all slamming doors and rushing winds- and the special effects-laden climax owes a great deal to *Poltergeist*. Although Tsutsumi checks all the Japanese teen drama staples- including love rivalry, the young and handsome male teacher, as well as ouija boards (known in Japan as kokkuri-san) and urban legends- he also avoids the childishness that often characterises teen-oriented films and manages to coax convincing performances from his young leads, both of whom also appeared in Matsuoka's version of the story. Like *2LDK* and *Forbidden Siren*, *Shinsei Toire no Hanako-san* is a lean, well-paced film, occasionally marred by the director's preference for flashy but meaningless camera tricks, but on the whole a superior example of the form.

With its cast of teenagers and middle school setting, Tsutsumi's film is intended for audiences older than those who enjoyed the *Haunted School* series and Jôji Matsuoka's *Toire no Hanako-san*. Japanese teen horror had begun to develop in the early '90s, initially as V-cinema products before progressing on to theatrical releases. The mainstay of the emerging teen horror industry was Norio Tsuruta, later the director of *Ring 0: Birthday* (2000), *Kakashi* (2001) and *Premonition* (2004). In the early years of the decade Tsuruta directed a string of V-cinema anthologies, including the long-running *Hontô ni Atta Kawai Hanashi* ('true fear stories') franchise, which eventually spawned its own TV series and included among its alumni Hideo Nakata and Hiroshi Takahashi. Most often set in a deserted school building, these films typically consisted of three or four short segments, as well as a wrap-around story that usually centred on a group of schoolgirls trying to frighten each other with spooky tales. As well as his three features, Tsuruta has contributed to almost every major TV and video horror franchise, including the *Haunted School* series and *Tales of Terror from Tokyo* (*Kaidan Shinmimibukuro*). Although these early works are largely typical of Japanese V-cinema/made-for-TV horror- mainly dull with occasional flashes of style and originality- Tsuruta was among the first to understand the potential of teen-oriented horror, and his stories prefigure the success of the *Ring* and *Juon* films. Also thanks in part to Norio Tsuruta, the anthology has become a staple of the Japanese horror, from Makoto Wada's *Kowagaru Hitobito* (1994), starring Hiroyuki Sanada and Hitomi Kuroki, to *Tales of the Unusual* (*Yo Nimo Kimyôna Monogatari: Eiga no Tokubetsuhen*, 2000), the theatrical spin-off of a heavily *Twilight Zone*-inspired TV series, featuring Mami Nakamura (*Tomie*), Megumi Okina (*Juon: The Grudge*) and Shinji Takeda (*Pulse*).

While the bulk of mid-'90s teen horror films were content to recycle the same clichés and conventions over and over again, occasionally a work of genuine originality appeared. The best of these pre-*Ring* efforts is Takahisa Zeze's *Kokkuri* (1997), a sober and thoughtful film built around a group of teenage friends struggling to find direction in their lives. Mio (Ayumi Yamatsu), Hiroko (Hiroko Shimada) and Masami (Moe Ishikawa) are

# Flowers From Hell

three Tokyo schoolgirls with typical teenage interests: boys, friendship, hanging around shopping malls. One of their favourite activities is listening to 'Michiru', a radio presenter who appears to be roughly the same age as the girls themselves. She's a confident, streetwise type, sexually experienced and open about her life. Unsurprisingly she's idolized by some of her more impressionable listeners. Unknown to her friends, 'Michiru' is none other than Mio, and her radio persona is almost entirely a sham. Hiroko has her own secret too: she's in love with Masami's boyfriend Akira, and Masami is beginning to suspect that her friend cannot be trusted. Following a suggestion from 'Michiru', the girls create a ouija board and prepare to ask the spirit to reveal some details about the

*Sleeve art for* **Haunted School**

22

# Vengeful Spirits, Part One

mysterious radio presenter (these are then supposed to be sent to the station, to see who comes up with the most accurate answers). However, with tensions between Hiroko and Masami nearing breaking point, few of the questions deal with 'Michiru'. Each of the girls receives a momentous revelation that night: 'Michiru' will be dead before her 18th birthday, less than a month away; Masami's relationship with Akira will not last much longer; and Hiroko will meet the love of her life soon. While Mio keeps quiet and shrugs off the portent of doom, Masami runs off in tears. The only one pleased with the result is Hiroko, who assumes that the person in question is Akira.

Naturally all three prophecies come true in the end and, this being a horror movie, not in the way the girls first think. Thankfully we are spared any *Wishmaster*-style twists-in-the-tail. Instead the emphasis is on the emotional responses of the girls, mainly Hiroko and Mio. These two share a deeper connection based upon separate past experiences. As a child, Mio saw her mother drown after saving her from a strong sea current, while Hiroko's friend Midoru accidentally drowned in her bathtub after the pair had been playing with a ouija board. Like many survivors, Mio feels that she was supposed to drown with her mother, and believes that Midoru had to die as well to take her place. As well as visions of her mother's death, Mio has also seen a small figure in a red rain slicker following her. Is it Midoru, returned to take revenge?

Although *Kokkuri* was commissioned by Nikkatsu to capitalize on the growing interest in teen-oriented horror, acclaimed pinku eiga veteran Takahisa Zeze has created a surprisingly mature and intelligent film. It has much in common with the excellent South Korean ghost story *Memento Mori* (1999), since both films use the trappings of the genre to explore the mental and emotional turmoil of their protagonists, rather than the supernatural events resulting from this psychological chaos. As well as the typical Japanese horror conventions, *Kokkuri* takes a certain amount of inspiration from Nicholas Roeg's *Don't Look Now* (1973), another unorthodox, heavily symbolic horror film about a drowning child. Zeze's Vengeful Spirit (for example) has the typical black hair and long white robe, but she's also wearing a red raincoat. In *Kokkuri* red is almost always associated with feelings of guilt and regret, underscoring the film's main themes. Red is the colour of Mio's guilt: the colour of her mother's lipstick on the day she drowned, and the colour of the raincoat worn by the phantom visitor. In a possible nod to Peter Medak's *The Changeling* (1980), a red bouncing ball makes an appearance too. Given that the majority of the film is shot either in partial darkness or in drab, brown surroundings- like a number of Kiyoshi Kurosawa films, *Kokkuri* seems to have been shot in many disused buildings- the flashes of bright red leap off the screen. The other prominent symbol is of course water, occurring in almost every scene, from the sea itself to fish tanks and leaking pipes. Although water plays a pivotal role in the psychological collapse of the protagonists, by the end Zeze returns to the more neutral concept of water as the ultimate physical and spiritual cleanser, embodying both destruction and subsequent rebirth.

*(Footnotes)*

1 *Finally published in English in 2003 under the curious title of Strangers.*

# CHAPTER TWO
# The 1980's: Splatter and Beyond

The history of the Japanese splatter movie is just as colourful and perhaps a little longer than its western counterpart. While H.G. Lewis' *Blood Feast* (1963) is generally acknowledged to be the first splatter movie, there's a case for suggesting that the genre's Japanese origins date back to Nobuo Nakagawa's acclaimed *Hell* (*Jigoku*), released by Shintoho three years earlier, in 1960. *Hell* certainly provides the necessary graphic dismemberments and decapitations to qualify, but after its initial- and unsuccessful theatrical run the film was caught up in Shintoho's subsequent collapse and remained unavailable for several years. Since the '70s *Hell* has been widely recognised as a landmark of Japanese horror cinema and a genuine cult classic. It's also been remade twice, once in 1979 by Tatsumi Kumashiro, and again twenty years later by veteran director Teruo Ishii, as *A Japanese Hell* (*Jigoku*, 1999). In Nakagawa's film a guilt-ridden young man finds himself condemned to Hell after he accidentally runs over a drunk one night. Half of the film is taken up with the events that lead him to the realm of the damned, setting the stage for Nakagawa's psychotropic tour of the inferno, complete with every kind of physical torture imaginable.

Nakagawa was best known for directing ghost stories in the traditional Japanese mould, and *Hell* was effectively a one-off production that would not be considered influential until years later. The roots of Japanese splatter are not to be found in the horror genre, but in the uniquely Japanese pinku eiga or 'pink films', soft-core sex movies that formed a substantial part of the domestic cinema scene in the '60s and '70s. Naturally, there are artistic precedents stretching back much further- in the same way that the Grand Guignol theatre of the late 19th century prefigured the appearance of cinematic splatter in the west, explicit brutality and violence were a common subject of Japanese ukiyo-e (woodblock prints) and paintings. The works of ukiyo-e master Yoshitoshi in the late Edo (1603-1868) and early Meiji (1868-1912) periods were dominated by scenes of mutilation, dismemberment, suicide and murder, often associated with the civil war gripping Japan at the time. It is not difficult to see the connection between Yoshitoshi's stylised depictions of samurai torturing ornately bound women and the faux-snuff *Flower of Flesh and Blood* (*Guinea Pig 2: Chiniku no Hana*, 1985), in which similar activities are portrayed.

Nudity and open sexuality began to appear in Japanese films in the mid-1950s. In some cases these elements were added to spice up existing genres, such as hardboiled detective thrillers or yakuza movies, but in others they were the entire focus of the film. New genres sprang up to accommodate them, including the popular 'pearl diver' movies, in which shapely and under-dressed girls spent much time frolicking in the water. Most of these trends were short-lived, and the films circulated at the lower end of the market, without the backing the major studios gave to more respectable fare. With the emergence of the pinku eiga in the mid-'60s, the situation changed; by the end of the decade pink films accounted for almost half of the films produced in Japan. Although frequently described as Japanese soft-core pornography, the comparison is not entirely accurate. In pink cinema the only taboo was the depiction of genitalia and the pubic region, and a variety of methods- from optical 'fogging' to the judicious placement of flowerpots, furniture and other objects- were used to conceal the offending areas. Unlike the earlier nudie films, the pinku eiga were often produced or distributed by major studios, most notably Nikkatsu, whose output would eventually be dominated by the form. Theatrically released and produced on an enormous scale, pink cinema was given a level of exposure rarely afforded to pornography in any other nation. The arrival of video pornography- referred to as AV or 'adult video'- in the 1980s dealt a serious blow to the pink industry, with audiences able to obtain hardcore material and watch it in the privacy of their own home. In the '90s the industry hit an all-time low, with many established production houses like Nikkatsu forced to shut down. In recent years the historical value of this uniquely Japanese genre has been re-assessed, leading to film festival retrospectives of important directors and a fair amount of critical study.

As well explicit sexuality (for the time, at least), pink cinema also promoted graphic violence. Efforts like Teruo Ishii's period-set anthology film *Joys of Torture* (*Tokugawa Onna Keibatsushi*, 1968) devoted equal attention to physical torture and sex, usually perpetrated on attractive young women. Kôji Wakamatsu's *Violated Angels* (*Okasareta Hakui*, 1967) took the true story of Richard Speck- who raped and murdered twelve nurses in 1968- as its inspiration, and the resulting film is predictably brutal. The combination of sexual and horrific imagery was frequently described as ero-gro ('erotic-grotesque'). Although the term was initially pejorative- it's shortened from 'erotic-grotesque nonsense'- it later came to represent a particular sub-genre that encompassed everything from the repellent *Guts of a Virgin* (*Shojo no Harawata*, 1986) to the multiple adaptations of the works of Edogawa Rampo, one of Japan's leading literary figures of the 20<sup>th</sup> century. At the same time splatter was becoming an increasingly popular aspect of the chanbara and jidai-geki (samurai films and period dramas respectively), such as the acclaimed *Lone Wolf and Cub* (*Kozure Ôkami*) series, edited and released in the west as the one-time 'video nasty' *Shogun Assassin*. However, while graphic violence made regular appearances in other films, it was taken to its furthest extent in pink cinema, where audiences were willing to accept anything as long as it had the requisite amount of sex and violence. For much of its history, the splatter movie has been largely indivisible from the pink film, and no examination of Japanese splatter is possible without an acknowledgement of its connection to the pinku eiga.

Many of the most important splatter movies of the 1980s were directed by pinku veterans, including Toshiharu Ikeda's excellent *Evil Dead Trap* (*Shiryô no Wana*, 1988). If Hideo Nakata's *Ring* (1998) is the archetypal Japanese horror film of the late 1990s, then *Evil Dead Trap* is its equivalent for the previous decade. Although dissimilar in content and execution, both films explore different ways of blending Japanese and western influences. Like Kazuo Komizu (a.k.a. Gaira), Kiyoshi Kurosawa and Shûsuke Kaneko, both Ikeda and Nakata started their careers working on pink films for Nikkatsu, and both were associates of Masaru Konuma, one of the studio's most important directors. While *Evil Dead Trap* cannot claim to be as popular or as influential as *Ring*, it is still an important landmark in the history of modern Japanese horror.

In loose terms, *Evil Dead Trap*'s plot seems to prefigure *Ring*. When Nami (Miyuki Ono, from Takashi Ishii's *Black Angel*)- presenter of 'Late Late Night', a trashy mondo-style clip show- receives a video that seems to show a woman being murdered she decides to investigate in the hope of finding a serious story and breaking out of her career rut. The tape also provides directions to an abandoned military base, so Nami gathers her production crew and heads off. From there the film's slasher movie roots become apparent, as the group splits up to search the derelict buildings. Predictably, one couple find somewhere to get intimate; needless to say, the woman (pink and AV star Hitomi Kobayashi) soon becomes the film's first victim. As she wanders off alone, she is impaled on wooden spikes that shoot from the walls and floor. The rest of the group are killed off one by one, eventually leaving Nami alone to face her antagonist, a smoothly dressed psychopath called Muraki.

It is the elaborate and brutal death scenes- including one that involves a crossbow, several tripwires and a huge swinging blade- that have made *Evil Dead Trap* a firm favourite with splatter fans across the world. However, despite the graphic and plentiful gore, the film is not simply a clumsy excuse for cheap-and-nasty exploitation, like Komizu's ero-gro efforts from the same period. For one thing, *Evil Dead Trap* is exceptionally well made, combining long, fluid tracking shots with careful editing to create a tangible atmosphere of tension and suspense. Much of the credit must go to cinematographer Norimichi Kasamatsu, whose excellent lighting and atmospheric camerawork help to make it one of the best-looking Japanese horror films of the decade. Aside from Miyuko Ono and her opponent Yûji Honma, the majority of the cast are drawn from the pinku/AV arena. Even so, Ikeda manages to coax credible performances from them, thanks in part to a well-written script from manga artist Takashi Ishii. Before they collaborated on *Evil Dead Trap* Ikeda had already directed several adaptations of Ishii's work, including the brutal revenge drama *Mermaid Legend* (*Ningyô Densetsu*, 1984) and *Angel Guts: Red Porno* (*Tenshi no Harawata: Akai Inga*, 1981), the fourth film in Nikkatsu's popular series. A keen fan of western horror, Ishii's script contains a number of references to genre classics, including several nods to Dario Argento- the maggots-on-the-ceiling scene is a direct lift from *Suspiria* (1977)- and some rapid 'knee-level' tracking shots reminiscent of Sam Raimi's *Evil Dead* (1983). Curiously, those same tracking shots, filmed in black & white across industrial wasteland, are also remarkably similar to Shinya Tsukamoto's *Tetsuo: The Iron Man* (1989). The western influences are even more apparent in Tomohiko Kira's excellent synth-based score, which recalls Claudio Simonetti's work with Goblin, as well as John Harrison's *Day of the Dead* (1984) score.

In the final act, *Evil Dead Trap* takes a sharp left turn into 'body horror' territory that owes a great deal to the films of David Cronenberg. In a scene that is highly reminiscent of Cronenberg's 1979 film T*he Brood* and Ridley Scott's *Alien* (1979), the killer's alternate personality bursts forth from Nami's chest, making her the surrogate mother Muraki was looking for all along. While Ikeda and Ishii cannot be accused of simply recycling the usual sub-*Halloween* clichés, it's hardly surprising that this abrupt change has provoked a mixture of confusion and irritation from fans and critics alike. Such themes- physical

*Sleeve artwork for* **Evil Dead Trap**

mutation and transformation- are fairly common in modern Japanese horror cinema (a similar scene occurs in Fujirô Mitsuishi's *Tomie: Replay*, 2000), but they do not sit comfortably alongside the rest of the film. Nonetheless, *Evil Dead Trap* is still superior to most of the similar movies coming out of the western world in the late '80s and deserves its status as a cult classic.

After a three-year gap, *Evil Dead Trap 2: Hideki* (*Shiryô no Wana 2: Hideki*) was released in 1991. Possibly because of his less-than-pleasant experiences with the first film (the director was hospitalized with nervous exhaustion after a gruelling shoot) Toshiharu

Ikeda was not involved this time, and neither was Takashi Ishii. Ikeda's place was taken by Izô Hashimoto, director of *Bloody Fragments on White Walls* (*Shiroi Kabe no Kekkon*, 1989), a nearly plotless but occasionally interesting splatter flick that has sometimes been mistakenly labelled as part of the *Guinea Pig* series. Aside from directing a handful of horror movies, Hashimoto has also provided scripts for a number of high-profile projects, including Katsuhiro Ôtomo's seminal anime hit *Akira* (1988). *Evil Dead Trap 2* was co-written by Chiaka Konaka, one of the most prolific genre scriptwriters in Japan. As well as a large number of anime screenplays (*Hellsing and Serial Experiments: Lain* among them), his works include Kiyoshi Kurosawa's *Door III* (1996), Takashi Shimizu's

**Evil Dead Trap 2** *sleeve artwork from Unearthed Films*

# The 1980's: Splatter and Beyond

*Marebito* (2005) and several instalments of the sprawling *Gakkô no Kaidan* (*Haunted School*) franchise.

Despite the reference in the title- Hideki was the name of Muraki's alternate personality- *Evil Dead Trap 2* is entirely unrelated to the first film. This time the focus is on Aki, a lonely and overweight film projectionist who enjoys reading picture books of corpses and mutilations. Her only friend is Emi, a glamorous and oversexed television reporter who delights in flaunting her boyfriends (including prolific cult favourite Shirô Sano) in front of Aki and making thinly veiled references to her non-existent sex life. What she doesn't know is that Aki has taken to slaughtering prostitutes, usually after clumsy and unsuccessful attempts to initiate sexual activity. The mutilated bodies are found on construction sites, with Emi covering the story every time a new one shows up. Meanwhile, Aki is having recurring visions of a small boy staring at her from the shadows.

The rivalry between Aki and Emi makes for compulsive viewing, but about forty minutes in, Hashimoto starts to pile on the surrealist touches. Although loosely tied in to the narrative, these scenes make less and less sense as the film progresses, eventually devolving into a series of fights between the two women in increasingly bizarre surroundings. These are excellently shot, with the influence of Dario Argento still obvious in terms of colour and light, and they're very gory, but are simply too abstract to hold much interest. It's perhaps a shame Hashimoto chose the route he did, because *Evil Dead Trap 2* had the potential to be an above-average splatter movie. The film's main theme- the disruptive effects of pregnancy and abortion- falls by the wayside after introducing a number of tantalizing and sinister elements. What's the significance of the boy Kurahashi's wife is talking to? Is it the same boy in Aki's visions? Frustratingly, the script makes little or no attempt to resolve any of these loose ends. Hashimoto is clearly a capable director, conjuring up a truly memorable picture of a Tokyo full of noisy construction sites, low-class hookers, bizarre cults and garish neon eyesores, but by the time the credits roll the film has become tiresome and frustrating.

A third film, *Evil Dead Trap 3: Broken Love Killer* (*Shiryô no Wana 3: Chigireta ai no Satsujin*) appeared in 1993, with Toshiharu Ikeda back at the helm, once again working from a Takashi Ishii script. Despite the presence of these two- as well as composer Tomohiko Kira and special effects man Shinichi Wakasa- the film bears little resemblance to the original or its unrelated sequel. When a pregnant student commits suicide- leaving behind a note claiming that one her professors is the father of her unborn child- the police initially treat it as an open-and-shut case. However, it's not the first time that professor Muraki (Shirô Sano again) has come to the attention of the police; five years before, another female student disappeared after telling her friends she was having an affair with a teacher. Furthermore, the good professor owns a holiday home in Irezumi, where a number of headless, limb-less torsos have been found dumped at the beach in recent years. Detective Yoko Mizuhashi (Megumi Yokoyama, from Ishii's *Gonin*) has a personal interest in the case- the girl who disappeared was a school friend of hers- and she becomes determined to prove there's a link between the professor and the dead girls.

As with many of the psycho thrillers of the '90s, the chief focus of *Evil Dead Trap 3* is the mind-games between the feisty young detective and the cold, intellectual suspected killer. Unlike the previous films, the violence is kept to a minimum here, with few of the killings taking place onscreen. Without the chief selling point of the first two movies- the graphic gore- *Evil Dead Trap 3* is left to survive on the merits of its plot, which is simply too derivative to sustain much interest. Ikeda remains a technically skilled director with a flair for eye-catching images, but his work here is simply proficient, rather than outstanding. The film's most interesting image is that of the axe-wielding killer clad in a white robe, wearing a white noh mask with long black hair and moving with the jerky, stylized movements of a bunraku puppet. It's remarkably similar to the appearance of Sadako and the ghosts that proliferated after *Ring*. For the most part however, *Evil Dead Trap 3* is just another '90s-style, *Psycho*-influenced serial killer thriller, with little to recommend it. Perhaps wisely, it was also the last in the series.

Throughout the '90s Ikeda remained an important figure on the cult and V-cinema scene, producing anything from women-in-prison thrillers (*Female Convict Scorpion: Death Threat*, 1991) to Riki Takeuchi yakuza flicks and (comparatively) high-profile pinku eiga, such as his 1997 version of *The Key* (*Kagi*), a Junichiro Tanizaki novel that had already been filmed by Tinto Brass in 1984. *The Key* achieved some historical significance as the first theatrically released film to portray full-frontal nudity. Among his better films from the period are the two erotic thrillers he contributed to Toei Video's XX series. The first, *XX: Beautiful Beast* (*XX: Utsukushiki Gakuen*, 1995) is a *Black Angel*-style revenge thriller co-written by Hiroshi Takahashi (*Ring*), while the second, *XX: Beautiful Prey* (*XX: Utsukushiki Emono*, 1996), is an S&M drama featuring Ren Ôsugi. It wasn't until 2001 that Ikeda returned to the horror genre, with *Shadow of the Wraith* (*Ikisudama*), a teen-oriented adaptation of a Nanaeko Sasaya manga. His best film in recent years is *The Man Behind the Scissors* (*Hasami Otoko*, 2004), a blackly humorous thriller about a serial killer who suspects that someone has stolen his 'signature'. With more than twenty films and thirty years of experience under his belt, Ikeda is slowly being recognized as the talented cult film director that he is. Although the majority of his films are still unavailable in the west, the situation is improving as the demand for Japanese cult films increases. *Evil Dead Trap* is his masterpiece, but Ikeda's extensive filmography contains a number of hidden gems waiting to be discovered.

Outside of the notorious *Guinea Pig* series, few Japanese horror films have managed to provoke quite as much revulsion as *Shojo no Harawata* (*Entrails of a Virgin*) and *Bijo no Harawata* (*Entrails of a Beauty*), both released in 1986 and directed by one of the leading figures of the mid-'80s wave of sex and violence, Kazuo 'Gaira' Komizu. The titles alone are enough to conjure up visions of mutilation and 'sexualized violence', which is not far from the truth; in a little less than two and a half hours (each film is the standard length for pink films, around 70 minutes), Komizu manages to serve up enough depravity and gore to fill the quotas of a dozen pink films. Appropriately enough, Komizu began his career in the early seventies, writing scripts for acclaimed pink directors like Kôji Wakamatsu and Masaru Konuma. Unsurprisingly, those early scripts, including Konuma's *Woman in a Box: Virgin Sacrifice* (*Hako no Naka no Onna: Shojo Ikenie*, 1985) and Yasuro Uegaki's *Female Market: Imprisonment* (*Ryûjoku Mesu Ichiba: Kankin*, 1986), were characterized by excessive violence.

In terms of plot, *Entrails of a Virgin* most resembles the slasher movie. A crew of glamour models and photographers are out in the wilderness setting up a series of soft-core shoots. When evening comes they take refuge in an isolated cabin, where the men try and sleep with as many of the women as possible (as in most slasher movies, the males are all sex-obsessed jerks while the women are all sex-shy virgins or promiscuous tramps). Most of the film is taken up with these encounters. Occasionally the 'monster'- apparently a mud-caked individual with a giant penis- shows up to ravish one of the women or murder one of the men. In the end he impregnates the last survivor, leaving her to wonder what her offspring will be.

It soon becomes apparent that *Entrails of a Virgin* is being played for laughs. Like many directors before him, Komizu encourages the cast to ham it up wildly in an effort to hide the fact that they're porn stars, not actors. The special effects are very poor indeed, but they're either deliberately bad- like the monster itself- or so ludicrous it's impossible to take them seriously. Perhaps the most infamous scene would be the one involving masturbation with a severed arm: it's tasteless and over-the-top, but it just about qualifies as a sick joke, with an apparent nod to *The Horror of Frankenstein* (1970) thrown in for good measure. There are plenty of casual lifts from more famous films too, mostly from *Friday the 13th* (1979) and *The Evil Dead* (1983). Credit must go to Komizu for finding some interesting ways of circumventing the Japanese censorship laws that forbade any depiction of the genitalia; at one point the camera cuts away to a silhouette of a gigantic penis. Pornographic shadow puppets, anyone?

So does this attempt to turn *Entrails of a Virgin* into a gory spoof pay off? Not really, since at least half of the film is taken up with sex scenes that will either titillate or bore, depending on the viewer's attitude. Once the horror and the gross humour make an appearance, it becomes a little more interesting, but *Entrails of a Virgin* is still only likely to appeal to a very selective audience. It's an interesting combination of western and Japanese genres however, even if the mix of pinku eiga and slasher movie doesn't entirely work.

A follow-up, *Entrails of a Beautiful Woman*, appeared soon afterwards. Rather than going over the same territory, Komizu took the rape-revenge movie as his template. The rape-revenge sub-genre, embodied in the west by films like Wes Craven's *The Last House on the Left* (1972) and the notorious *I Spit on Your Grave* (1978), is characterized by (predictably enough) by prolonged rape scenes followed by less protracted scenes of the heroine brutalizing and murdering her former tormentors. The majority of rape-revenge films are simple exhibitions of brutality and violence, although rare efforts like Takashi Ishii's *Freeze Me* (2000) manage to deal with the subject matter with intelligence and insight. Needless to say, *Entrails of a Beautiful Woman* is not one of those films.

A group of yakuza kidnap and rape a young woman. She eventually manages to escape, but not before they can pump her full of a drug called 'Angel Rain', intended to increase her sexual appetite. After her escape she confides in a young doctor, Dr Hiromi, but later commits suicide. Hiromi decides to seek revenge for the death of her patient, and devises a plan to turn the yakuza against each other.

**Entrails of a Beautiful Woman**

Unfortunately her efforts result in her being captured by the group, who inject her with 'Angel Rain' and begin to brutalize her. It is here that *Entrails of a Beautiful Woman* takes a turn into deeply strange territory, as Hiromi's body begins to merge with the corpse of a murdered yakuza, apparently because of the drug. After a gruesome transformation, a new being is revealed: a grotesque hermaphrodite monster that can kill with either one of its enlarged sexual organs. Bloody chaos ensues.

For the most part, *Entrails of a Beautiful Woman* does not waver from the pattern set down by its predecessor. Despite a little more character development, the film is just one sex scene after another; sadly they're predominantly rape scenes, something that quashes any minor titillation value they may have had. The final reel explodes into showers of gore and bright-red blood, and like the earlier film, things become a lot more entertaining when it does. The production values here are a little better, with improved lighting and camerawork, but the acting is still porn-standard and the special effects cheap and amateurish. The most significant difference is the absence of humour; Komizu has removed the slapstick and the gross gags that appeared in *Entrails of a Virgin*, and replaced it with a repellent storyline, making this film even harder to watch, despite the technical improvements. For better or for worse, Komizu has pushed the boundaries of bad taste even further.

Komizu continued his exploration of sex and splatter with 1987's *Female Inquisitor* (*Gômon Kifujin*). AV star Keiko Asano and her band of sadomasochistic followers kidnap and torture criminals until they hand over their ill-gotten gains, which Asano plans to use to purchase a sprawling estate for them all. They set their sights on a corrupt banker who embezzled a fortune from his former employees, subjecting the man and his girlfriend to a variety of physical and sexual tortures. Despite the stated aim of Asano's organization, the sadism here is mainly limited to the opening and closing scenes. For the most part the film focuses on the (allegedly) erotic rather than the grotesque, including some ludicrous episodes involving machines and eels. Clearly the budget was much bigger here, and the production values are the highest of Komizu's 80s films, but it remains effectively a glossy-looking porn movie that is unlikely to interest horror fans. Both *Entrails of a Virgin* and *Female Inquisitor* were shot by Akihiro Itô, who worked on *1/2 Mensch* (1986), Sôgo Ishii's documentary about German noise collective Einstürzende Neubaten. Surprisingly, Komizu's next film was the Takeshi Kitano-produced *Hoshi O Tsugomono* (1990), a nostalgic drama about childhood experiences during the Second World War. *Battle Girl* (1991), perhaps Japan's first zombie movie, was Komizu's last horror film and perhaps his most entertaining. In 1993 he directed *XX: Beautiful Weapon* (*XX: Utukushiki Kyôki*), the first in the series of violent and erotic action thrillers, including two directed by Toshiharu Ikeda, another associate of Masaru Konuma. The series rarely moves above the average, but *Beautiful Weapon* is the worst of the lot. Since then Komizu has retired from directing, concentrating his efforts on his AV production house, Gaira Shock.

The zenith- or the nadir, depending on your point of view- of the '80s splatter wave is the *Guinea Pig* series. Consisting of six original films- one is a combination of new and recycled footage from the rest of the series, while another is essentially a behind-the-scenes featurette- the *Guinea Pig* collection has become something of a Holy Grail to fans of explicit blood and gore. Although some of its impact has lessened in the twenty years since the first one was released- not all of the special effects hold up too well- the cruelty and physical nastiness that lies at the heart of the early films can still make for deeply uncomfortable watching. The series remains as controversial today as it ever was, even though some of the popular legends are not wholly accurate. The story about Charlie Sheen mistaking a *Guinea Pig* film for real snuff and contacting the FBI is probably apocryphal, but the second episode, *Flower of Flesh and Blood*, did indeed form the basis of one of the few successful prosecutions involving snuff movies. In the late 1990s a British man pleaded guilty to charges of distributing obscene material, even though the film is an obvious fake. His guilty plea seems to have been intended to ensure that the jury did not get to see the film; perhaps the defendant and his barrister were concerned that the jurors would assume it was a real snuff movie, as the tabloid media did. The film's director, popular horror manga artist Hideshi Hino, also became involved with the law in 1989 when the Japanese police received a tip claiming that the events depicted on the tape bore a surprising similarity to the recent- then unsolved- murder of a schoolgirl. Although the police eventually dismissed Hino as a suspect, the controversy resurfaced when journalists began to claim that a copy of *Flower of Flesh and Blood* had been found in the real killer's video collection. Once again, the story was later debunked, but by then the notoriety of the *Guinea Pig* films was assured.

The first *Guinea Pig* film, *Devil's Experiment* (*Akuma no Jikken*, 1984), is perhaps the most extreme of the series, an atrocity exhibition consisting of roughly 45 minutes of torture inflicted upon a young woman by a group of anonymous men. There is no plot; the victim is tied a chair and brutalized in a variety of different ways- beaten, cut, burned, mutilated- most of which are presented in close-up for maximum effect. *Devil's Experiment* is most definitely a deeply unpleasant movie, but its impact is actually lessened by the constant stream of cruelty; it quickly becomes tedious and rather pointless instead of horrifying. Despite claiming that *Devil's Experiment* is a snuff movie, the makers made no attempt to create a realistic experience and utilize a number of artificial cinematic techniques, from slow motion shots to rapid-fire editing, fades and dissolves. Combined with the comparatively primitive special effects, these make it unlikely that anyone could mistake it for a genuine snuff movie. Since *Devil's Experiment* does not include any cast or crew credits, it's difficult to know who directed the film, although the film's producer Satoru Ogura is one possibility. It has been suggested that Hideshi Hino, director of the next *Guinea Pig* movie, also handled the first one, but there seems little reason why he would happily admit to directing *Flower of Flesh and Blood* and not *Devil's Experiment*.

Like the previous film *Flower of Flesh and Blood* is based around the torture, mutilation and murder of a woman, this time by a man wearing a samurai helmet and leather apron. After kidnapping his victim and pumping her full of drugs, he proceeds to dismember her little by little, over the course of around 50 minutes. Although the special effects and general production values are higher that those of *Devil's Experiment*, the film suffers from much the same flaws: the effects are largely unconvincing, and the cumulative effect is more likely to provoke boredom and irritation than genuine horror. Ironically enough, while the advent of DVD and the interest in Asian horror has made these films far more accessible than they have ever been, *Devil's Experiment* and *Flower of Flesh and Blood* were probably more effective when seen on fuzzy nth generation videotapes. The added clarity of digital media does them no favours. Obviously their appeal depends on your appreciation for extreme violence and gore (free from the restraints of plot and character), but both of these items work better as promo reels for the special effects technicians than as actual films.

Apparently as a reaction to the controversy inspired by the earlier films, the subsequent *Guinea Pig* entries chose deliberately fantastic subjects, and injected a dose of humour into the mix. This is most obvious in the third film, *He Never Dies* (*Guinea Pig: Senritso! Shunanai Otoko*, 1986). Like *Devil's Experiment* and *Flower of Flesh and Blood*, *He Never Dies* is essentially just a series of graphic tortures inflicted upon one hapless individual, but this time the material is being played for laughs rather than shock and disgust. The unfortunate victim is Hideshi, a typical Japanese salaryman whose life has suddenly begun to crumble. He's not particularly handsome, so his girlfriend has dumped for a better-looking colleague, and he's not very good at his job either, so it looks like he's about to get fired. Eventually Hideshi comes to the obvious conclusion, and decides it's time to commit suicide, but his attempts to end it all do not go according to plan. After slashing his wrists, Hideshi discovers that not only is not feeling any pain, he's not actually bleeding either. In a panic-stricken frenzy he hacks his entire hand off- but still no pain, no blood and no imminent demise. Realising that he may not actually be able to die, Hideshi embarks on a desperate orgy of self-torture and mutilation. Thanks to the added humour and surrealistic material, *He Never Dies* is considerably easier to watch than its more nihilistic predecessors. It's also the first episode in the series that functions as a genuine film, complete with established characters and a developing plot. Not all of these elements are entirely satisfactory- the characters are barely two-dimensional and the story is effectively a bad joke stretched out for fifty minutes- but they're an improvement on the isolated scenes of brutality that characterised *Devil's Experiment* and *Flower of Flesh and Blood*.

Hideshi Hino returned to write and direct the next instalment, *Mermaid in a Manhole* (*Guinea Pig: Manhole no Naka no Ningyo*, 1987), a film that has more in common with his own manga than *Flower of Flesh and Blood*. Looking for inspiration, struggling artist Hayashi returns to a river he came across in his younger days. On his earlier visit he found a mermaid swimming in the water, and ended up painting her picture; when he returns he finds the river has become a sewer, but the mermaid is still there, now suffering from some disgusting disease picked up from the filth that now pollutes her home. Taking her back to his house, Hayashi puts the mermaid in the bath and begins to paint her again. As her body begins to decompose into multicoloured, iridescent slime, the artist uses her bodily fluids to paint her portrait. As the synopsis suggests, *Mermaid in a Manhole* is more interested in stomach-churning special effects than torture and brutality. On that level the film certainly succeeds, and few people are likely to come away without some sense of revulsion. Whether Hino succeeds in his attempts to find beauty in decay and to convey the tragedy in the decay of beauty- as seen in the river's transformation from natural beauty to sewer and the mermaid's decline into diseased sludge- is open to debate, but it's the only *Guinea Pig* film that comfortably supports any deeper analysis. Despite being hampered by the same budgetary restrictions that characterised the other instalments, it's certainly the most interesting- and arguably the most memorable- of the entire series.

Unfortunately the next film, Kazuhito Kuramoto's *Android of Notre Dame* (1989), is noticeably less interesting, not least because it's also the most mainstream of the *Guinea Pig* movies. Another variation on the Frankenstein tale, *Android of Notre Dame* is the story of a scientist (unhinged, of course) trying to find a cure for the disease that is killing his sister. Naturally his experiments require recently deceased test subjects, and a fair amount of the film (which is just as short as its predecessors) is taken up with the quest to find the necessary materials. Despite being derivative, poorly made and badly acted, *Android of Notre Dame* does possess some interest thanks to the presence of cult favourite Tomorowo Taguchi (*Tetsuo: The Iron Man*) and Mio Takaki from *Wizard of Darkness* (*Eko Eko Azarak*, 1995), but it's not enough to recommend the film to anyone other than *Guinea Pig* completists. The sixth and final film in the series, *Devil Woman Doctor* (*Peter no Akuma no Joi-san*, 1990), is the least serious of them all, being effectively a combination of camp overacting and over-the-top splatter scenes. The title character is played by transvestite actor Peter, best known for his appearance in Toshio Matsumoto's homosexual reworking of the Oedipus legend, *Funeral Procession of Roses* (1969). The film follows the *Devil Woman Doctor* as she 'treats' her patients, including a family who apparently explode when they get angry. And the doctor's preferred course of treatment? Abuse them until they do literally explode. Problem solved. The rest of her patients suffer from similarly unlikely conditions, and the doctor's methods much the same as before. Occasionally humorous but mostly pointless, *Devil Woman Doctor*'s most interesting aspect is the presence of popular comic actor Naoto Takenaka, years before his star-making turn in Masayuki Suô's *Shall We Dance?* (1997).

The *Guinea Pig* controversies and the decline of the pinku eiga industry in the 1990s left the Japanese splatter movie in a difficult position, with many directors choosing to concentrate on more commercially viable and less contentious areas. Toshiharu Ikeda's output from the period consists mainly of yakuza movies and erotic thrillers like Toei Video's *XX* series. He did direct an *Evil Dead Trap* sequel in 1993, but dropped the body horror and gore in favour of a straightforward police procedural/psycho movie, while Kazuo Komizu focussed on his own AV production company. However, the fading fortunes of pink cinema had the surprising side effect of allowing a handful of directors far more creative freedom than they might otherwise have enjoyed. With the industry apparently on its last legs, there seemed little point in resolutely churning out commercial material, so four directors- Hisayasu Satô, Toshiki Satô (*Perfect Blue: Yume Nara Samete*), Kazuhiro Sano and Takahisa Zeze (*Kokkuri*)- chose to use the pink framework to explore their own individual cinematic approaches and concerns. For Hisayasu Satô this included a sizeable amount of graphic violence, as typified by perhaps his most extreme film, *Splatter: Naked Blood* (*Megyaku: Naked Blood*, 1996).

A partial remake of one of Satô's earlier pinku eiga, *Splatter: Naked Blood* is often described as another example of *Guinea Pig*-style Japanese ultraviolence, but the association is not entirely warranted. In summary the plot certainly seems akin to *He Never Dies*- a teenage genius invents a new painkiller that turns sensations of pain into pleasure and tests it on three unsuspecting women, leading to an orgy of self-mutilation- but *Naked Blood* is more than just a showcase for grotesque special effects, and those expecting another *Devil's Experiment* are likely to be frustrated by the film's slow pace and lengthy non-violent scenes. The patient will be rewarded however, as the unwitting guinea pigs (no pun intended) discover the pleasurable sensations now produced by physical injury. One woman begins piercing her skin with every available sharp object;

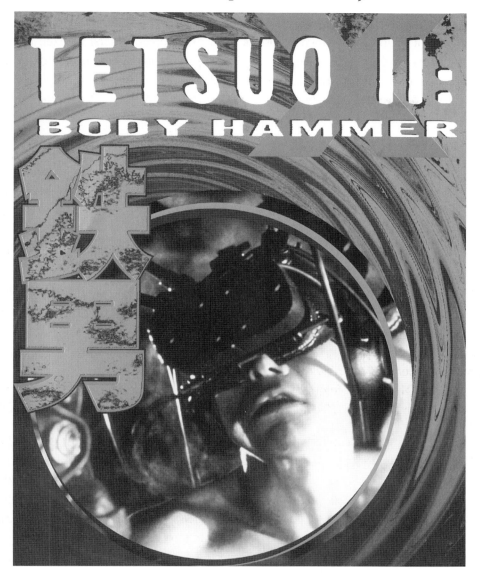

**Tetsuo 2: Body Hammer**

another accidentally scalds herself while cooking and thrusts her hand into the deep fat fryer, eventually biting her own fingers off, and the brutality escalates from there.

In contrast to the explicit gore, much of *Naked Blood* is infused with an odd, dream-like atmosphere supported by the many references to artificial and altered states of reality: drug-induced ecstasy, virtual reality, psychotic delusions, as well as memories and traumatic flashbacks (seen through home movies), dreams and nightmares. Video plays a key role, partly in its capacity to record and confirm reality but also in its ability to establish a bond between the individuals behind the camera and those in front of it. Many of these elements- most notably the conflict between reality and fantasy, psychological trauma and breakdown, psychotropic drugs, video and voyeurism- are recurring features of Satô's work, both in his pinku eiga and his more experimental V-cinema work like *Naked Blood*. Although he has yet to achieve the same degree of mainstream success as his contemporary Takahisa Zeze, Satô's profile has been slowly rising over the past few years. In 2005 he directed a segment of *Rampo Noir* (*Rampo Jigoku*), a four-part anthology of Edogawa Rampo adaptations, with indie favourite Tadanobu Asano starring in all of them. Two of the segments were directed by Atsushi Kaneko and Suguru Takeuchi, with the late Akio Jissôji, director of *Tokyo: The Last Megalopolis* (*Teito Monogatori*, 1988), handling the remaining one.

There has been a certain amount of crossover between the splatter film and the 'cyberpunk' movies that appeared in the mid-'80s and early '90s, with the primary cyberpunk theme- the conflict and hybridisation of flesh and metal- affording plenty of opportunity for graphic and grotesque special effects. The cornerstones of the genre are Shinya Tsukamoto's *Tetsuo* films, *Tetsuo: The Iron Man* (1989) and its follow-up *Tetsuo II: Body Hammer* (1992). *Tetsuo: The Iron Man* is a black-and-white montage of hallucinatory images, loosely based around the character of an individual whose body is slowly transforming into scrap metal. Shot on a very low budget and created by enthusiastic amateurs rather than skilled professional, *Tetsuo* avoids realistic, gory special effects in favour of erotica and old-fashioned (and cheap) stop-motion techniques. Although often criticised for being more mainstream than its predecessor, *Tetsuo II: Body Hammer* is a more expensive and more confident reworking of the original. Working in colour this time, Tsukamoto manages to make the film more cohesive and coherent, removing the abrasive elements of *Tetsuo* without compromising its impact.

Although they are frequently horrific, neither of the *Tetsuo* films can be properly considered horror movies. The same cannot be said for *Organ* (1996), the directorial debut of Kei Fujiwara, one of Shinya Tsukamoto's early collaborators and a cast and crewmember on *Tetsuo: The Iron Man*. *Organ* is not an easy film to watch and it's almost impossible to enjoy. In terms of its power to disgust or disturb, it's in a category with the early *Guinea Pig* instalments and the ero-gro films of Kazuo Komizu. But unlike those films, it's not a bland attempt to shock or gross out, but a complex portrait of moral, physical and psychological decay. After a failed bust a cop is captured by a black market organ smuggling ring, and kept alive as an experimental plaything by the insane brother and sister who run the group. The cop's brother heads up the investigation to find his twin- or whatever is left of him. Writer-director Fujiwara takes every opportunity to push the material to its limits, resulting in a barrage of gore, brutality, body fluids and festering disease. Unsurprisingly, the result is an incredibly downbeat movie. Everything in the film- from the locations up to the protagonists' morality and even their own bodies- is a state of decay. For those with a high tolerance for the grotesque and the gruesome *Organ* is an interesting and surprising film, but everyone else will probably just feel an overwhelming urge to take a shower afterwards. Despite releasing twenty minutes of footage from *Organ 2*, the full sequel has yet to materialise, although Fujiwara did return to these themes in her next film, 2005's *Id*.

Although the days of blood-soaked nihilistic brutality in the *Guinea Pig* vein seem to have come to an end, Japanese splatter is far from dead. Over the past decade graphic blood and gore has become a powerful tool of many filmmakers, appearing in such disparate works as *Audition* (2000), *Suicide Club* (2002) and *Junk* (2000), as well as crossover movies like *All Night Long* (1992) and *Battle Royale* (2000). Takashi Miike's

# The 1980's: Splatter and Beyond

**Ichi the Killer**

*Ichi the Killer* (*Koroshiya 1*, 2001) certainly rivals anything produced in the 1980s in terms of violence and sheer nastiness, in its tale of a psychopathic yakuza (Tadanobu Asano) and his quest to track down the weedy, unassuming title character who slaughtered his boss. In his quest to create one of the most extreme films ever made, Miike packs as much jaw-dropping violence into his two-hour running time as he possibly can. However, unlike the faux-snuff of *Flower of Flesh and Blood*, Miike also creates plot and characters, providing a context to ensure that his outrageous splatter achieves the maximum impact. The same can be said about *Audition* and *Battle Royale*, in which the graphic blood and gore is put at the service of interesting stories and memorable characters, as opposed to the anonymous atrocities of the early *Guinea Pig* films. Like many established genres, the Japanese splatter movie has undergone a process of metamorphosis, moving away from the 'pure' splatter movies of the 1980s and closer to genre hybrids like *Suicide Club*, *Kichiku* (*Kichiku Dai Enkai*, 1997) and *Versus* (2001).

# CHAPTER THREE

## Demons, Monsters and the Living Dead

Although they have been a staple of anime since the mid-'80s, the vampire (kyûketsuki) has never been a regular feature of Japanese live-action horror. Mainly represented by occasional cash-ins like Nobuo Nakagawa's *Onna Kyûketsuki* (1959) that use the name of the creature but little else, and Michio Yamamoto's trilogy of early '70s Hammer pastiches- *The Night of the Vampire* (*Chi o Suu Ningyô*, 1970); *Lake of Dracula* (*Chi O Suu Me*, 1971); *Evil of Dracula* (*Chi O Suu Bara*, 1975)- the vampire's presence in Japanese cinema has been at best erratic. However, with the growing influence of western horror in the late '80s, it's not entirely surprising that the vampire was (ahem) resurrected once more for Shûsuke Kaneko's *My Soul Is Slashed* (*Kamitsukitai*, 1991). Ken Ogata stars as Ishikawa, a typical company man in every respect: he works insanely long hours for a pharmaceutical company, rarely sees his wife, while his teenage children ignore him completely, mostly because he's never at home. One day Ishikawa discovers that company executives have been indulging in a number of dodgy deals, and makes the mistake of telling one of his superiors; soon afterwards he meets with an unfortunate 'accident', and ends up in intensive care while doctors fight to save his life. In the same hospital doctor and vampire obsessive Yuzuko (Narumi Yasuda) is receiving a consignment of blood from Romania, where the fall of Ceausescu's regime has opened up trade links. The blood is reputed to have belonged to Dracula himself, and Yuzuko intends to use it to resurrect her dead father as a vampire. Unfortunately there's a mix-up during surgery, and shortly before dying Ishikawa is given a transfusion of Dracula's blood. Figuring she might as well make use of the new situation, Yuzuko tells Ishikawa's daughter that she can bring her father back to life by spilling her own blood on his ashes- provided she's a virgin, of course. The grieving daughter does as she's told, but nothing happens- until a year later, when her father crawls out of his grave and heads off home, completely unaware of what has happened.

My Soul Is Slashed is the genre debut of former pinku eiga director Kaneko, later famous for helming the revived *Gamera* trilogy and the smash hit *Death Note* films. The horror elements are balanced by a fair amount of humour- although not quite enough to push the film into comedy territory- and most of the film is taken up with Ishikawa's quest for revenge upon the corrupt executives responsible for his death. Kaneko uses the contrast between man and vampire to present a fairly ham-fisted message about human cruelty- Ogata's monster is more 'human' than his former employers- but *My Soul Is Slashed* is more successful when satirising family and company life. Ishikawa is possibly the perfect employee, since he keeps working until he dies (literally), while he's actually a much better father once he's been turned into a blood-sucking monster. When he was alive, his daughter never saw him; now that he's dead she gets a lot more quality time with him. The movie ends with Ishikawa publicly exposing the criminal dealings of the

# Demons, Monsters and the Living Dead

pharmaceutical company, before he and Yuzuko head off together to set up their own mobile blood donation service. The best joke in the film has nothing to do with plot or characters, however- the 'cigarette burns' (reel markers) are actually drops of blood.

In 1993 Kaneko became the first of the contemporary Japanese horror directors to make his English-language debut when he directed a segment of the anthology film *Necronomicon*. Co-produced by Brian Yuzna, Samuel Hadida and Takashige Ichise (who also acted as Kaneko's second unit director), *Necronomicon* comprises three short tales inspired by the works of H.P. Lovecraft and a wraparound piece starring genre favourite Jeffrey Combs as Lovecraft himself. The other segments are directed by Brian Yuzna (*Beyond Re-Animator*) and Christophe Gans, director of the excellent *Brotherhood of the Wolf* (2001) and computer game adaptation *Silent Hill* (2006). Written by *Ghost in the Shell* (*Kôkaku Kidôtai*, 1995) scriptwriter Kazunori Itô, Kaneko's segment stars David Warner as a scientist who has discovered a means of extending his life infinitely, as long as he remains in a perpetually cold environment.

The vampire didn't return to the live-action arena until 1996 and Kiyoshi Kurosawa's *Door III*, coincidentally written by Chiaki Konaka, who also penned the *Hellsing* anime. An in-name-only sequel to Banmei Takahashi's *Door* (1988) and *Door II* (1991), Kurosawa's film is set in the joyless world of insurance sales, with Minako Tanaka starring as struggling saleswoman Miyako. After accidentally bumping into him, Miyako makes the acquaintance of Mitsuru (Akiharu Nakazawa), a sinister, mascara-wearing lothario who claims to work for another company. However, his permanently fog-bound office and the pale, drifting women that make up his 'staff' suggest his pastimes are a little more exotic than insurance sales; even if he isn't a true vampire- it's never made entirely clear- Mitsuru is certainly an interesting late 20th-century remix. *Door III* is one of the genre exercises that dominated Kurosawa's career before *Cure* (1997), and like *The Guard from the Underground* (*Jigoku no Keibiin*, 1992), it presents established genre conventions against a backdrop of Japanese corporate life. Also like the earlier film, Kurosawa ends up struggling against financial difficulties. He does the best he can, but at times the film's low budget becomes distractingly obvious, most notably in the choppy editing and the often-indistinct sound. However, *Door III* does contain a handful of effective moments that prefigure the ghostly manifestations in both *Séance* (*Kôrei*, 2000) and *Pulse* (*Kairo*, 2001). True vampires would later appear in a non-horror setting with Takahisa Zeze's hit sci-fi movie *Moon Child* (2003), a well-made but ultimately hollow vehicle for rock stars HYDE (from L'Arc en Ciel) and Gackt.

Appropriately enough, *My Soul Is Slashed* was followed by *Last Frankenstein* (1992), Takeshi Kawamura's revisionist reading of Mary Shelley's classic novel. Based on a play performed by Kawamura's 'Dai 3 Erotica' theatre group, *Last Frankenstein* features a number of actors with connections to the Tokyo theatre scene, including Akira Emoto (The *Eel*) and Tsukamoto regular Naomasa Musaka (*Tetsuo: The Iron Man*). In the near future Japan has been decimated by a virus that causes its victims to commit suicide years later. While scientists struggle to find a cure, bizarre cult groups propose mass suicide. Professor Sarusawa (Emoto) has a personal motivation for finding a cure- he also has the virus- and this drives him into contact with a former colleague, Aleo (Yoshio Harada),

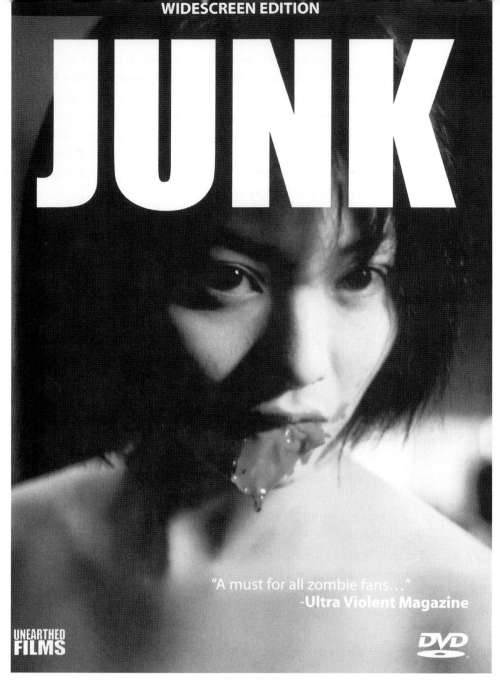

*Sleeve art for* **Junk**

who was fired because of his unpleasant research into artificial life. Recruiting Sarusuwa's assistance with his Frankenstein-style experiments, Aleo promises to reveal what he knows about the origins and cure for the disease. Unsurprisingly, things do not run according to plan, the situation becomes very bloody indeed. One of the better Frankenstein tales of recent years, Kawamura paints a compelling portrait of a world without a future, where the only hope rests with an increasingly unstable scientist. Both Akira Emoto and Yoshio Harada deliver great performances, including Harada at his scenery-chewing best. Like many Japanese horror films from the 1990s, *Last Frankenstein* is almost entirely unknown outside Japan, but it deserves to be rediscovered.

# Demons, Monsters and the Living Dead

Despite the popularity of the zombie movie in Europe and America following George Romero's *Night of the Living Dead* (1968), the walking dead never became a staple feature of Eastern horror films. Hong Kong filmmakers threw zombies into their usual brand of martial arts, horror and fantasy on a handful of occasions, such as *Kung Fu Zombie* (1982) and *Zombie vs. Ninja* (1989), but the creatures bear little resemblance to Romero's rotting hordes. A single Thai zombie movie- Rotar Ru-Tar's *Ginseng King*- appeared in 1989, but failed to inspire any others despite boasting an undead blood-sucking Nazi. Even though *Dawn of the Dead* (1978) was a box office hit in Japan, it wasn't until 1991 that Japanese zombies first appeared, in Kazuo Komizu's cheap and silly *Battle Girl* (a.k.a. *The Living Dead in Tokyo Bay*). A radioactive asteroid is turning the citizens of Tokyo into walking corpses, but Komizu is far more interested in showcasing the shapely charms of female wrestler Cutey Suzuki- now an AV idol- who spends most of the movie squeezed into a tight black PVC outfit. In a change from the days of *Godzilla* (1954), the Self-Defence Forces have turned on the civilians, and it's up to our heroine to take out their lunatic general and rescue the survivors. Suzuki (who was popular enough to warrant her own computer game, 'Ringside Angel') may not be a particularly good actress, but the black PVC and leather help to make up for her dramatic shortcomings. It was another eight years before the Japanese zombie movie began to proliferate however, inspired by the success of the Resident Evil computer games and *Ring* (1998).

The main issue facing Japanese zombie films is a religious one. In keeping with Japanese funerary practices, corpses are usually cremated, leaving very little behind to resurrect. Komizu dodged the problem by infecting living people with radiation from an asteroid (the same explanation that was added to Japanese prints of *Dawn of the Dead*), and Tetsuro Takeuchi's *Wild Zero* (1999) also blames the Enemy From Space. Aliens have landed on Earth and begun turning people into zombies, so teenage punk Ace (Masashi Endô) teams up with Guitar Wolf- his favourite greasy rockabilly band- to help save the planet and hopefully find true love. On the way they run into a Cutey Suzuki-like weapons expert and the usual bunch of yakuza weirdoes that end up getting in the way. Abandoning any pretence at horror, Takeuchi throws in everything he can think of: gore gags, bad taste, romance, the Power of Rock 'n' Roll (well, guitars that shoot bullets) and even a feel-good message about the universal nature of True Love. Just how universal it gets you'll have to wait and see- *Wild Zero* boasts at least one jaw-dropping, hilarious revelation.

Released just a few months after *Wild Zero*, Atsushi Muroga's *Junk* (*Junk: Shiryôgari*, 2000) uses reanimated gaijin ('foreigner') soldiers instead. Obviously inspired by *Return of the Living Dead* (1985) and the Resident Evil games- which are known in Japan by the more appropriate title of Biohazard- the re-agent is a chemical weapon mothballed years ago by the US Army and accidentally uncovered by a bunch of amateur bank robbers. Muroga keeps the pace moving faster than his zombies, but like his other films the end result is effectively a collection of clips from other movies (including his own), stitched together with occasional ingenuity. Like his earlier *Score* (1996), *Junk* kicks off with a raid and a trip to a deserted factory to divide the loot. In both films the robbers end up having to fight to keep hold of the takings- in Score, against thieves; in *Junk*, against gangsters-

but in the latter the squabbles are interrupted by the newly reanimated living dead. Like Muroga's spaghetti western pastiche *Gun Crazy Vol. 1- Woman From Nowhere* (2002), *Junk* is saddled with a surplus of terrible gaijin non-actors, recruited from the local area (Thailand, in this case) and enlisted to play the US soldiers, forcing at least one Japanese actor to read his lines in broken English.

None of the recent Japanese zombie films are particularly serious, and like *Wild Zero*, Naoyuki Tomomatsu's *Stacy* (2001) is primarily a spoof, although it's a pretty gory one too. This time there's no need for aliens or space viruses, because the problem is confined to teenage girls- girls between the ages of 15 and 17 are, after a brief period of ecstasy, turning into zombies, or 'stacies'. The only option after that is to dismember the body completely, preferably with a chainsaw, and leave the remains in bags for the garbage men to pick up. In true *Day of the Dead* (1985) style, a group of scientists have captured and imprisoned a number of stacies for research into a possible cure or treatment. Sure enough, they don't stay imprisoned for long. For a low-budget splatter spoof, *Stacy* has a surprising number of literary connections. It's based on a novel by former rock star-turned-writer Kenji Ôtsuki, who appears on TV in the film selling 'Bluce Campbell's Right Hand 2', the latest convenient device for dismembering your daughter. Shungiku Uchida, author of the controversial autobiographical bestseller Father Fucker (filmed by Genjirô Arato in 1995) also makes an appearance, as does Yasutake Tsutsui, the science-fiction writer whose works have formed the basis of Satoshi Kon's excellent *Paprika* (2006) and the multiple adaptations of *The Girl Who Leapt Through Time*, including one by Nobuhiko Obayashi and Mamoru Hosoda's 2007 version. Two different Eko Eko Azarak alumni-Natsuki Katô and Hinako Saeki- also appear, as well as handful of well-known genre players. Although the cameo appearances and some of the gags are entertaining enough, *Stacy* is leaden-paced and unfunny much of the time, with little of the laugh-out-loud humour and vitality of *Wild Zero*. Tomomatsu is not untalented- he wrote the excellent Junji Itô adaptation *Love Ghost* (2000)- but *Stacy* is a misfire.

The brief craze for zombie movies hit its peak with Ryûhei Kitamura's *Versus* (2001), a volatile mix of gore and martial arts that's equally influenced by *The Evil Dead* (1983), *The Matrix* (1999) and brutal 70's chambara (samurai films). Based on the director's earlier short (*Down to Hell*), *Versus* subscribes to what might be termed the Sam Raimi/Peter Jackson Theory of Low-Budget Filmmaking: if you haven't got the budget for stars, expensive sets and complex special effects, keep the pace fast and make sure you go completely over the top with whatever you can afford (usually gags and gore). The premise is straightforward. Prisoner KSC2-303 (played by Tak Sakaguchi) is on the run, having escaped from prison. His route takes him through a forest where he meets a gang of yakuza and their female hostage. A dispute arises, and soon KSC2-303 is running from the cops and yakuza, but now accompanied by The Girl (Chieko Misaka). Someone else is waiting for him in the forest too- a group of smartly dressed assassins commanded by The Man (Hideo Sakaki). Just to keep things interesting, the forest is actually the Forest of Resurrection, which happens to be over the 444th gate into the world of the dead, and anyone who dies in the forest will be coming back to life soon afterwards.

With the film effectively one long free-for-all, Kitamura and co-screenwriter Yûdai

# Demons, Monsters and the Living Dead

Yamaguchi introduce just enough plot to explain the presence of various characters- the cops are chasing the convict, and so forth. As *Versus* builds to the climactic showdown between KSC2-303 and The Man, we discover that the pair, with The Girl in tow, have been fighting it out for thousands of years, endlessly reincarnated and thrown together for purposes that are never entirely explained. The plot itself is of secondary importance, however; what really matters is the action- the John Woo-style gunplay, the faux-*Matrix* camerawork, the parade of fake blood, severed limbs and exploding headshots. Blessed with more vitality than half a dozen Hollywood blockbusters, the only real flaw is the two-hour running time- after 90 minutes *Versus* threatens to wear out its welcome before reaching the final stretch. After securing a US distribution deal Kitamura shot a further ten minutes of footage for the special edition DVD, a decision that does the film no favours. Nonetheless, *Versus* soon became an international cult favourite, propelling Kitamura towards the mainstream.

Just as KSC2-303 and The Man are destined to replay their fight in different times and places throughout eternity, Kitamura has spent the past few years trying to apply the dynamic of *Versus* to a variety of different settings: science-fiction (*Alive*, 2002), period drama/samurai flick (*Azumi*, 2003, and *Aragami*, 2002), horror (*Skyhigh*, 2003) and even a daikaiju eiga ('giant monster movie') with *Godzilla: Final Wars* (2004). Although these

attempts have not always been successful, the thematic similarities between them confirm Kitamura's status as an auteur, supported by his consistent use of the same regular crew: scriptwriters Yudai Yamaguchi and Isao Kiriyama, cinematographer Takumi Furuya, editor Shuichi Kakesu and composers Nobuhiko Morino and Daisuke Yano.

Based on a manga by Tsutomu Takahashi, *Alive* allows Hideo Sakaki to take on the hero role. After murdering the men who raped his girlfriend, Tenshu (Sakaki) is sentenced to die in the electric chair. After his execution is mysteriously cut short, Tenshu is dragged off to a separate chamber, apparently having avoided the death sentence. He is not alone: his new 'cell' is also occupied by another death row convict (Tetta Sugimoto from Takashi Shimizu's *Reincarnation*). Their new wardens- played by genre stalwart Jun Kunimura and Koyuki, from *Pulse* (2001) and *The Last Samurai* (2003)- inform them that they have been spared and can now serve out their sentence in the metal chamber, but before long they're increasing the temperature in the room and reducing their food in an attempt to push the pair into conflict. The wardens, it emerges, are actually scientists studying an alien lifeform currently possessing the body of a young woman; since the creature only changes host when it finds a creature of superior strength and savagery, they intend to use whichever of the convicts survives as a means of rescuing the young woman. Naturally the military has other ideas, and neither the alien nor the prisoners are terribly keen to go along with the plan either. The material is pure pulp sci-fi, but it's not without potential. Unfortunately *Alive* suffers from the same problem as *Versus*- it's far too long- but while the earlier film was supported by Kitamura's breakneck pacing and inventive fight scenes, *Alive* is left to survive on more than an hour of dialogue in two small rooms. Kitamura does eventually unleash some excellent effects-driven combat, but *Alive* descends into tedium long before it arrives.

Created as part of a wager between Kitamura and director Yukihiko Tsutsumi, *Aragami* utilizes the same formula but is at least only 80 minutes long. The wager was to produce a movie featuring two characters in conflict, taking place in one location and shot in a week. Tsutsumi chose two competing actresses for his excellent *2LDK* (2002); Kitamura uses a wounded samurai (Takao Osawa) who looks for shelter in an old temple, occupied by a strange warrior (Masaya Katô) and his silent servant (Kanae Uotani). The warrior claims to be a god of battle, and challenges the samurai to provide him with the first decent fight he's had in centuries. The outcome is never in doubt, and as his prize the samurai becomes the next occupant of the temple. The film ends with the arrival of another competitor, played by Tak Sakaguchi.

Takao Osawa and Kanae Uotani also star in *Skyhigh*, Kitamura's attempt to find a story strong enough to match his exhilarating action scenes. Adapted from another Tsutomu Takahashi manga and accompanied by a TV series directed by Norio Tsuruta, *Skyhigh* stars Yumiko Shaku as Izoku, a woman murdered on her wedding day. Given the option to either return to the world of the living as a ghost, sacrifice her chance to get into heaven by punishing her murderer or become the Keeper of the Gate of Souls, Izoku chooses the third way, hoping to find some way to track down her killer before her cop fiancé takes justice into his own hands and blows his chance at gaining entry to heaven. The murderer (Osawa) is a multi-millionaire geneticist who's collecting hearts from souls destined to become Gatekeepers as part of a ritual intended to bring his own fiancé back to life. He is assisted by a lithe female swordsman (Uotani), who just happens to be one of the few people on earth who can kill Gatekeepers. Although it's is a potentially interesting mix of Kitamura's typical sword-fighting action with a Vengeful Spirit plot, neither one is particularly well represented. Burdened with too many characters (Eihi Shiina appears briefly as another of the Gatekeepers) and an excess of complicated but predictable plot developments, *Skyhigh* struggles to maintain any kind of momentum and collapses long before the final stretch.

The best of Kitamura's post-Versus work is *Azumi*, an adaptation of Yu Koyama's popular manga. Defiantly tongue-in-cheek, *Azumi* showcases some of Kitamura's finest fight choreography, supported by solid pacing and offbeat humour. Unlike *Alive* and *Skyhigh*, the plot is not so ponderous that it sinks the rest of the film, but neither is it quite as minimalist as *Versus*. Pop idol Aya Ueto stars as Azumi, a member of an elite squad

# Demons, Monsters and the Living Dead

of assassins, trained since childhood by their grizzled mentor Yoshio Harada (*Another Heaven*; *Nightmare Detective*) to take on any troublemakers and rebellious types who threaten the peace and stability of 14th century Japan. Glossing over the more dubious aspects of this setup (Azumi and her pals are just a period goon squad, jumping on anybody who disagrees with their bosses), Kitamura sets his heroes against a variety of villains, from the expected samurai and ninja types to a family of moronic thugs (including Tak Sakaguchi) and Jô Odagiri's master swordsman- a rose-sniffing weirdo who giggles like a schoolgirl while he's chopping his enemies into little pieces. The attractive Ueto is the weak link here, often coming across as more than a little wooden. However, she carries the action scenes well, and the pulp material is not crying out for virtuoso performances. She's supported by a handful of veterans, including Harada and Naoto Takenaka, as well as some capable younger performers. While not a huge box office success, *Azumi* was well received by cult movie fans around the world. With Kitamura taking over the reins of the Japan's most famous monster franchise for *Godzilla: Final Wars*, Shûsuke Kaneko (director of 2001's *Godzilla, Mothra, King Ghidorah: Giant Monsters All-Out Attack*) stepped in to helm *Azumi 2: Death or Love* (2005). With Chiaki Kuriyama (*Battle Royale*) and Mikijirô Hira taking over as the chief villains, *Azumi 2* follows much the same pattern as its predecessor, with more emphasis on plot and the heroine's love life. However, while Kaneko's fights are professionally staged, they lack the spark and vitally that characterised Kitamura's efforts, and much of the humour has been reduced. *Azumi* was solid pulp entertainment, but *Azumi 2* is merely competent. After *Godzilla: Final Wars*, Kitamura travelled to the USA to make his Hollywood debut with *The Midnight Meat Train*, an adaptation of a Clive Barker short story included in The Books of Blood.

Kitamura's regular collaborators have since become something of a self-contained cottage industry. *Versus* scriptwriter Yûdai Yamaguchi directed the oddball comedy *Battlefield Baseball* (*Jigoku Kôshien*), starring the ubiquitous Tak Sakaguchi as a rebellious loner with a talent for combining martial arts and sports. His unique style and incredibly powerful throwing arm lands him a position on his high school baseball team, who dream of making it all the way through the regional championship. Unfortunately their main competition is the Gedo team, who are not just first-rate baseball players- they're also undead psychos whose opponents don't always make it home alive. Yamaguchi's mixture of sports, martial arts, zombies and musical numbers is certainly an acquired taste, although it does contain moments of inspired insanity, and Tak Sakaguchi is obviously having fun spoofing the tough guy roles he's played in so many other films.

Yûdai Yamaguchi also directed *Meatball Machine* (2006), a bizarre low-budget sci-fi film about two people (Issei Takahashi and Aoba Kawai) who get taken over by alien parasites. The pair are then converted into human-machine hybrids and forced to fight for the aliens' entertainment. Based on a short film directed by Junichi Yamamoto, *Meatball Machine* was then re-scripted by Yamaguchi and his *Battlefield Baseball* co-writer Junya Katô before being remade on a larger budget. Generally entertaining and occasionally inventive, the resulting film is equal parts *Tetsuo: The Iron Man* (1989) and Robert Heinlein's novel The Puppetmasters.

Even Yûji Shimomura, the fight director of *Versus*, got in on the act with the Junya

# Flowers From Hell

Katô-scripted *Death Trance* (2006), a martial arts fantasy influenced by spaghetti westerns and Hong Kong kung fu flicks. Tak Sakaguchi (again!) stars as Grave, a wandering fighter who has stolen a relic from a temple (in a *Django*-inspired touch, he drags it around in a coffin). Pursued by temple priests eager to get their possession back, Grave is chased across the countryside, fighting every step of the way. With set design and costumes inspired by both period dress and gothic fantasy, plus a first-rate rock score by Japanese goth/metal stars Dir en grey, *Death Trance* is very much style over substance. Despite the elaborate combat scenes (co-directed by Sakaguchi himself), Shimomura doesn't manage to do anything particularly original with the *Versus* template.

The influence of western horror did not manifest itself only in Japanese versions of western classics like *Dracula* and *Frankenstein*; it also resulted in western conventions and concepts appearing in typically Japanese settings. A notable early example of this is the late Akio Jissôji's *Tokyo: The Last Megalopolis* (*Teito Monogatari*, 1988). Like the following year's *Sweet Home*, *Tokyo: The Last Megalopolis* was Toho's attempt to replicate the big-budget, special effects-driven Hollywood horrors of the '80s, such as Tobe Hooper's *Poltergeist* (1982). For *Sweet Home* Kiyoshi Kurosawa hired American effects maestro Dick Smith; Jissôji recruited eccentric Swiss artist H.R. Giger, creator of Ridley Scott's alien. Like Dick Smith, Giger also contributed to the *Poltergeist* franchise, providing some unusual monsters to the otherwise unremarkable *Poltergeist II* (1986) before performing the

*Artwork for* **Wizard of Darkness**

# Demons, Monsters and the Living Dead

same service for Jissôji's film. Based on Hiroshi Aramata's popular novel and scripted by Kaizô Hayashi, *Tokyo: The Last Megalopolis* is set during the Taisho era (1912-1926), a time of transition for the city. Western suits are slowly taking the place of Japanese dress, while cars are becoming a frequent sight. City planner Shibusawa (played by the original Zatoichi himself, Shintarô Katsu) struggles to achieve his dream of remaking Tokyo as a truly modern city, rebuilt in a contemporary style with high-rise, earthquake-resistant building and an underground railway system. While Shibusawa dreams of the future, militarist and evil magician Katô (Kyusaku Shimada) has his own plans for the capital: he intends to summon the spirit of long-dead psychopath Masakado and use his power to attack the city. Aware that Tokyo is headed for a supernatural disaster, civil servant Keiko (Mikijirô Hira, from *Azumi 2: Death or Love*) tries to unravel the portents and omens and discover exactly what Katô is planning to do.

Taking place over a number of years and a couple of generations, *Tokyo: The Last Megalopolis* is a densely plotted, complex tale. While the strong supporting cast, the unusual setting, and the contrast between modern science and traditional mysticism make for interesting viewing, the film struggles to build up any momentum. Weighed down by a great amount of exposition and secondary characters, only the flamboyant special effects-driven sequences have anything resembling pace, although that improves as Jissôji drives towards his appropriately apocalyptic finale. Thanks to solid performances,  excellent special effects and first-rate production design *Tokyo: The Last Megalopolis* retains a fair amount of entertainment value, but its ponderous plot and pacing difficulties prevent it from being the bona fide cult classic it could have been.

A sequel, *Teito Taisen*, appeared a year later, with Shimada reprising his role as the demonic Katô, supported by Kaho Minami (*Angel Dust*) and the late great Tetsurô Tanba. *Teito Taisen* was the directorial debut of producer Takashige Ichise, who would later become one the major players in the post-*Ring* Japanese horror boom. This time the special effects were handled by American effects technician Screaming Mad George, who also worked on the Ichise-produced *Necronomicon*. *Teito Taisen* did not achieve the same degree of critical approval and box office success as its predecessor, and a further sequel did not arrive until 1995, with the V-cinema release *Teito Monogatari Gaiden*. Written by Rika Yamagami and directed by Izô Hashimoto (co-writer of *Akira* and director of *Evil Dead Trap 2: Hideki*), *Teito Monogatari Gaiden* takes a more overtly grim and horrific approach to the material than the earlier films. This change of tone was probably influenced by Toei Video's 1992 OVA (direct-to-video anime), released in the west as *Doomed Megalopolis*. More graphic and explicit than Akio Jissôji's film, the anime has echoes of the notorious *Urotsukidôji*- particularly the demonic impregnation- although it does not plumb quite the same depths. A popular franchise in all its forms- novel, films and anime- its influence can still be seen today, most notably in Koei's Shin Megami Tensei computer games.

Japanese superstitions and folklore also play a significant part in Shinya Tsukamoto's *Hiruko the Goblin* (*Hiruko: Yôkai Hantâ*, 1991). Based on the Daijirô Morobashi manga, *Hiruko the Goblin* is a respectable and entertaining horror film that is often passed over in favour of the director's more experimental films such as *Tetsuo: The Iron Man* (1989) and its follow-up *Tetsuo II: Body Hammer* (1992). Kenji Sawada stars as an archaeologist who discovers that his nephew's school is built over a tomb designed to imprison an ancient demon. When the demon is accidentally released and begins killing off schoolchildren, the archaeologist and his nephew head down into the underground caverns to seal the creature within its tomb. The word yôkai- here translated as 'goblin'- refers to any one of a variety of different supernatural creatures, from playful, mischievous spirits to outright malevolent demons. Hiruko is one of the latter kind, taking the form of severed head with several spindly legs and using her hypnotic voice to ensnare her victims, who are then dispatched in geysers of blood. Although *Hiruko the Goblin* is the most mainstream film from a unique director, it boasts enough genuine weirdness and originality to lift it above many of its contemporaries. A handful of Tsukamoto's stylistic flourishes are in evidence- including the rapid ground-level tracking shots- while the archaeologist's home-made demon hunting devices are reminiscent of the DIY special effects used in *Tetsuo*. It's also possible to see elements of that film's theme of bodily transformation and mutation- every time Hiruko takes a victim, an image of their face appears on the nephew's back, almost branded onto the skin. One of the demon's first victims is Tsukamoto regular Naoto Takenaka, who also appeared in *Tokyo Fist* (1995) and *Gemini* (1999).

Tales of the yôkai have not been particularly common since the 1960s, when Daiei released classic films like *The Great Goblin War* (*Yôkai Daisenso*, 1968), but periodic attempts are made to resurrect the style and sell it to the now-middle-aged audiences who enjoyed the originals. The renewed interest in horror after *Ring* prompted Warner Bros.- through their subsidiary Towani Inc.- to produce *Sakuya: The Slayer of Demons* (*Sakuya Yôkaiden*, 2000), a yôkai revival piece directed by special effects technician Tomoo Haraguchi. Given the large number of special effects needed to portray the dozens of different kinds of fantastic creatures- including the one-eyed umbrella monster, the bakeneko or 'ghost cat' and the onryo-musha ('demon warriors')- it's appropriate that the film should be the brainchild of effects expert. The human component of *Sakuya* is well represented too, with supporting roles filled by Kyusaku Shimada (*Tokyo: The Last Megalopolis*), *Tetsuo* director Shinya Tsukamoto, Naoto Takenaka and cult icon Tetsurô Tanba. Nozomi Andô (*Tomie: Final Chapter- Forbidden Fruit*) stars as Sakuya the demon slayer, a young warrior determined to drive back the demons that have taken over Mt. Fuji. Her opponent is the demon queen, played by Keiko Matsuzaka. While the decent special effects and the solid cast ensure that *Sakuya* is reasonably entertaining, the film is undermined by the fact that although giant cats might have been mildly scary back in the '60s, when placed alongside truly frightening characters like Sadako they are simply comical. More successful when approached as a children's film, it still lacks the rollercoaster-ride pacing and contemporary references of the *Haunted School* films. Despite selling well on video, the proposed sequel did not materialize, and neither did the intended resurrection of the yôkai sub-genre.

However, this did not prevent Kadokawa, Japan's largest publishing company and a major movie production house, from celebrating their 80th anniversary with a loose remake of *The Great Goblin War* (2006). Although the appointment of Takashi Miike- the enfant terrible of Japanese cinema- as director might have been interpreted as a desire

# Demons, Monsters and the Living Dead

on Kadokawa's part to push the envelope a little, the thoroughly routine results suggested otherwise. Lonely city kid Takashi (Ryunosuke Kamiki) is stranded in the countryside with his divorced mother (Kaho Minami from *Angel Dust*), and hating every minute of it. Things start to improve when Takashi is selected to be the hero of the yôkai world and help to defeat the evil wizard Kato (Etsushi Tokoyama, also from *Angel Dust*) and his goblin henchwoman, played by Chiaki Kuriyama. Like the earlier yôkai films, this is strictly for the kids, although Miike keeps the pace fast and throws in some welcome humour along the way. Kuriyama and Mai Takahashi make attractive pixies, and there's a welcome appearance from Bunta Sugawara, a Kinji Fukasaku favourite and icon of Japanese cinema in the '60s and '70s, but on the whole there's little here that hasn't been done before. *The Great Goblin War* will probably score points for nostalgia and keep the younger viewers happy, but that's about it.

One of the most popular strands of Japanese fantasy-horror is the 'magical teenager' sub-genre. Most often described as the Japanese equivalent of *Buffy the Vampire Slayer* (1992), the central concept is effectively the same: a teenager- generally a schoolgirl- discovers that she has magical or supernatural powers, and the school becomes the battleground for the resulting showdown between the forces of good and evil. Although teenagers with magical powers have been a common feature of manga and anime since the 1970s, the roots in cinema date back to the early '80s. One of the first examples is Nobuhiko Obayashi's *Nerawareta Gakuen* (1981), an effects-driven tale of psychic teenagers and a secret organization looking to use their powers to take over the world. Equal parts sci-fi and horror, *Nerawareta Gakuen* is a slick, stylish film that showcases Obayashi's love of grandiose fantasy sequences and up-to-date special effects. His failure to provide much substance to support the style means that the film does not rank among Obayashi's best work, but it did earn a sizeable cult following over the years, and was later remade during the mid-'90s heyday of the 'magical teenager' films. The influence of *Nerawareta Gakuen* can also be seen in Jôji Iida's hit TV series and movie *Night Head* (1994), starring Etsushi Toyokawa (*Loft*) and Shinji Takeda (*Pulse*) as pair of troubled psychics, and in Shûsuke Kaneko's *Crossfire* (2000)

The pinnacle of the 'magical teenagers' sub-genre is the *Eko Eko Azarak* series. Based on the manga by Shinichi Koga, the *Eko Eko Azarak* series is built around the adventures of Misa Kuroi, a teenage girl in possession of magical powers that she uses to combat the forces of evil, wherever they may appear. There's a definite touch of romance to her story, but it's tinged with tragedy. A perpetual tenkosei (transfer student), she's always moving on to new schools and new battlegrounds, but frequently leaving behind a pile of corpses after each clash with the supernatural. Misa's powers always save the day, but she rarely manages to save everyone else; on many occasions, Misa is the only one to walk away from the fight. Although the rest of the series has never quite managed to equal the brilliance of the first instalment, it has become a perennially popular franchise, spawning to date six features and two television series, as well as the obligatory merchandising, from Misa Kuroi dolls to rugs inscribed with magical symbols.

The first film in the series, Shimiko Satô's *Wizard of Darkness* (*Eko Eko Azarak*, 1995) is a classic of modern Japanese horror, managing to be everything teen horror films aren't supposed to be in the 90s: bloody, controversial, sexually-charged, intelligent and serious. Although conceptually similar to *Buffy the Vampire Slayer* it takes a much grimmer view of teenage existence. Compared with the sexual abuses, classroom rivalry and thinly-veiled atmosphere of violence that characterize school life in *Wizard of Darkness*, Sunnydale High's vampires and demons seem mercifully straightforward. On her first day alone, Misa has to contend with a perverted teacher that likes to 'check' the girls' skirts at the school gate, a predatory lesbian teacher who's having an affair with a student (the pair provide the film's memorably steamy sex scenes) and an occult-obsessed geek who carries a craft-knife- the weapon of choice for delinquent Japanese schoolchildren- and resents Misa because she knows more about witchcraft than he does but isn't a marginalized otaku (nerd) like him. On top of that, there is her real purpose: to find out who at the school is using magic to commit a series of bloody murders. In *Wizard of Darkness* Misa is played by Kimika Yoshino- an attractive, wide-eyed actress with a steely gaze and a cool demeanour- who is, for many fans, the definitive Misa Kuroi. The supporting cast includes a number of genre veterans, including Miho Kanno, who played the title role in Ataru Oikawa's *Tomie* (1999), and Kanori Kodamatsu (*All Night Long*).

    *Wizard of Darkness* opens at a cracking pace, following a woman running frantically through Tokyo's glitzy Shibuya district. We cut between the woman and a group of red-robed figures chanting around a candle-strewn altar. In the centre of the altar is doll made of wood and sackcloth. As the woman runs, the figures complete their chant and raise a knife above the doll; when the knife falls, the woman is hit by a falling girder that splatters her head across the pavement. This sequence sets the tone for the rest of the film: fast-paced and punctuated with graphic brutality. Director Satô- who made her genre debut with British horror flick *Tale of a Vampire* (1993), starring Julian Sands- overcomes her budgetary restrictions by setting the entire film (aside from the opening scene) within the confines of the school, and mainly over the course of one day and night, as thirteen students find themselves trapped inside with all doors and windows magically sealed. The same spell also prevents Misa from using her powers, allowing Satô to save the costly computer-generated special effects for the apocalyptic climax, rather than dissipating them over several smaller scenes. This in turn became a standard feature of the movies that followed, with Misa unable to make full use of her magical powers, either because of other magicians (*Misa the Dark Angel*, 1997) or in the case of the prequel *Birth of the Wizard* (1996) because she hasn't yet acquired them.

    As the group separates to look for ways out, the red-robed figures begin to pick them off, using the voodoo dolls to engineer their bloody deaths: one student is made to fall down a flight of stairs and smash his head on the stone wall, while another leans out of a window only to find it slamming shut, decapitating her in a geyser of blood. A number appears on the blackboard, counting down from thirteen every time one of them dies. Eventually only Misa is left to face the leader of the red-robed villains, who is using the blood sacrifices to summon Lucifer in the hope of being granted incredible powers. The setting is another classroom, with a pentacle drawn in human blood, a naked schoolgirl staked out on a makeshift altar, and an axe-wielding Satanist teacher. Rather than stage the typical wizard vs. wizard duel, Satô gives the flashy special effects to the

# Demons, Monsters and the Living Dead

THE FUTURE IS AT THE MERCY OF THIS LITTLE GIRL

**Birth of the Wizard** *artwork*

villain, who summons the angel Lucifer- an enormous, winged, armour-clad figure- and tries to consume his power, only to find that her fragile human body is torn apart in the process. Misa's magic is more discreet- and considerably more powerful, too- and tempered by her own humane impulses; even after all that's happened, she still tries to warn her enemy about the dangers of summoning Lucifer, but to no avail. The climax of *Wizard of Darkness* is typically cruel: having failed to protect any of the students- including the handsome baseball player who asked her on a date- Misa discovers that the one responsible for the magic and the murders is her only friend, the class representative (Miho Kanno). Evil has been defeated, but Misa is the only one who leaves the school alive.

Satô and Yoshino returned a year later with *Birth of the Wizard* (*Eko Eko Azarak 2*), a prequel that explains how Misa came to understand her powers. Her opponent this time is a century-old witch, formerly imprisoned in her tomb, but now free, thanks to a group of unsuspecting archaeologists. Able to jump from body to body, the witch is looking for the one host that will allow her to utilize her vast destructive power: Misa Kuroi. Unaware of her own magical heritage, Misa is assisted by Saiga, the last survivor of a tribe wiped out by the witch one hundred years ago. Having been kept alive simply to protect Misa in the future, it is his mission to ensure that the witch never gets possession of the girl's body. Although it maintains the same fantasy-horror approach as the previous film, *Birth of the Wizard* is effectively a combination of James Cameron's *The Terminator* (1984) and Jack Sholder's cult classic *The Hidden* (1988). While the high school milieu of *Wizard of Darkness* allowed Satô to exploit the sexual tensions and violent undercurrents, *Birth of the Wizard* has only the fast-paced action and bloody fights to rely upon. Satô's confident handling of the material ensures that the film is never less than entertaining, but it lacks the incisive insights into teenage life that elevated its predecessor above the typical run-of-the-mill teen horror movie.

A third film, *Misa the Dark Angel* (*Eko Eko Azarak 3*), was released in 1998, directed by Katsuhito Ueno and starring Hinako Saeki (*Spiral* and *Uzumaki*) as Misa Kuroi. Essentially a retread of the first film, *Misa the Dark Angel* finds the heroine attending a new school in order to track down the source of a series of supernatural murders. Following up on her only clue, Misa joins the drama club (which includes Hitomi Miwa in her debut role), who are rehearsing a fantasy story for a later performance. Part of the process involves the entire cast moving into an old school building for a few days of intensive rehearsals before the big day. Naturally the group soon find out that they can't leave, and end up being picked off one by one, in *A Nightmare on Elm Street*-influenced fashion that usually reflects their deepest fears. The methods range from dumb- the obsessively clean girl finds herself dumped in bathtub full of slime- to borderline tasteless- one girl finds herself back in her room with her abusive father at the door- or simply derivative, as in the infamous 'tree assault' scene recycled from *The Evil Dead* (1983). Equally ham-fisted are the attempts at psychological insight, including the lengthy shots of Misa running happily through tree-lined meadows- in slow-motion, of course- intended to show how happy she is having finally made some friends. Naturally it's destined to end badly, as Misa is forced to erase the memory of only other girl who survives so she never finds out the secret of her birth. Writer-director Ueno resurrects the lesbian theme of *Wizard of Darkness* and marries it to some fairly pointed comments about classroom rivalry and favouritism, as the drama club's chief manipulates her actors both on and off stage. *Misa the Dark Angel* scores points for drawing its fantasy elements from an unusual source (for a Japanese film, at least); in contrast to Satô's references to Milton and Christian mythology, Ueno's wizards pray homage to Lovecraft's Old Ones, sacrificing their victims to Cthulhu and Yog-Sothoth.

Despite the success of an *Eko Eko Azarak* TV series starring Hinako Saeki- including episodes directed by (amongst others) Ueno and Higuchinsky, later the director of *Uzumaki* (2000)- a fourth instalment didn't appear until 2001. Simply titled *Eko Eko Azarak*, the film takes a noticeably different approach to the earlier movies, replacing the fantasy with a grimly serious exploration of media manipulation and deceit. When a cluster of mutilated corpses are found in a forest, with only one survivor- the nearly catatonic Misa Kuroi (now played by Natsuki Katô)- the media quickly decides that she is a dangerous psychopath. When Misa's friends sneak her out of the hospital, television reporters waste no time in crucifying her and using any underhanded means necessary to prove their point, from subtle manipulation of facts to outright lies. Following on from fiction works like Kim Newman's short story 'The McCarthy Witch Hunt', director Kôsuke Suzuki uses the literal 'witch hunt' to explore metaphorical media witch-hunts.

# Demons, Monsters and the Living Dead

The conceit is clever and unusual, but the execution is heavy-handed and obvious. By the time Suzuki gets around to his blood-drenched climax, Misa has been reduced to the status of a supporting character, pushed aside by the director's need to hammer home his message and spending most of the film in a trance.

Misa returned to television in 2004 with the hit series *Eko Eko Azarak: Me*. Like the first series, the bulk of the episodes were written by Chiaki Konaka (*Marebito*) or Sadayuki Murai (*Perfect Blue*), and directed by Atsushi Shimizu, Iwao Takahashi and Mitsunori Hattori. All three had cut their teeth on the V-cinema *Angel of Darkness* (*Injû Kyôshi*) series in the mid-90s. Based on an anime of the same name, the *Angel of Darkness* films (and the many others like it) are effectively an attempt to fuse the 'magical teenager' formula with the notorious 'tentacle rape' genre epitomized by *Urotsukidôji*. This uniquely Japanese concept arose from stringent censorship regulations forbidding the depiction of genitalia and the pubic region. In order to circumvent these rules, filmmakers began portraying women being 'raped' by monsters with large phallic tentacles. Typically the plot revolves around a teacher- male or female- who becomes possessed by a demon and ends up raping and often eating various schoolgirls. Amounting to little more than soft porn, these films have attracted harsh criticism from western commentators, but it's actually quite difficult to take seriously the sight of a woman squealing in horror as a vacuum cleaner hose wiggles suggestively at her. Among the more flamboyant heroines of this disreputable but occasionally hilarious subgenre is Sister Maria Cruel, the leather-clad, sharpened-crucifix-wielding star of Takao Nakano's *Exorsister* series (called *Uratsukidoji*, in a conscious echo of the anime), played by manga artist Ban Ippongi.

Although overshadowed by the success of *Ring* and *Juon*, the 'magical teenager' has remained a prominent aspect of Japanese fantasy/horror cinema since the mid-90s. Hinako Saeki's appearance in *Misa the Dark Angel* was prefigured by her starring role in the 1997 remake of Nobuhiko Obayashi's *Nerawareta Gakuen*, directed by Atsushi Shimizu and released to capitalize on the success of the first *Eko Eko Azarak* films. Saeki also starred in the subsequent TV series, with episodes directed by Shimizu, Iwao Takahashi and Katsuhito Ueno. Takahashi returned to the field in 2004 with *Mail*, an internet-released series based on the manga by Hôsui Yamazaki. Takamasa Suga and Chiaki Kuriyama star as a 'psychic detective' and his mysterious 19-year-old assistant who specialize in helping earth-bound spirits to pass over to the other world. This reasonably interesting premise is undermined by the need to present the story in 15-minute chunks, a format that is even more restrictive than the usual 26-minute television slot. With little room for character development and the need to present at least one scene of Suga exorcising a ghost per episode, *Mail* quickly becomes formulaic.

The majority of the 'magical teenager' films follow the template established by *Wizard of Darkness* fairly closely, but Ryû Kaneda's *Boogiepop and Others* (*Boogiepop wa Warawanai*, 2000) uses it as the starting point for a surprisingly complex collection of interrelated stories that range from science-fiction to teen romance and all stops in between. Released as a prequel to the equally convoluted anime series *Boogiepop Phantom*, the film's title refers to a mysterious blue-cloaked being seen perched on the roof of various school buildings. Since there have been a number of disappearances in

# Flowers From Hell

the area, the local children mistakenly believe it to be a shinigami- a 'god of death', or grim reaper. The disappearances are in fact the work of a creature called the Manticore, who has taken over the body of a schoolgirl (Ayama Sakai) in order to get close to its victims. Like the Manticore, the being known as 'Boogiepop' has also possessed a student called Tôka (Sayaka Yoshino), but her/its mission is to track down and destroy the creature preying on the schoolchildren. Although the conflict between a schoolgirl with magical powers and her demonically-possessed enemy could have come from any number of other films, writer-director Kaneda's approach to the material prevents it from becoming another *Eko Eko Azarak* clone. *Boogiepop and Others* is actually a lengthy (over two-and-a-half hours long) ensemble piece that builds up the story through several chapters, each focussing on a different character and revealing different elements of the main plot, with the significance of the events taking place only fully understood at the end. As well as the two beings and their hosts, others are drawn into the mystery: Tôka's boyfriend suspects that her changes in mood and personality might be a sign of mental illness; the cold, aloof Masami (Hassei Takano from *Uzumaki*) is in love with the girl possessed by the Manticore and agrees to help her procure more victims; the headstrong Kirima Nagi (Maya Kurosu) is determined to discover the cause of the disappearances, even if it means risking her life.

Kaneda's characters are not two-dimensional clichéd archetypes; in contrast to many teen-oriented films, he is not interested in simply charting their role in the main story, but also in exploring their psychological makeup and personal lives. One girl suffers from survivor's guilt after discovering that she was to be the next victim of a serial killer who was caught before he could accomplish his goal; another finds his unrequited love overwhelming his moral standards. Although this means that the film sacrifices the tension and sense of urgency that drove *Wizard of Darkness*, it also results in realistic, believable characters whose actions are informed by their own emotions and experiences. Like *Battle Royale* (2000), *Boogiepop and Others* benefits from the casting of actors only a few years older than their characters, particularly Asumi Miwa, who delivers an excellent performance as the over-confident, unhappy Naoki. Rather than trying to mimic the dark expressionistic feel of the anime, Kaneda bathes the much of the film in a nostalgic dusky glow that makes even the more unpleasant scenes take on the quality of half-remembered childhood memories. The result is a gentle and often ambiguous movie that lacks the power to scare or horrify, but conjures up a number of memorable, heartfelt images. Many of Kaneda's other films touch on the same teen-fantasy territory: *Video Girl Ai* (*Denei- Shôjo Ai*, 1991), adapted from Kazuhara Keisho's popular manga, features a shy teenager who gets landed with a gorgeous girl who steps out of a soft-core video, while *Full Moon Kiss* (*Mangetsu no Kichizuke*, 1989) is about a group of girls who accidentally summon a demon with a ouija board.

**Boogiepop and Others**

# CHAPTER FOUR

## Psychos and Serial Killers

In Japan, as in many countries, the psycho movie enjoyed great popularity during the 1990s. Part of this was due to the success of several recent Hollywood films, most notably Jonathan Demme's *The Silence of the Lambs* (1991), David Fincher's *Seven* (1995) and Wes Craven's *Scream* (1996). All big hits in Asia, they inspired a wave of domestic reworkings and follow-ups, including psycho thrillers such as the South Korean *Tell Me Something* (1999) and Hong Kong's *Koma* (2004), or supernatural slashers that combined the twin influences of *Scream* and *Ring* (1998), like *Nightmare* (2000). Japan's most significant contribution to the genre was Kiyoshi Kurosawa's *Cure* (1997), a tense detective thriller that takes the western police procedurals as a starting point before heading off in its own cerebral, challenging direction. Although *Cure* had little in common with the mass-produced ghost stories that followed in the wake of *Ring*, the renewed interest in horror that followed Nakata's film also lead to a number of psycho thrillers getting green-lighted in the years afterwards.

The other significant factor in the popularity of the Japanese psycho movie was the rising crime levels within Japan itself. Although the early 1980s were a time of economic growth and prosperity, the later part of the decade saw the levels of violent and apparently motiveless crime rising to all-time highs. Many column inches were devoted to the 'sickness' within Japanese society, in particular the growing number of suicides and violent incidents involving children and young adults, from schoolyard stabbings to teenage serial killers. It is no coincidence that *Cure* and many of the films that followed it featured killers who were to all intents and purposes entirely normal, until some unseen trigger turned them into psychopaths or suicides. However fantastic some of them might be, these films are an attempt in cinematic terms to deal with the increasing violence and crime within a country that had previously enjoyed the reputation of being one of the safest in the world. Other films addressed the issue of delinquent youth, from Kinji Fukasaku's controversial but sympathetic masterpiece *Battle Royale* (2000) to Toshiaki Toyoda's violent, oddly poetic *Blue Spring* (*Aoi Haru*, 2002) and the nihilistic misanthropy of the *All Night Long* series. *Ring* might be the archetypal Japanese horror film of the late 20th century and beyond, but these films- with their themes of youth, violence, friendship and despair - explore the flipside of the post-'bubble economy' generation.

As *Cure* begins, dozens of white-gloved detectives are crowded into a narrow corridor and a single hotel room. The victim, a woman, lies on the bed; she has been bludgeoned to death. Even more unusual is the large 'X' carved into her neck and upper chest. The officer in charge of the case, detective Takabe (Kurosawa regular Kôji Yakusho, who also appeared in *Charisma*, *Séance* and *Pulse*) begins exploring the scene. After opening a maintenance hatch in the corridor, Takabe finds a naked, shivering man huddled inside- the killer apparently, although he was not hiding from the police, but simply hiding. The dead woman is the third victim in this peculiar 'series', all of them found with the distinctive 'X' mutilation. Although they were murdered in different ways, the circumstances were generally the same: all of them were killed by a person they were close to- a husband or wife, business partner, and so on- and in every case the killer made no attempt to flee the scene or to cover up the murder, in effect simply waiting for the police to show up. When apprehended all of them displayed the same confusion and semi-amnesia, showing little memory of the incident and no idea why they were motivated to commit murder. Although there are no links between the separate victims, the method and circumstances are too similar for them to be purely random incidents. As the body count rises, Takabe and police psychologist Sakuma (Tsuyoshi Ujiki) struggle to understand the meaning behind these bizarre murders. It doesn't help that Takabe's private life is also in difficulty, since his wife (Anna Nakagawa) is mentally ill. She is receiving treatment at a nearby hospital, but her condition is growing noticeably worse, making it harder and harder for Takabe to take care of her himself. As he becomes more and more involved

*Artwork for* **Chaos**

in the investigation and his wife's fragile stability declines even further, Takabe is forced to admit defeat on the latter front and check her into the hospital.

In many psycho thrillers the capture of the murderer is the logical climax, but Kurosawa is not particularly concerned with the mechanics of identifying and apprehending the killer. In *Cure* the capture of the murderer- and here it echoes *Seven* to a certain extent- is actually the beginning of the film's main section rather than the end. It does not take Takabe and Sakuma long to realise that the culprit is Mamiya, a rootless drifter played by Masato Hagiwara, star of Yôichi Sai's grim police procedural *MARKS* (*Mâkusu no Yama*, 1995) and Hideo Nakata's convoluted kidnap thriller *Chaos* (2000). However, it is not as easy to figure out how or why Mamiya is inducing people to commit murder, mainly because he talks in nonsensical riddles, never answering questions but constantly repeating his own plaintive inquiries: "Who are you?" "What do you do?" Mamiya's soporific delivery and listless movements make him an unlikely killer, but before long it becomes apparent that he has a very real power that he is content to use for his own inscrutable purposes. Kurosawa never fully explains the source of Mamiya's abilities- like his detective, we are kept largely in the dark- although it seems likely that he came across something in his studies of psychology and hypnotism.

A surprising battle of wills emerges between Takabe and Mamiya, as the detective fights not only to understand the nature of the murders but also to prevent himself falling prey to Mamiya's hypnotic powers. After establishing Takabe as the audience identification figure- a hard working, conscientious husband and policeman- Kurosawa deliberately pushes him into a position where there is only one possible solution. Having studied Mamiya's powers and his crimes, the detective realises that he does not dominate or 'brainwash' his victims, but simply awakens something in them; he addresses that aspect of everyone's personality that is capable of brutal, senseless violence. As a detective, it's part of Takabe's work to find a way to ensure that these crimes do not continue, but even from his cell Mamiya is able to manipulate and control, and it's impossible to engineer a situation where he has no contact with other human beings. In *Seven* Brad Pitt has to make the choice between personal vengeance and official justice, but either way, the killer's career is over. Takabe does not have the luxury of such a choice- either he can stop Mamiya, or the man will stay in an institution and turn everyone he meets into a murderer. The detective takes the only option available to him as both a policeman and a human being, springs the prisoner out of his cell, takes him to an abandoned building and shoots him several times. Takabe has certainly closed the case, but he's also done the one thing that Mamiya has spent half the movie trying to force him to do and tacitly underlined the notion that everyone, under the right circumstances, is capable of murder- including those of us who identified with the harassed detective. If Kurosawa's ending lacks the emotional punch of David Fincher's, it's perhaps because his conclusion is entirely inevitable; *Cure*'s impact derives not from the choices the hero makes, but from the fact that he has absolutely no choice.

Kurosawa's first foray into the psycho genre was 1992's *The Guard from the Underground* (*Jigoku no Keibiin*), a rare Japanese attempt at a slasher movie. Set in a typical office building, the film follows a young art consultant Akiko (Mikako Kuno) in her first few days at a new job. Among her colourful co-workers are the perverted Ren Ôsugi, toadying Tarô Suwa and the fearsome head of Human Resources. The main problem however is the new security guard, a tall, powerfully built man who never says a word but appears to have developed a fixation on Akiko- he even wears a single earring that she dropped. Unknown to Akiko and her co-workers, the new guard is in fact a psychotic sumo wrestler who murdered his girlfriend and her lover. Having escaped punishment once thanks to a mistrial, the police intend to arrest him a second time but are unaware of his current whereabouts. At night the employees find themselves trapped in the building, as the guard begins to kill anyone who stands between him and the object of his obsession, Kurosawa stages his violent murders well, with more than a few echoes of western horror films like John Carpenter's *Halloween* (1978). A long-time fan of cult director Tobe Hooper, Kurosawa used Hooper's *Poltergeist* (1982) as the model for his own *Sweet Home* (1989), and *The Guard from the Underground* takes much of its inspiration from the director's greatest work, *The Texas Chainsaw Massacre* (1974). Although Kurosawa's film is certainly violent, budgetary limitations prevented the use of expensive special effects, which ironically brings the film closer in tone to the surprisingly gore-free *Chainsaw Massacre*. Thanks to his status as a respected lecturer in film studies, Kurosawa was able to recruit crewmembers from his students, including two future directors of note: Shinji Aoyama, director of the excellent *Eureka* (2000)- which also starred Kôji Yakusho- and Makoto Shinozaki, director of *Okaeri* (1995), the film that inspired Kurosawa to include the character of Takabe's mentally ill wife in *Cure*.

Although not as influential as *Ring* or *Juon*, the central aspects of *Cure* were appropriated by a number of subsequent films. Modelled on the standard police procedural, these generally follow the same pattern: a pair of detectives (one older and experienced, one younger and energetic) find themselves swamped by a rising tide of apparently motiveless murders or suicides, committed by otherwise ordinary individuals. The beleaguered heroes eventually determine that some kind of supernatural/ extraterrestrial/subluminal agency is at work, but fail to apprehend the villain or stop the incidents. Like Shûsuke Kaneko's *Crossfire* (2000) they can be read as broad criticisms of the Japanese police and comments on the increasing levels of violent crime, but only Sion Sono's *Suicide Club* (*Jisatsu Circle*, 2002) attempts to examine these themes in any depth. Significantly, most of these films ignore *Cure*'s implication that the capacity for violence and destruction lurks within us all, preferring to portray their victims/murderers as innocents corrupted by an external force.

In Masayuki Ochiai's *Hypnosis* (*Saimin*, 1999) the self-destructive urges manifest themselves in spectacular fashion- one victim runs faster and faster until her bones snap and her heart gives out, while another sets fire to his face- and the victim's final words are always the same: midoru no saru ('green monkey'). The police, assisted by psychiatrist Saga (played by SMAP pop idol Goro Inagaki, also in Ochiai's *Parasite Eve*), suspect that a flamboyant television hypnotist may be the perpetrator. Around the halfway point Ochiai, working from Keisuke Matsuoka's novel, changes focus from the police investigation to Saga's romantic interest in a girl (Miho Kanno) who may or may not be an alien (it's never made entirely clear). Although the influence of *Cure* is obvious, Kanno's character allows for the introduction of a *Ring*-style Vengeful Spirit: she is apparently possessed by a supernatural intelligence that physically manifests itself as a woman in a white dress with long black hair. A few misguided attempts at humour- the phone rings after the detectives have been watching some grainy, black-and-white of the Vengeful Spirit, causing everyone to look at the phone in horror- suggest that Ochiai isn't taking much of this seriously. Despite an incoherent conclusion, the material was tapped for a short-lived TV series, also starring Goro Inagaki, while *Senrigan* ('clairvoyance'), a semi-sequel adapted from another of Matsuoka's novels, appeared in 2000. This time the suicides have turned into suicide bombers, and with the military now involved, the focus is on action rather than horror.

Jôji Iida's *Another Heaven* (2000) is an attempt to graft the director's characteristic sci-fi sensibilities onto the *Cure* framework, although the resulting film is far closer to Jack Sholder's underrated cult favourite *The Hidden* (1988) than to Kurosawa's work. Based on Iida's novel, *Another Heaven* starts out in the usual fashion, with grizzled veteran detective Yoshio Harada and his handsome young partner Yôsuke Eguchi investigating a string of extremely brutal and apparently motiveless murders in which the victim's brains have been cooked and eaten. The killer turns out to be a body-hopping creature from the future visiting 21st century earth to have the kind of fun you can't have in his own time any more. In *Bounce KoGals* (1997) Yukiko Okamoto was charging a high price for her company, but in *Another Heaven* she's graduated to picking up drunken dates in nightclubs, sexually assaulting them and beating them to death. As well as some surprising violence, the film boasts a few nicely ghoulish gags, mostly about the alien's dietary peculiarities. Unfortunately Iida can't resist the same maudlin sentimentality that plagued his *Ring* sequel *Spiral* (1998), and the silly but undeniably entertaining sci-fi theatrics soon give way to humourless, drawn-out attempts at emotional resonance. If nothing else, the first half of *Another Heaven*- dominated by handheld camerawork, flashy MTV-style editing and well-choreographed action scenes- suggests that Iida could make the transition to Hollywood with little difficulty, and might well benefit from the tighter, studio-imposed guidelines. As with *Hypnosis*, it was followed with a TV series (*Another Heaven: Eclipse*) starring several people from the movie and some well-known guest stars, including genre favourite Hinako Saeki.

Yôsuke Eguchi also stars in Toru Matsuura's *Synesthesia* (2005), this time as Shinsuke, a hacker who discovers that someone is using a popular new computer game to dominate people and eventually force them to commit suicide. The title refers to a rare neurological disorder that causes the subject to register sensory stimulus through different sensory organs: colours and shapes can be tasted, for example, or music can be seen. After stumbling across a series of clues, Shinsuke realizes than the killer- like himself- might well suffer from synesthesia, and recruits his best friend (Masanobu Andô from *Battle Royale*) to track down the creator of the computer game. With his long hair, leather trousers and cowboy hat, Eguchi makes for an unlikely computer nerd- much like he did in *Shichinin no Otaku* (1993)- and the rest of the casting is equally slapdash. Ryûhei Matsuda is the blank-faced villain, while Aoi Miyazaki plays another mute, traumatized girl, effectively reprising her role in Aoyama's *Eureka*. The gimmicky inclusion of an exotic medical condition seems to suggest a psychological connection between hero and villain, but the idea is never explored and synesthesia itself turns out to have almost no impact on the film at all.

Both *Hypnosis* and *Another Heaven* feature grotesque death scenes, but they are easily outclassed by Sion Sono's *Suicide Club*, which opens with the jaw-dropping sight of fifty-four giggling schoolgirls cheerfully throwing themselves in front of the Tokyo express as it roars through the station. Scouring the area, the police discover a holdall containing square segments of human skin, all sewn together to form a long strip. The rest of the film follows similar lines: groups of schoolchildren excitedly jump from the roof of their school; a housewife casually slices her hand into little pieces; a mangled car crash victim is discovered to have a small square area of skin missing from his back. On the basis of these images alone, *Suicide Club* manages to be surprising, disturbing and very memorable.

*Suicide Club* is on reasonably safe ground when it's pointing the finger at commercialism and the ludicrous fashion-following tendencies of Japanese youth: many of the suicides are apparently being provoked by a curious pre-teen girl group, but hundreds of other people are topping themselves simply because they don't want to look out of step with the current trends. Unlike many of the other films that followed *Cure*, *Suicide Club* suggests that the roots of this wave of self-destruction are already present in the Japanese psyche, simply waiting for the right trigger. Sono's detectives, played by Ryô Ishibashi (*Audition*) and Masatoshi Nagase (*The Hidden Blade*), represent the establishment: efficient, well meaning, and completely helpless in the face of society's new-found nihilism. Hampered by their insistence that they are dealing with an ordinary crime, they do not understand that there is a much deeper problem manifesting itself. Ishibashi believes his family to be almost perfect- wife and two children greet him as he comes home from work, he smiles indulgently as the kids tease him for not being up-to-date with the latest fashions- until he finds them all dead one day. Having failed to realise that his own family were at risk, he too kills himself.

Unfortunately *Suicide Club* is let down by Sono's failure to assemble these themes into a coherent narrative. The police procedural format gives him plenty of room to explore his deeper concerns, but it also sets us up to look for answers we're never going to get. The actual detective work- the discovery that a cutesy gang of pre-teen pop idols are apparently responsible- is done by a secondary character in the film's final twenty minutes, and even then no explanation is given as to how or why the mass suicides are being caused. While Sono's grotesque humour and impeccable timing ensures that the suicides themselves retain their impact even when not directly relevant to the plot, the same cannot be said for some of the less visceral scenes. At its worst the film descends into parody: a protracted scene in which a ludicrously camp glam-rock star serenades a kidnap victim in a bowling alley is both self-indulgent and ultimately pointless. By the time *Suicide Club* grinds to a halt, the film has become tedious and irritating. Having opened with a truly astonishing scene and littered the first half with surprising violence and intriguing clues. Sono finds himself unable to construct a resolution worthy of the incredible setup.

Although obviously not blockbuster material, *Suicide Club*'s graphic brutality and topical subject matter attracted a great deal of attention, both domestically and internationally, spawning a couple of imitators of its own, *Suicide Manual* (2003) and *Suicide Manual 2: Intermediate Stage* (2003). The films claim to be based upon Wataru Tsurumi's non-fiction book The Suicide Manual, a 'beginner's guide' to the art of killing oneself, providing helpful tips and suggestions for those considering putting an end to it all (just for the record, the author's personal preference is to wander out into the middle of nowhere, sink a few bottles of sake and lie down in a snowdrift). Needless to say, the book became an instant bestseller and provoked a media controversy, being cited as further evidence of the spiritual and psychological crisis gripping Japan as a whole and Japanese youth in particular. The film *Suicide Manual* tries to justify its appropriation of the book's title by

*Artwork for* **Another Heaven**

inserting scenes of Nozomi Andô discussing the act of suicide while walking past metallic 'suicide machines' that are never demonstrated, but in truth it's a gore-free rip-off of *Suicide Club* with elements of *Ring* thrown in. Browbeaten TV cameraman Kenji Mizuhashi- best known as the first victim in Kiyoshi Kuosawa's *Pulse* (*Kairo*, 2001) and the masochistic schoolboy in Akihiko Shiota's *Moonlight Whispers* (*Gekkô no Sasayaki*, 1999)- tries to uncover the reasons behind the recent spate of mass suicides, while struggling with his own self-destructive tendencies. Although this set-up provides a potentially interesting opportunity to examine the suicidal urge from an insider's perspective, director Osamu Fukutani (who also helmed the awful cannibal drama *Last Supper*) ignores this approach in favour of a *Ring*-influenced investigation into a mysterious DVD that the suicides all possess. Fukutani does assemble a solid cast- as well as Mizuhashi, there's Yûko Nakamura (*Hotaru*), Hideo Sakaki (*Versus*) and Chieko Misaka, the female lead from *Versus* and also one of the many suicides in *Suicide Club*- but avoids openly exploiting his gruesome theme, as if unwilling to risk the kind of controversy that accompanied Tsurumi's book, even though that would seem to be the entire point of a film like *Suicide Manual*. If so, he is not alone- the UK distributor of the DVD coyly changed the title to *The Manual*.

Sono's official follow-up- *Suicide Club 2: Noriko's Dinner Table* (*Noriko no Shokutaku*)- appeared in 2005. More plot-and character-driven than its predecessor, Noriko's *Dinner Table* lacks the immediate impact of the first film, with the suicides themselves taking a back seat to Sono's psychological and sociological concerns. Despite his best efforts, the method and motive behind the epidemic remains as inscrutable as before. More interesting is *Strange Circus* (*Kimyô na Sâkasu*, 2005), a hallucinatory psychosexual drama that suggests Sono's talent for controversy extends to more than over-the-top splatter. Masumi Miyazaki stars as Taeko, a writer of torrid erotic novels whose latest work may or may not be an autobiographical account of the twisted relationship with her unpleasant husband (Hiroshi Ôguchi) and her teenage daughter. As her assistant (Issei Ishida) digs into Taeko's background he begins to question how much truth there is in the supposedly fictional novel, and precisely what role Taeko played in the dark secrets of her past. Like *Suicide Club*, *Strange Circus* is a confusing, psychedelic mixture of contradictory or apparently random events, but this time Sono's approach is entirely suited to the film's feverish conflict between reality and fantasy, truth and fiction, giving his calculated weirdness a direct relevance was lacking in *Suicide Club*. Released in a much shorter version in several territories- including the USA- *Strange Circus* is essentially a contemporary update of the ero-gro formula pioneered by the writer Edogawa Rampo, fusing the erotic and the grotesque into a surprisingly powerful mixture that both titillates and unsettles, often at the same time.

In recent years there has been something of an ero-gro revival, with many of the works comfortably straddling the boundaries between erotica, horror and mystery. The four-part anthology *Rampo Noir* (*Rampo Jigoku*, 2005) went directly the author's works for inspiration, while others crafted their own stories with a definite *Rampo* influence. Takashi Miike's *Box*, an episode of the anthology *Three... Extremes* (2004), is perhaps the most sedate film the director has ever produced, but it's no less effective for it. As in *Strange Circus*, the lead character is a writer whose past in rooted in a mystery. Using the minimum amount of cuts, dialogue, music and sound, Miike creates an atmospheric, quietly disturbing tale of death and perversion that ranks as one of the director's most interesting works. He returned to ero-gro territory for *Imprint* (2006), an episode of the first *Masters of Horror* series and Miike's English-language debut. Given his reputation, it's not entirely surprising that the finished work- as well as being far longer than the other episodes- was deemed too extreme to be shown on US TV, although it was broadcast uncut in the United Kingdom and later released on DVD. While it is satisfying to know that Miike did not compromise on the material, that are elements in *Imprint* that would have benefited from alteration. The main barrier is one of language; even though most of the cast are Japanese, the film was shot in English, leaving the cast to muddle through in halting phonetic line readings. Not only does this make it sometimes difficult to under what's being said, it also interrupts the flow on the movie. Given that *Imprint* made its debut on DVD and that Miike's fans are no doubt used to subtitles, it wouldn't have been too much of a stretch for the film to be shot predominantly in Japanese. It doesn't help that Billy Drago, playing a sailor looking for a prostitute he fell in love with many years ago, overacts horribly throughout the film. Although *Imprint* is every bit as brutal and unpleasant as the director's most extreme works, it's also rambling, unfocussed and cursed by poor acting, leaving it far behind his best films.

In the same way that the Manson Family murders and the Jonestown massacre inspired a number of American films, in the wake of the 1995 sarin gas attacks on the Tokyo subway system by the Aum Shinrikyo cult, similar pseudo-religious cult groups appeared in several Japanese movies, both within and outside the horror genre. Jûzô Itami's *Woman of the Police Protection Program* (*Marutai no Onna*, 1997) is the serio-comic tale of a pampered actress who finds her life thrown into turmoil after she witnesses a group of cult members murdering a nosy lawyer- a direct reference to a murder committed by the Aum cult- while Shinji Aoyama's *An Obsession* (*Tsumetai Chi*, 1997) deals with the fall-out from a police raid on a cult stronghold and the gun battle that followed. Although both films are inspired by the Aum Shinrikyo incidents, the directors find different ways of approaching the subject. Itami uses the topicality of the events and the horror they provoked in the Japanese public to give his story an extra measure of relevance, while Aoyama- whose cult is simply part of the backdrop to the main story- seems to suggest that such groups will be one of the defining elements of the era.

The cult leader with the power to compel his brainwashed followers to commit murder has much in common with *Cure*'s blank-faced hypnotist, and there has been a certain amount of overlap between the two themes. Takashi Miike's six-part surrealist horror opus *MPD Psycho* (*Tajû Jinkaku Tantei Saiko- Amamiya Kazuhiko no Kikan*, 2000) explores both concepts through the framework of a police procedural, although the result bears little similarity to the average made-for-TV detective thriller. Films like *Cop* (1987) suggest that their heroes are as unstable as the psychopaths they're trying to catch, and Miike confirms the diagnosis by presenting a detective who suffers from Multiple Personality Disorder and is- in clinical terms at least- every bit as unhinged as the cult leader he's chasing. However, next to the parade of oddballs, freaks and weirdoes that Miike brings to the screen- including a young cop who makes detailed, delicately carved models of each victim (with removable body parts of course) for the morning briefing, a one-eyed snuff movie director and another typically loopy performance from Ren Ôsugi- detective Amamiya comes across as one of the more level-headed characters.

Amamiya and his team are investigating a series of exceptionally gruesome murders and suicides in which the victims/killers all bear a barcode tattoo. This symbol connects them to a missing architect-turned-rock star and cult leader called Lucy Monostone, who has apparently orchestrated the kidnapping of Amamiya's new wife. As Amamiya's investigation progresses Miike draws attention to the darker, more violent side of modern existence: murderous cults, serial killers, snuff movies and *Guinea Pig*-style

# Flowers From Hell

**Evil Dead Trap 2**

faux-snuff, mass teen suicides that prefigure *Suicide Club* (including a key role played by Chiaki Kuriyama). Naturally the police are at least several steps behind the perpetrators, and if Amamiya is the only one who can prevent and even attempt to understand this wave of annihilation, it's because he's not hampered by the rationality and normality that separates the other detectives from the criminals.

Although the level of gore on display would be enough to make most TV channels run for the hills- perhaps the most extreme example involves the murder of several pregnant women in which the foetus has been removed and replaced with a mobile phone belonging to the next victim- *MPD Psycho* would still be difficult viewing without it. Working from the manga by Eiji Ôtsuka, Miike has created a series of ludicrous complexity, peppered throughout with deliberately surreal touches, including multi-coloured snow and digitally crafted artificial backgrounds. Despite the graphic nature of the material, no censorship was incurred; although it is often assumed that the digital mosaics occasionally present on screen were added to comply with censorship guidelines, they were in fact added by Miike himself. Not only do they not conceal anything graphic or unpleasant, but they also suggest that the 'hidden' images are considerably worse than what is on display. Although intended as a sly dig at Japanese censorship, the main result seems to have been irritated protests from Miike fans who fear they have been fobbed off with censored material.

A more realistic view of cults can be found in *EM Embalming* (1999), Shinji Aoyama's first (and only) foray into the horror genre. Reiko Takashima stars as an embalmer ordered to prepare the body of a young man who committed suicide, only to find herself caught up in a sequence of ever-more bizarre events, the least of which is that the deceased may have been murdered. Apparently he was also a follower of a local cult leader, who turns up at the mortuary in person, claiming that what Takashima plans to do to the body- the embalming process- is evil and strictly forbidden under their religion. Their wishes soon become academic, as the corpse's head is stolen shortly afterwards, leaving the embalmer to follow the thread of unlikely clues. Aoyama touches upon a controversial subject: the political power that cult and pseudo-cult groups can muster. The police chief is reluctant to intervene because the cult leader is a major campaign supporter who provides both financial assistance and votes during local elections. Although such instances have declined in the wake of the Aum Shinrikyo incidents, the idea that religious groups can amass political- and even in some cases put forward their own candidates and win seats- remains a contentious issue. In *EM Embalming* the cult is simply a red herring, another twist in a story that also takes in murder, missing twins and black market organ smuggling rings. This complex, over-plotted framework is part of the film's homage to film noir, along with the smoky jazz score, femme fatales (including

Hitomi Miwa), cops in crumpled raincoats and the deliberately artificial rear-projection backgrounds. However, *EM Embalming* is far more convincing as a detective story than as Cronenberg-inspired body horror, and although the many scenes of autopsies, embalming and dismemberments are appropriately squirm-inducing, they can't hide the fact that the films runs out of steam long before the end. It does benefit from another of co-scriptwriter Izô Hashimoto's compelling portrayals of the dark underbelly of urban life, a concept that supports Hashimoto's status as an auteur, appearing in both his own directorial efforts-such as *Teito Taisen* (1989) and *Evil Dead Trap 2: Hideko* (*Shiryô no Wana 2: Hideki*, 1991)- and his script work (including Katsuhiro Ôtomo's seminal *Akira*).

Equally interesting are the references to cult groups that pre-date the Aum Shinrikyo attacks. In *Evil Dead Trap 2: Hideki* fraudulent cults are presented as another seedy, unpleasant aspect of modern Tokyo, along with noisy construction sites, enormous neon advertisements and prostitutes from a variety of other Asian countries. Typical of the disenfranchised losers who seek refuge in such groups is Aki, a lonely, overweight projectionist who turns up to cult meetings to kill time before she heads out in search of prostitutes to butcher. The cult itself is a ludicrous mish-mash of other religions, offering a variety of 'psychic services'- for a reasonable fee, of course. Hashimoto's cult leaders are not the type who exhorts their followers to acts of violence or self-destruction; they're cynical opportunists, guilty of fraud and mercenary exploitation but little else.

The so-called 'self-help gurus' in Sôgo Ishii's *Angel Dust* (1994) are much more dangerous however; they're the kind who dominate every aspect of their followers' lives and face endless lawsuits from distressed families who have lost all contact with relatives once they've joined the cult. Released a year before the Aum Shinrikyo attacks, *Angel Dust* has taken on a sinister significance since then. The plot is oddly prescient: the film deals with a string of murders on the Tokyo subway system, the victims injected with a poison during the hectic rush hour period when commuters are packed in like sardines. Setsuko Suma (Kaho Minami), a psychologist called in to assist the police, discovers that the several of victims were once members of a 'self-help' cult, and initially suspects the group. Digging deeper, she discovers that they also visited Dr. Rei Aku, a psychiatrist whose controversial methods of 'de-programming' cult members are not entirely dissimilar to the brainwashing techniques used by the cults themselves. Dr. Aku is also Suma's old lover, and his penchant for manipulative mind games leads her to think that he might be behind the murders. Unfortunately, as she is drawn back into his orbit, Suma finds herself increasingly unable to separate her identity from those of the victims. Stylistically *Angel Dust* is breathtaking, and Ishii's portraits of the urban Tokyo landscapes, dominated by the ghostly Mount Fuji, are powerful stuff indeed. The problems start to emerge when Ishii attempts to shift focus onto the plot and bring the film to an appropriate resolution. Not only is the much of the material rather derivative, the climax feels forced, and does not sit comfortably with the established characters. *Angel Dust* is not necessarily a bad film, but the conflict between ambiguous art film and plot-driven thriller does cause problems towards the end.

Closely related to the cult-oriented psycho movies is Kazuyoshi Kumakiri's *Kichiku* (*Kichiku Dai Enkai*, 1997), perhaps the most memorable portrait of group's collapse into violence and brutality seen in recent years. *Kichiku* echoes the real-life Asama Lodge incident in 1972, when the police laid siege to a mountain lodge where a group of terrorists belonging to the Japanese Red Army were holed up, along with their hostages. After ten days the police finally gained entry to the lodge, only to discover that half of the terrorists had been killed by their own comrades, apparently as punishment. The events have been documented in three films: Masato Harada's *The Choice of Hercules* (*Totsunyûseyo! Asama Sansô Jiken*, 2002), Banmei Takahashi's *Rain of Light* (*Hikari no Ame*, 2002) and Kôji Wakamatsu's *United Red Army* (2007), as well as Kazuhiko Hasegawa's long-mooted, oft-delayed version of the story. *Kichiku* documents the spectacular implosion of a left-wing student group, set at some unspecified point during the 1970s. Like the Asama Lodge revolutionaries, the group is dominated by a woman, Masami (Sumiko Mikami), who uses her sexual favours to ensure the loyalty and compliance of the others. Their real leader is Aizawa (Yûji Hashimoto), but he is currently languishing in prison, leaving the day to day running of the group to his girlfriend. Their numbers are bolstered by the presence of Fujihara (Kentarô Ogiso), a cellmate of Aizawa's, sent to 'check on' his comrades. Unfortunately soon afterwards they hear that their leader has committed suicide in prison, and the cracks in their fragile alliance begin to show. Desperate to maintain her position, Masami uses violence to strengthen her hold, selecting one of them as a scapegoat and ordering him to be viciously beaten. From there the situation rapidly spirals out of control, leading to orgy of mutilation, murder and bloody retribution.

*Kichiku*'s abrupt shift into ultraviolence is as harrowing as it is unexpected. Although Kumakiri's low-budget special effects are not as convincing as they could be, the director's unflinching approach and careful staging heighten their impact. Since *Kichiku* is in many respects intended to emulate student films from the 1970s- shaky camerawork, erratic sound and so forth- the old-fashioned practical special effects seem quite appropriate. While *Kichiku*'s graphic brutality has garnered the film an appreciative reception from splatter movie aficionados, Kumakiri cannot be accused of simply pandering to gore fans. The first half is entirely free of gore, used primarily to set up the group dynamic and establish characters, something that 'pure' splatter movies- like the *Guinea Pig* films- rarely bother to do. When Kumakiri does unleash the violence, it's intended to compliment a strong plot, rather than using the plot as a means to introduce the splatter scenes.

The most memorable Japanese psychos of recent years have been predominantly female. The first of note is *Evil Dead Trap 2*'s Aki, whose colourful, murderous insanity is the logical reflection of the garish, sleazy city she dwells in. Aki's only friend is an oversexed television journalist who regales her lonely, unattractive companion with endless stories about her conquests but becomes insanely jealous when one boyfriend (Shirô Sano) conceives a passion for Aki instead. Unlike many female movie psychos who are driven to murder because of masculine exploitation and abuse, Aki takes her rage out on women. Her victims are prostitutes who flaunt their sexuality in a way that she will never be able to, while her main opponent is the supposed friend who cannot accept Aki as competition.

Almost the polar opposite of Aki is Asami Yamasaki, the antagonist of Takashi

Miike's *Audition* (2000). Played by former Benetton model Eihi Shiina (who also appeared in Shinji Aoyama's *Eureka* and Ryûhei Kitamura's *Skyhigh*), Asami is everything Aki is not- slender, pretty, demure and cultured. However, she too is dangerously unhinged, although her victim this time is mild-mannered widower Aoyami, played perfectly by former rock star Ryô Ishibashi (*The Grudge*). Since his wife died seven years ago, film producer Aoyama has remained single, living alone with his now-teenaged son (played by Tetsu Sawaki, who starred in *Boogiepop and Others*, and also appeared with Eihi Shiina in Akihiko Shiota's *Harmful Insect*). At the prompting of his son, Aoyama decides it is time for him to find a new wife. Since he is unsure how to proceed, a friend and business colleague (Jun Kunimura) conceives of a way in which Aoyama can find his ideal bride: cultured, demure, intelligent- the perfect Japanese woman, in fact. The pair decide to set up a fake audition, advertising for candidates to star in a phoney forthcoming TV drama, with Aoyama selecting his favourite applicants and inviting them to come for an audition. At this point *Audition* seems to be a fairly average romantic comedy-drama, built around the typically ludicrous methods the heroes of such movies use to secure a girlfriend. This impression is supported by the snappy editing and quirky music that accompanies the audition scenes, and in one of Aoyama's secretaries Miike even provides a character who seems to be another favourite of romantic comedies: the friend of the hero who has always been in love with him, but he's too blind to see the little attempts she makes at getting his attention. Aoyama does find the woman he's after, a former ballet dancer called Asami Yamasaki, and is so taken with her that he ignores all the other girls that attend the audition. A few days later he arranges to meet with Asami, telling her that because of funding problems it doesn't look like the 'project' is going to get made at all. She accepts his apology and the pair begin meeting regularly.

Although Miike's handling of these scenes is competent, it's almost restrained to the point of absurdity; by the time *Audition* is halfway through, most viewers will be wondering when, if at all, anything is going to happen. However, Miike quietly introduces elements that **Audition**

hint at a much darker reality behind the trappings of a romantic comedy. After spending the night with Aoyama at a holiday resort, Asami disappears. His friends have already warned him

against becoming involving with the girl- her details did not check out, and the individual she gave as a reference disappeared mysteriously some time ago- but Aoyama is distraught and determined to track her down. While following up every detail about her life that Asami ever told him, Aoyama makes a number of alarming discoveries, including an elderly, wheelchair-bound man who may have tortured and abused Asami when she was younger. He also finds out that the owner of the bar where Asami claimed to work was brutally murdered, and several other body parts- not belonging to the bar owner- were found at the scene.

Here *Audition* appears to be following in the footsteps of Adrian Lyne's *Fatal Attraction* (1987) or Clint Eastwood's *Play Misty For Me* (1971), with Asami revealed as a disturbed, and possibly murderous, individual who will undoubtedly attempt to kill her unfortunate lover. However, while this is essentially correct, anyone expecting a sanctimonious, reassuring, *Fatal Attraction*-style conclusion is likely to be surprised, to say the least. In the film's final half-hour Miike unleashes a nightmarish torrent of torture and mutilation that includes some of the most sadistic images ever filmed. It may even be a literal nightmare, since it isn't clear how much of it is taking place in Aoyama's own tormented psyche. Some have suggested that the entire sequence is a hallucination, conjured up by Aoyama's guilt over his 'infidelity' to his deceased wife. Either way, he ends up drugged and paralysed on the floor of his apartment, while Asami- clad in a PVC apron and full-length gloves- inserts acupuncture needles into his face before cutting his foot off with cheesewire. These scenes are presented with an obvious glee that almost dares the viewer to continue watching (not all of the critics who saw *Audition* at festivals took up the challenge, and headed for the exits instead).

Based on a novel by Ryû Murakami and scripted by Daisuke Tengan (the son of respected director Shôhei Imamura), *Audition* has unsurprisingly become one of the most controversial and heavily discussed Japanese films of recent years. Attempts have been made to read the film as a critique of patriarchal Japanese society, but in truth Miike's main intention is simply to shock the audience. This might not be a particularly noble ambition, and it's certainly something the director has tried before, but *Audition* is the most effective and successful attempt, partly because he goes to such great lengths to set up the story and provide the essential contrast between the banal and almost tedious first half and the gruelling final act. Even if Miike does value style over substance, with *Audition* he has created a truly unforgettable film and a landmark of exploitation cinema.

If *Audition* is Miike's take on *Fatal Attraction*, Takashi Ishii's *Freezer* (2000) is the Japanese version of the rape-and-revenge drama, a staple of 70s exploitation cinema. Although the plot has much in common with films such as Meir Zarchi's abhorrent *I Spit On Your Grave* (1978), *Freezer* is not voyeuristic trash that delights in portraying violent multiple rape, but a disturbing and surprisingly sympathetic account of one woman's descent into madness. Former model Harumi Inoue plays Chihiro, a young woman with a handsome fiancé and a promising career ahead of her. But she also has a dark secret: five years before, Chihiro was raped by three men, who also videotaped the assault. Afraid of the public shame that might result, she did not report the incident to the police and the rapists went unpunished. Late at night one of them shows up at her apartment and forces his way inside, claiming that the other two are on the way and bringing the tape, to show her new fiancé. Still afraid to go to the police and unable to count on the help of her cowardly boyfriend, Chihiro decides that her only option is kill the three rapists. Unlike the heroine of *I Spit On Your Grave*, Chihiro is not motivated by a desire for bloody revenge upon the men who raped her. Instead she is an increasingly fragile woman trying to preserve what little stability and sanity she has left, unable to turn to her loved ones for help and desperate to avoid the shame that attaches itself to even the victims of rape. After the blood-soaked climax of Sam Peckinpah's *Straw Dogs* (1971), uptight mathematician Dustin Hoffman walks away from the carnage with a grin on his face, suggesting that he has achieved a degree of self-realisation through violence, but Chihiro finds no such liberation. Her murders are the final step in her decline into insanity, with the film's title referring to the large freezers that she stores the bodies in.

*Freezer* aspires to be more than exploitation, and succeeds, but Katsuya Matsumura's *Kirei: The Terror of Beauty* (*Kirei?*, 2004) revels in all its sleazy glory. Although less sadistic and cruel than his notorious *All Night Long* series, *Kirei* is still infused with Matsumura's profound contempt for humanity. This time he leaves the teenagers behind and focuses on Yoko Noguchi, a twenty-something plastic surgeon played by Asuka Kurosawa (*A Snake of June*). With her own clinic and a staff of beautiful nurses- every one of whom is an advert for her skill with the scalpel- as well as a handsome fiancé, Yoko would seem to be the epitome of a successful young woman. Until Yoshie (Yukiko Okamoto from *Bounce KoGals*) shows up at her clinic demanding extensive plastic surgery, that is. Although the patient is quite obviously mentally unstable, Yoko accepts the challenge of turning Yoshie into an attractive woman. However, once the surgery is completed, Yoshie will not leave her alone, apparently blaming Yoko for the fact that her new face has not brought her the new happiness it was supposed to.

Matsumura (who co-scripted with Rusher Ikeda) spends the opening scenes establishing Yoko as a character to be desired for her beauty and envied for her success, fiancé and material wealth. He takes a voyeuristic delight in lingering over the lovely Asuka Kurosawa's naked body while she takes a shower and stages a lengthy sex scene that's shot entirely from her lover's point of view, so that all you see is the topless Kurosawa. Yoshie on the other hand is physically unattractive, socially inept and mentally unstable, to be pitied or reviled rather than lusted after. Any serious point Matsumura might be trying to make about society's ludicrous worship of beauty is undermined by frequent nude scenes aimed precisely at the people he is apparently condemning. Equally suspect is his portrayal of Yoshie, in which he equates her physical ugliness with her psychological instability: "When a man is ugly, maybe he does ugly things" says Boris Karloff in the 1935 film *The Raven*, and Matsumura doesn't seem to have moved on much from there. *Kirei* does boast some memorable and shocking scenes, but like the *All Night Long* films the main effect of all this misanthropic nihilism- in Matsumura's world view, everyone is worthless- is to leave the viewer with an urge to shower.

*Evil Dead Trap 2* and *Kirei* portray conflicts between unattractive, marginalized women and those that successfully pander to male fantasies- prostitutes, a sexy reporter, a plastic surgeon whose work transforms women into more pleasing shapes. This theme also

TARTAN ASIA EXTREME

**"A FILM THAT HURTS, DISTURBS AND OVERWHELMS"**
Fantasia

FREEZER

**"A WALK ON THE VIOLENT AND NASTY SIDE"**
Japan Times

18

DVD
VIDEO

*Sleeve art for* **Freezer**

features in Satoshi Kon's anime classic *Perfect Blue* (1998), one of the best Japanese psycho-thrillers of recent years, live-action or otherwise. Loosely based on Yoshikazu Takeuchi's novel, *Perfect Blue* covers some of the same ground as *Evil Dead Trap 2* and *Kirei*, but Kon is a much better director. Unlike Hashimoto, Kon puts his graphic gore and delirious fantasy sequences to work in the service of a strong plot, and avoids Matsumura's heavy-handed moralizing and repellent nihilism. Kon's interest lies first and foremost in the psychological state of his heroine, rather than the seamy world of pop idols, celebrity stalkers, 'glamour' photography and gory movies that forms the backdrop to his story. Mima Kirigoe is a struggling pop idol who decides to move into acting to kick-start her career, taking a small part in TV serial killer drama. As Mima struggles to come to terms with the demands of her new career- including a graphic rape scene- others are equally unhappy with the situation: her agent Rumi, a former pop idol herself, thinks Mima is being exploited, while a hulking obsessive fan known only by his internet handle 'Mr. Me-Mania' resents her new sexually-charged image. Someone has created a website that claims to be written by Mima herself, describing with surprising accuracy her innermost thoughts and her dissatisfaction with the work. The line between fantasy and reality begins to blur as Mima finds herself tormented by a phantom that looks just like her, dressed in her old pop idol costume; furthermore, the writer of the TV show is brutally murdered, and Mima suspects that like her character, she may have developed a second personality to exact her revenge.

# Psychos and Serial Killers

As *Perfect Blue* progresses, Kon deliberately undermines the viewer's grasp on the plot, portraying scenes from the show as reality before pulling back to reveal the events being viewed on a television screen, and then blending the two together, making it impossible to establish where one ends and the other begins. For the climax Kon cuts between Mima's increasingly hallucinatory perspective and 'reality', allowing us to see her shape-shifting, tutu-clad doppelganger as it really is: Rumi, her middle-aged agent, clad in her own pop idol costume. Having used Mima to relive her own failed ambition of becoming a pop idol, Rumi is now punishing anyone who tarnishes her proxy's squeaky-clean image: the screenwriter who wrote the rape scene, a photographer who coaxed her into posing nude for a sexy magazine spread, and finally Mima herself, whose own ambitions now conflict with Rumi's. Despite a surprisingly twee final sequence, *Perfect Blue* is a masterpiece that confirms anime's status as an art form to rival live-action cinema. Kon sets his horrors in a realistic, recognizable world that would easily make the transition to live-action, saving the limitless possibilities of animation for Mima's psychological terrors and delusions. This approach enhances both sides of the equation, with the 'normal' scenes gaining impact from their realistic portrayal, and the fantasy sequences benefiting from the contrast with them. Having crafted a first-rate psycho-thriller, Kon also includes a few pointed comments about less original efforts: the TV show is a derivative *Silence of the Lambs* rip-off, relying on the clichéd 'multiple personality' trope that *Perfect Blue* toys with before discarding in the climax.

In 2002 a live-action remake was released, directed by noted pinku filmmaker Toshiki Satô. Whereas Satoshi Kon and scriptwriter Sadayuki Murai (*The Dimension Travelers*) discarded most of the source novel except for the three elements the producers wanted kept- the pop idol, the stalker, and the horror theme- Satô's film is largely faithful to Takeuchi's work. The resulting film, titled *Perfect Blue: Yume Nara Samete* ('*perfect blue: if it's a dream, wake up*'), is substantially different to the anime version in content, tone and quality. This time Mima is an aspiring model whose pushy manager decides that should release a single and start marketing herself as a pop idol. Aside from dealing with the difficulties of breaking into the music business- she can't sing, for one thing- there are other problems emerging. In a convenience store Mima meets a young man who claims to be her biggest fan. Although she's initially flattered, she soon becomes suspicious of the amount he knows about her. His obsession with her dates back to long before her professional career began: he's been following her (in both senses of the word) since they were in middle school together. Equally disturbing is her manager's wife; she bitterly resenting sharing her husband with attractive young girls and drops heavy hints about the 'disappearance' of the last client he got too attached to. A real-life stalker was the basis for Ataru Oikawa's *Tokyo Psycho* (*Tôkyô Densetsu: Ugomeku Machi no Kyôki*, 2005), as Sachiko Kokubo attends a school reunion only to find that one of the less savoury aspects of her past life has returned too.

Kazuya Konaka's *Lady Poison* (1994) pits a female serial killer (Tomoko Mayumi, from Kiyoshi Kurosawa's *Door III*) against an obsessive and equally deranged writer. Yuka Miroku is a classy photographer who enjoys murdering men she picks up in bars and posting pictures of the mutilated victims on the Internet, where they are seen by Sogabe

# Flowers From Hell

(Ren Ôsugi, in one of his best psycho performances), a successful writer and violent sadist. After discovering Yuka's identity, Sogabe decides to kidnap her for a marathon torture session. Scripted by Chiaki Konaka, *Lady Poison* is a defiantly sleazy film in which the only remotely normal characters are the two ineffectual detectives pursuing the killer. Far more attention is lavished on the attractive and demure Yuka, however. Sogabe's violent and perverted tendencies are made explicit from the start, as he gropes, fondles and hits a PVC-clad girl, leering over her with his video camera. In contrast, Konaka deliberately avoids showing Yuka slicing up her victims, who are typically middle-aged men with a few kinky sexual preferences. After being kidnapped by Sogabe, Yuka becomes the traditional woman-in-peril. Eventually she is rescued by her young stalker, who ends up with the hero role, if only because he's more presentable and less twitchy than Sogabe.

Equally tongue-in-cheek is Toshiharu Ikeda's *The Man Behind the Scissors* (*Hasami Otoko*, 2004), the director's first venture into psycho territory since his landmark '80s splatter movie *Evil Dead Trap* (*Shiryô no Wana*, 1988). This time Ikeda foregoes the graphic blood and gore entirely, in favour of complex plotting and black humour. Kumiko Asô (*Ring 0, Pulse*) stars as Chinatsu, a shy and put-upon OL ('office lady') who falls in love with the tall and handsome Yasunaga, played by former heartthrob Etsushi Toyokawa, star of Jôji Iida's *Night Head*. Unfortunately Yasunaga is also a psychopath, and Chinatsu quickly finds herself helping to locate and procure his schoolgirl victims. Their murderous career becomes considerably more complicated when they track down their next prospective victim only to discover that someone has already killed her, leaving behind Yasunaga's 'signature', a pair of scissors thrust into the neck. To make matters worse, the police show up moments later, and suddenly the pair are witnesses to the latest crime of the infamous 'Scissor Man'. With the police dangerously close, Chinatsu and Yasunaga try to find out who wants to frame them for the one murder they didn't commit. By providing a steady supply of plot twists and surprising revelations, all shot through with a streak of dark humour, Ikeda creates an oddly compelling pastiche of police procedurals and serial killer thrillers.

Delinquent youths became a regular feature of psycho movies in the early '90s, not long after they started to grab headlines. One of the first to exploit this particular social concern was documentary filmmaker Katsuya Matsumura, director of *Kirei*. Matsumura's *All Night Long*, the first in a series of five thematically linked films, appeared in 1992, having secured a theatrical release (the distributors withdrew the film soon afterwards, and the rest of the series was released direct-to-video). All of them follow a similar story arc- an otaku character is transformed from nerdy recluse into violent psychopath- that the director uses to underline his central message: everyone is capable of violence. The first film is undoubtedly the most accessible, thanks to the comparatively small amount of graphic brutality, although it is still a grim and nihilistic work. After witnessing the murder of a schoolgirl, three students find themselves drawn together by their shared trauma. When one of their number is beaten up and his would-be girlfriend raped, the trio take it upon themselves to punish the gang responsible, leading to a bloodbath that leaves two of the friends dead and the third- the otaku- murderously unhinged. *All Night Long: Atrocity* followed in 1994, with the levels of cruelty significantly increased. Shinichi, a bespectacled manga enthusiast, becomes involved with a gang lead by an effeminate rich-kid psychopath. Initially he is the gang's victim, but soon their homosexual leader takes a fancy to the boy and invites him to hang out with them. All the time trying to seduce him, the psychopathic gang leader pulls Shinichi into an orgy of brutality and violence, including mutilation, rape and murder. Eventually the boy snaps, slaughtering everyone left alive- both perpetrators and victims. The third film, *All Night Long: The Final Chapter* (1996), is just grim and unpleasant as its predecessor. Kikuo is a typically nerdy individual who works as a cleaner at a 'love hotel', where rooms are rented by the hour. During the course of his work, Kikuo sifts through the rubbish he finds in the rooms, assembling information about the guests from the trash they leave behind. This obsession with the detritus of human life reaches breaking point when his co-workers rape one of the guests at the hotel. After apparently rescuing her, Kikuo takes her to his home; but rather than freeing her, he chains her to the bed and begins torturing her for more information about her life.

*The Final Chapter* states the central theme of the *All Night Long* series succinctly: human existence is defined by the garbage we leave behind, because human beings are garbage. Unfortunately, Matsumura's argument is not particularly convincing, mainly because he's not actually interested in portraying the nihilism of human existence; instead the *All Night Long* films read like a conservative view of everything that's wrong with Japanese youth today. His characters are stereotypical in every way, and could easily have come straight from the pages of a tabloid newspaper: otaku whose reclusive lifestyle masks obsessive and psychopathic tendencies, bored rich kids in search of increasingly brutal thrills, sex-obsessed schoolgirls. Rather than attempting to understand his characters or present some kind of explanation for their behaviour, Matsumura is simply exploiting and confirming the paranoid fears of the older generation. The fact that each of the first three films ends with the surviving otaku grinning to himself suggests that Matsumura is influenced by Sam Peckinpah's *Straw Dogs*, in which Dustin Hoffman does the same thing after slaughtering the yokel thugs who are victimising his family, but there the similarities end. Hoffman's explosive violence possesses an emotional impact because we see his internal struggles and watch him being pushed closer and closer to the edge until he is left with no other choice than to fight back. For Matsumura's characters violence is not a last resort, but an inevitable result. There is no moral conflict, since most of them give in to their murderous impulses quite voluntarily. Hoffman grins because he's found a degree of liberation through his actions; in *All Night Long* the survivors grin because they're having fun.

As well as the five *All Night Long* films (the final two have not yet been released outside of Japan) Matsumura also directed *Joshikô Konkuriito Dume Satsujin Jiken* (1995), an account of a notorious true-life 1988 murder case, in which a gang of youths kidnapped, tortured and murdered a girl before dumping her body in a oil drum and covering it with concrete. Equally unpleasant was the revelation that during the girl's six-week captivity, not one person reported the incident to the police- including the dozens of friends who passed through the house, and the gang leader's mother and father, who were at home the whole time. Needless to say, the story fits comfortably into Matsumura's oeuvre, providing plenty of support for his usual sensationalist portrayals of juvenile delinquency. A more fictionalised version of the story can be found in *Alice Sanctuary* (1995), the debut feature from documentary filmmaker Takaaki Watanabe, and in Hiromu Nakamura's *Concrete* (2004).

Few teen-oriented movies have created the same impact as Kinji Fukasaku's *Battle Royale* (2000), perhaps the most well-known Japanese film of the past twenty years. Although it has yet to receive a legitimate release in a number of countries- including the USA- *Battle Royale* has amassed a massive worldwide following. Based on Kôshun Takami's equally controversial bestseller and scripted by the director's son Kenta, Fukasaku's film has been condemned as a sick fantasy and praised as one of the most powerful movies of recent years; it's certainly one of the most memorable. As the final film from one of Japan's most popular filmmakers- who was 70 at the time- *Battle Royale* is a fitting end to a long, influential and highly successful career. The premise itself is simple: forty-two high school students are drugged and transported to a deserted island, provided with a variety of weapons and told that only one person will be allowed to leave. The time limit is three days- if there is more than one survivor left at that point, then all of them be killed. This is achieved by detonating a metal collar all of the 'contestants' wear. As well as allowing those in charge of the game to monitor the location and progress of each contestant, it also contains an explosive charge that can be detonated by remote control. Each time a student dies, their name and number is displayed on screen, informing us how many 'players' are left.

Needless to say, the resulting film is very violent indeed, and intentionally so, since Fukasaku was determined that *Battle Royale* should be realistically bloody, as opposed to the fantastic, ludicrous violence of Hollywood action movies. In another contrast with Hollywood-style filmmaking, the cast are all the same age as their characters, which lends another degree of realism to the film. Despite the graphic blood and gore, Fukasaku is primarily interested in the different ways the characters respond to their new situation. Some refuse to fight and commit suicide immediately, while others quickly decide to play the game 'for real' and begin slaughtering their classmates. One of the most dangerous characters is the silent psychopath (Masanobu Andô from Shinya Tsukamoto's *Nightmare Detective*) who signed up for just for fun. Old schoolyard squabbles are dredged up and used to justify murder, something that might cause viewers to reflect and question exactly how their own classmates would have behaved. The central characters are basketball player Shûya (Tatsuya Fujiwara from *Death Note*) and the pretty Noriko (Aki Maeda), two friends who decide to look for a way off the island without fighting their classmates, but find themselves drawn into the conflict out of self-defence. Other memorable characters include Mitsuko (Kô Shibasaki from *One Missed Call*), who uses her sexuality to lure her male victims closer so she can cut their throats with a scythe, and the athletic Chigusa, played by Chiaki Kuriyama. After seeing her in *Battle Royale*, Quentin Tarantino hired Kuriyama to play the ball-and-chain-wielding schoolgirl assassin Go Go Yubari in the first *Kill Bill* film. Top billing goes to 'Beat' Takeshi Kitano, the iconic Japanese actor (and director, writer, comedian, talk show host, etc), who delivers a fine performance as the hated Kitano, former schoolteacher and overseer of this year's game.

Despite the knee-deep blood and gore, *Battle Royale* is not simply an excuse to show kids in school uniform slaughtering each other, and neither is it a childish attempt to generate controversy. Partially informed by the director's own experiences as a child working in a munitions factory during the Second World War-where he

*Sleeve art for* **Battle Royale**

and his co-workers were forced to compete for space in the bunker when the air raids started- *Battle Royale* is infused by Fukasaku's staunch anti-establishment sympathies and his empathy for younger generations struggling against the policies and attitudes of their predecessors, a sentiment that teenagers of any culture and background can associate with. It is to the director's credit that he manages to embrace a positive message amongst all the bloodshed and chaos: love and friendship are worth fighting for, and it is possible to triumph against the odds without compromising your principles.

Although ultimately not enough to lessen the impact of the film, *Battle Royale* does come up against a few plot difficulties. First of all, no explanation is given about the game's origins and purpose- why was the game instituted in the first place? Takami's novel is set in alternate history, where the Japanese empire survived the Second World War. The country is still ruled by the same military dictatorship, who use the game as a means to inspire mistrust and competition between its citizens, in the same way that other dictatorships reward those who report their friends' and neighbours' to the authorities. But no mention of this is made in the film, and aside from inflated unemployment figures, it is assumed that the world of *Battle Royale* is effectively the same as ours. It seems likely that this was deliberate, since Fukasaku was aiming for as much realism as possible, and setting the film in an alternate fantasy world might have distanced the audience from the events on screen; however, it does create a little confusion. Even more problematic is the film's prologue, showing the arrival of the previous year's winner, a blood-spattered little girl, grinning maniacally and clutching a teddy bear. Despite the media frenzy that greets her arrival, none of the students seem to have any idea what has happened to them. It is later confirmed that the *Battle Royale* game has been running for a number of years, so why are they confused? In Fukasaku's defence, the novel does not provide an entirely satisfactory explanation for this either.

Thanks in part to the intense media coverage that had surrounded the film, *Battle Royale* was a strong commercial success. Having been forced to defend his film to a committee of politicians- some of whom backed down when the director pointed out that censoring movies was something the wartime government had been fond of- and struggle against the R-15 rating imposed by Eirin, the Japanese ratings board, Fukasaku's hard work had paid off, and Toei had a major hit on their hands. Soon afterwards an extended version of the film was released, with the Eirin-imposed cuts reinstated and a handful of extra scenes inserted, including a lengthy basketball match and background details about certain characters. The reinstated violence is fair enough, but the extra scenes are largely superfluous and have a negative impact on the film's pacing. Needless to say, Toei

**Battle Royale**

were keen to see if they could repeat their success, and shooting of *Battle Royale II- Requiem* (*Battle Royale II- Chinkonka*) began in January 2003, with the director's son Kenta once again providing the script. Having made the decision to forego treatment for cancer in order to work on this film, the 72-year-old Fukasaku collapsed after a single day's shooting, dying in hospital soon afterwards. Production continued, with Kenta Fukasaku stepping in as director.

*Battle Royale II- Requiem* picks up three years after the first film, with Shûya now leading an armed rebellion against the Japanese government. In an effort to stop him, the powers-that-be have amended the rules of the *Battle Royale* game- rather than fighting each other, the new contestants will be armed with military weapons and sent to deal with Shûya's rebels. Haunted by the deaths of his comrades, Shûya has become jaded and paralyzed, unable to commit fully to the war and unwilling to withdraw completely. His rhetoric now sounds hollow- he claims to be acting in

**Battle Royale**

defence of the abused and exploited youth of Japan, but by the time he realizes who he's fighting there are only a dozen or so contestants left. The morality of the situation has become increasingly muddled. Shûya and his supporters are terrorists, and while their cause has some justice to it, it's hard to rationalize the innocent lives that have been lost in their attacks on urban areas. The Japanese government develops even harsher methods to deal with society's problems, still unable to understand their children, let alone control them. For the first hour, Battle Royale II is compelling viewing indeed, its sharp observations about guerrilla warfare supported by intense and violent action sequences. The standout scene is a bloody beachhead invasion that paints an accurate picture of the horrors of war, with dozens of lives lost amid the chaos of blood, smoke and noise. These scenes are generally handled well by the film's youthful cast, which includes Ai Maeda, sister of Aki Maeda, playing schoolteacher Kitano's daughter.

**Battle Royale**

# Flowers From Hell

**Battle Royale**

Fukasaku regular and Japanese action legend Sonny Chiba also appears in a brief cameo.

Unfortunately not all of the film is up to the same standard. In place of 'Beat' Takeshi Kitano we now have V-cinema favourite Riki Takeuchi, giving a ludicrous, scenery-chewing performance completely at odds with Kitano's chuckling menace. Even more damaging are the lengthy monologues delivered by the morose Shûya, bringing the film to a complete halt while he spouts repellent sentimentality over real-life footage of giggling Afghan children. Worst of all is the streak of pointless anti-Americanism that runs through much of *Battle Royale II*. The opening scene includes footage of an office block being destroyed in an obvious parallel with the 9/11 attacks, while the stated motive behind the Japanese government's brutal actions is to forestall the American invasion that will follow should they not be able to deal with their domestic terrorism. As part of his motivational speech, Takeuchi provides a list of countries that have been subjected to American military 'intervention'. Not only is this rather ridiculous, but it also undermines the film. Sending schoolchildren up against terrorists just about works as an attempt to make the enemy kill those people it claims to be fighting for, but as part of a last-ditch attempt to prevent an invasion of your own country it's just pathetic. These motives also let the Japanese government off the hook; they're no longer killing children for sport, but desperately trying to save their nation from the real enemy- the Americans. Whereas *Battle Royale* dealt with very personal considerations that most people can at least understand, by addressing real political concerns- anchored to a specific time period- *Battle Royale II* loses a great deal of the impact of its predecessor, and winds up looking more like a confused critique of the Bush administration than a successor to a milestone of contemporary cinema.

REINCARNATION

DER FLUCH
THE GRUDGE 2

www.grudge2-film.de

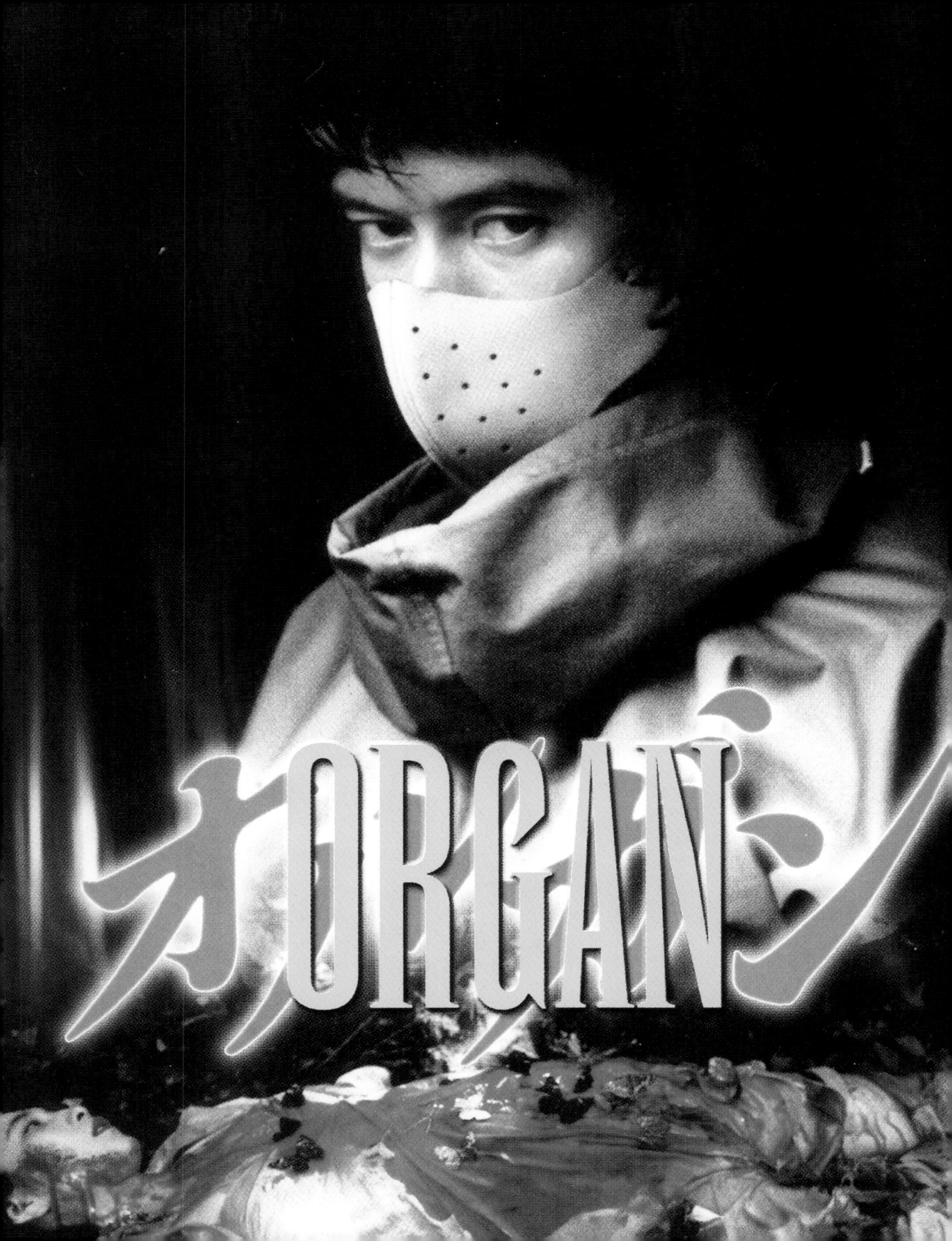
ORGAN

entrail
of a
beautiful
Woman

Ichi the Killer

Organ

Juon The Grudge

AMBER
**TAMBLYN**

JENNIFER
**BEALS**

SARAH
**ROEMER**

SARAH MICHELLE
**GELLAR**

# DER FLUCH
## THE GRUDGE

CONSTANTIN FILM SAM RAIMI PRÄSENTIEREN EINE GHOST HOUSE PICTURES PRODUKTION EINEN FILM VON TAKASHI SHIMIZU „DER FLUCH - THE GRUDGE 2" AMBER TAMBLYN ARIELLE KEBBEL
JENNIFER BEALS EDISON CHEN SARAH ROEMER UND SARAH MICHELLE GELLAR MUSIK CHRISTOPHER YOUNG SCHNITT JEFF BETANCOURT SZENENBILD IWAO SAITO
KAMERA KATSUMI YANAGIJIMA MICHAEL KIRK DREW CREVELLO SHINTARO SHIMOSAWA HERSTELLUNGSLEITUNG BILL BANNERMAN AUSFÜHRENDE PRODUZENTEN JOE DRAKE NATHAN KAHANE ROY LEE DOUG DAVISON
BASIEREND AUF JU-ON: THE GRUDGE" BUCH UND REGIE TAKASHI SHIMIZU DREHBUCH STEPHEN SUSCO PRODUZENTEN SAM RAIMI ROB TAPERT TAKA ICHISE REGIE TAKASHI SHIMIZU

GHOST HOUSE

www.grudge2.film.de

Constantin Film

## KIMURA YOSHINO    KUROSAWA YU    ISHIGURO KEN

สาวผี
แผ่นดินไหว

瞳 創 忍 殊
千 幸生 陽子 範 悠 理陶 満
尋 瞭子 子 ナ 子

# ISOLA

RATING 70

**JAPANESE/HORROR**

199
บาท

Freezer

Spirit of Vengeance

A Horie Kei Film

# SPIRIT OF VENGEANCE
## SHIBUYA KAIDAN

You may not be able to withstand
this horrific incident....

嬰
魂

Dark Water

The Ring 2

One Missed Call

DER FLUCH
THE GRUDGE **2**
www.grudge2.film.de

parasite EVE

It's Not A Virus...
IT'S EVOLUTION.

# 猛鬼勿語

One Missed Call 2
着信アリ2

日本賣座究極恐怖猛片
穿針引血 縫製「咀」咒

日本人氣女星 瀬戶朝香

新晉美少女 Mimula

Juon: The Grudge 2

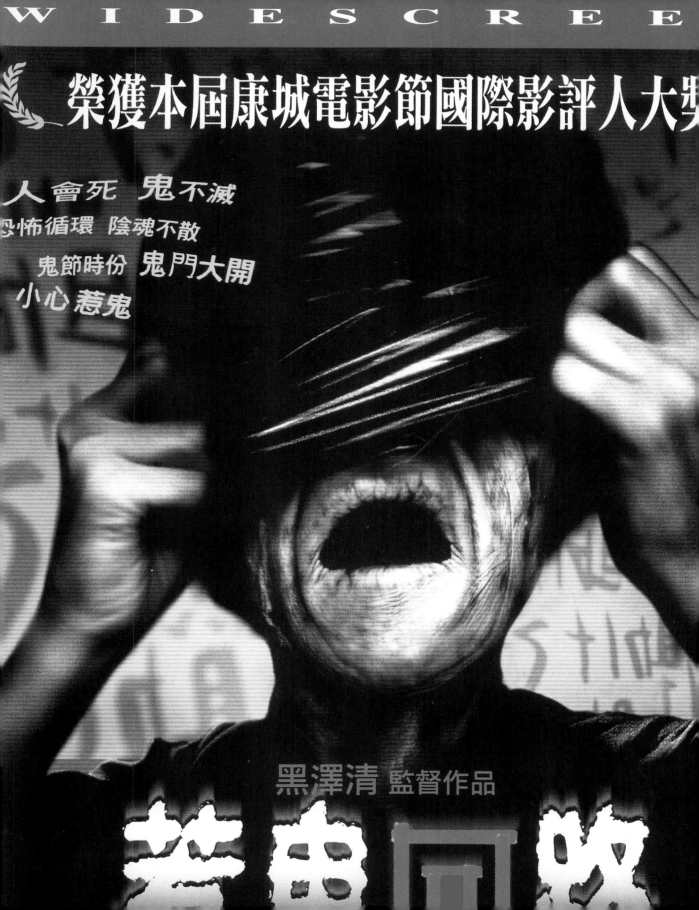

Dark Water

Audition

DER FLUCH
THE GRUDGE **2**
www.grudge2.film.de

*Constantin Film*

Ichi the Killer

ANAMORPHIC · WIDESCREEN

SHUSUKE KANEKO'S

PYROKINESIS

Chaos

Top: Juon: The Grudge 2
Bottom: Juon: The Grudge

One Missed Call

Top: The Ring 2
Left: One Missed Call

TURN

2:16

《大逃殺》 柴崎幸 全新鬼異體驗
《夢想飛行 GOOD LUCK!!》

最恐怖手機留言...凶靈準時索命！

# 鬼來電
着信アリ
ONE MISSED CALL

Top Left: Ghost Train
Top Right: Juon: The Grudge 2
Bottom Left: Juon: The Grudge 2
Bottom Right: Junk

Middle: Ichi the Killer
Right: The Ring
Middle Right: The Ring
tom Left: The Ring

DER FLUCH
THE GRUDGE 2
www.grudge2.film.de

Constantin Film

Constantin Film

ブギーポップは笑わない

Boogiepop
and
Others

entrails
of a
Virgin

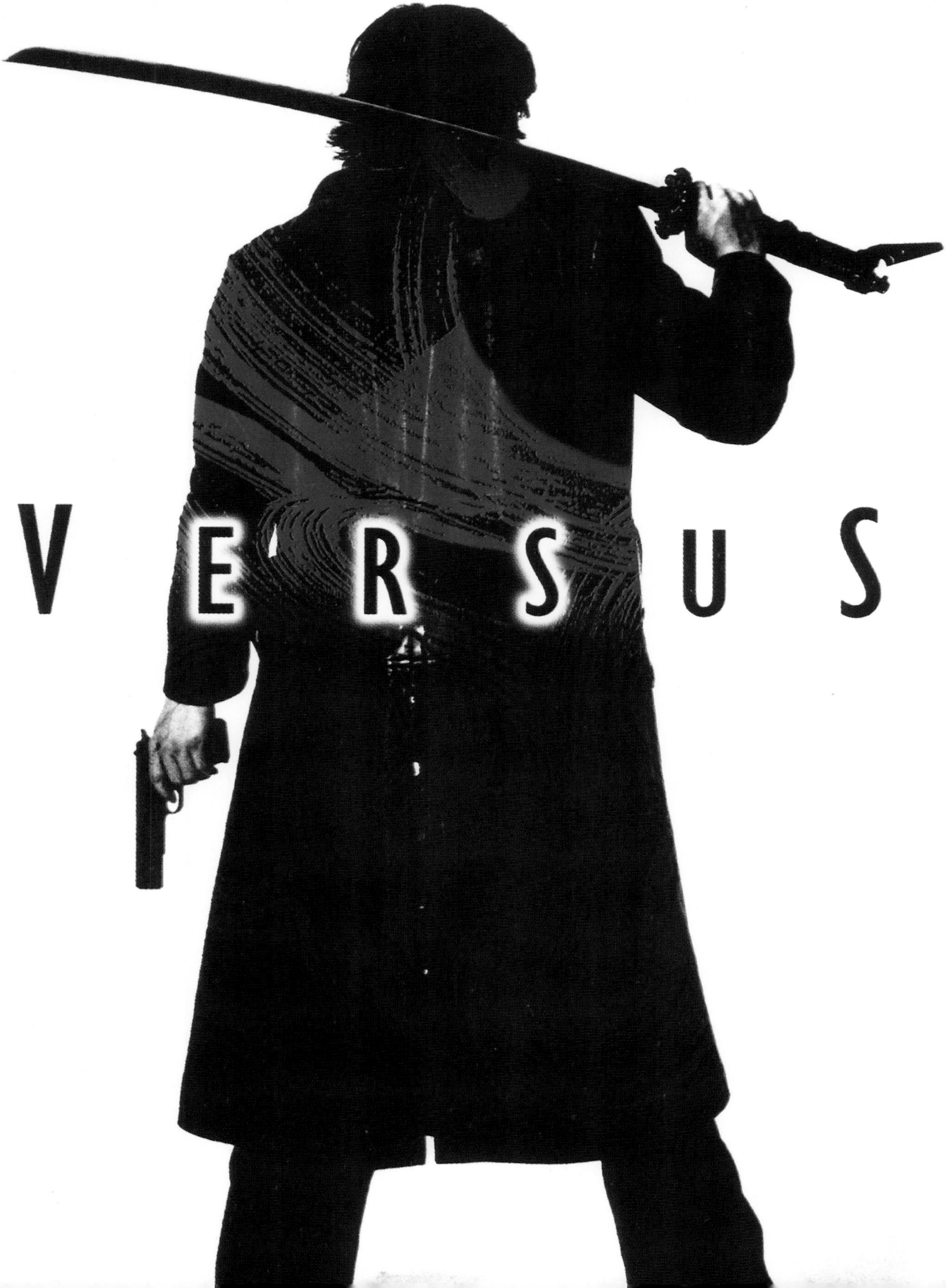
VERSUS

The Golden Raven
24th Brussels International Festival Of Fantastic Film
榮獲
2005全球最大奇幻影展「布魯塞爾影展」
最佳恐怖片金獎

稀

FROM THE DIRECTOR OF THE CULT HIT **THE GRUDGE**
**A FILM BY TAKASHI SHIMIZU**
《咒怨》導演清水崇挑戰驚嚇極限

MAREBITO

STARRING CULT DIRECTOR **SHINYA TSUKAMOTO**
《鐵男》怪雞導演塚本晉也飾演

# EKO EKO AZARAK
# WIZARD OF DARKNES

# CHAPTER FIVE
## Hideo Nakata and the Ring Cycle

The film opens with scenes of a black, turbulent sea, accompanied by a low metallic wailing, and a few brief cast and crew credits. A moment later, the black water and white surf dissolve into a close-up of a television, and we see two girls, Masami and Tomoko, deep in conversation. Their talk focuses on the two favourite topics of horror movie teenagers everywhere: scary stories and the opposite sex. Masami (Hitomi Satô, from *Bounce KoGals*, 1997) has heard a story about a video tape that kills you if you watch it; but such stories are fairly common, and she thinks it's more funny than terrifying. Tomoko (Yûko Takeuchi) is less amused, however; in a quiet voice she tells her friend that she's seen that tape, at a sleepover with a few friends last week. The room goes momentarily quiet; then Tomoko begins to laugh. The joke worked, but more importantly, Tomoko has spent the night with her boyfriend, and Masami wants to hear all about it.

Of course, it's not a joke, and Tomoko really did watch the tape. Their conversation is the first red herring; the second arrives soon afterwards, when the phone rings- ear-piercingly loud at first, but getting quieter with every ring- just like it does in Masami's story. But it's only Tomoko's parents saying they'll be home late, and the pair laugh at their own foolishness. Moments later the television switches on by itself, but there's no get-out clause this time; something really is happening. As Tomoko prepares a drink for herself and Masami, a scratching noise sounds behind her, causing her to pause and shudder briefly, before slowly looking back over her shoulder. A freeze-frame and a sudden shift into negative black and white, and it's all over.

So begins Hideo Nakata's *Ring*, released on 31st January 1998 and arguably the most famous Japanese horror film ever made. Based on the best-selling novel by Kôji Suzuki and scripted by Hiroshi Takahashi, *Ring* is the film credited with kick-starting the Japanese horror boom of the late 90s, although initially it's perhaps not obvious why. After all, it's not an entirely original opening- countless teen-oriented horror films from all over the world have begun with teenagers trying to freak each other out with scary stories or swapping notes on their latest conquests- but it's certainly an effective one. In the space of that one brief scene, Nakata manages to introduce all the key plot elements- the urban legend, the video tape, the dynamics of the curse itself- and pique the viewer's curiosity about what exactly happens to the victims, in preparation for the devastating climax. Perhaps most significantly, it underlines the importance of sound, whether it's the sudden, piercing phone ring, or the eerie insect-like skittering that Tomoko hears just before her death.

The next scene begins with yet more children recounting the legend of the noroi no bideo ('cursed video'), but this time it's for the purposes of an article being written by journalist and single mother Reiko Asakawa (Nanako Matsushima). Initially it seems to be just another in a long series of human interest stories about ghostly sightings and supernatural curses. However, a remark made by one of the children suggests that there might be a link between this seemingly commonplace urban legend and the mysterious death of Reiko's niece Tomoko. Digging a little deeper, she discovers that Tomoko and three friends recently spent the night in a holiday cabin, where they supposedly found an unmarked tape. Like Tomoko, the other three are also dead, having passed away on the same night, seven days after their sleepover.

Initially spurred on by her concern over the death of her niece, Reiko's journalistic curiosity soon takes over. Finding the tape turns out to be relatively easy- after the holiday cabin was cleaned it was put with all the rental tapes available at the reception desk- but after viewing it she begins to realize that her casual scepticism might have been misplaced. Although there's nothing on the tape that is overtly frightening- it runs for less than a minute and consists of a series of grainy, black & white images, including several writhing figures, a page of jumbled newsprint and a single close-up of someone's eye- there seems little doubt that it isn't entirely normal. Worse still, just after Reiko finishes watching the tape, the phone rings, but there's no voice on the line, just a thin metallic screeching. Finally convinced that she has stumbled onto something out of her league, Reiko turns to Ryûji (Hiroyuki Sanada), her coolly intellectual ex-husband and the father of her six-year-old son Yôichi (Rikiya Ôtaka), for help. A lecturer in mathematics, Ryûji's response is predictably disdainful, especially when the phone doesn't ring after he watches the tape. Even so, he asks Reiko to make him a copy and agrees to investigate further.

As a former protégé of 'Sonny' Chiba and perhaps the most famous member of Chiba's 'Japan Action Club' (a training ground for future action movie stars), Hiroyuki Sanada might not seem to be the obvious choice to play the role of a cerebral university lecturer. Before appearing in *Ring*, he spent much of the 80s and early 90s playing heroic men of action in films like Kinji Fukasaku's *Samurai Reincarnation* (*Makai Tensei*, 1982) and *Legend of Eight Samurai* (*Satomi Hakkenden*, 1983), including a brief- and fruitless-attempt to market him to western audiences as 'Henry Sanada'. In recent years however his profile has increased outside Japan, earning him roles in Danny Boyle's *Sunshine* (2007) and the Jackie Chan/Chris Tucker comedy *Rush Hour 3* (2007). It was Sanada who recommended Nanako Matsushima for the role of Reiko, having appeared with her in a TV drama. Originally a model, Matsushima has remained predominantly a television actress despite the success of Ring and its sequel.

Like a number of the western ghost stories that inspired it- *The Amityville Horror* (1979), for example- *Ring* relies partly upon parallel plot developments. Typically the parallel plot involves a young child being terrorized or influenced by a supernatural force while his or her parents are distracted by other events. Having watched the video Reiko is too busy trying to track down its origins to notice that her son is behaving oddly. During Tomoko's funeral Yôichi is drawn upstairs by a fleeting vision of his cousin, only to be found staring at the television in a scene reminiscent of Tobe Hooper's *Poltergeist* (1982). Later on he tells his mother that Tomoko watched the cursed video. It's clear that the now-malevolent Tomoko has been telling him about the tape, but Reiko fails to realise the danger Yôichi is in. When she finally finds him watching it, she asks him why he would do that. His answer is simple: "Tomoko told me to."

For the first half of his running time, *Ring* is an exceptionally well-constructed exercise in suspense. It's not a particularly fast-moving one- the film doesn't pick up any real pace until Yôichi watches the tape- and it certainly doesn't provide anything more than the bare minimum of plot details; in fact, there's barely an extraneous word in the entire movie (for example, Reiko's status as Ryûji's ex-wife is only mentioned once, and their marriage and divorce not at all). Instead Nakata uses these early scenes to establish the atmosphere of unease that permeates throughout the film. His greatest asset is Kenji Kawai's highly unusual score. Already well-known for his collaborations with Mamoru Oshii- he has scored most of the director's best work, including the *Patlabor* films, *Avalon* (2001) and both *Ghost in the Shell* (*Kôkaku Kidôtai*) movies- Kawai provides a truly exceptional soundtrack for *Ring*, composed of a variety of industrial crashes, chimes and poundings, all manipulated and digitally processed beyond recognition. Although it is occasionally melodic and simple, at its most extreme it seems to resemble the frenzied buzzing of a swarm of bees, filtered through the avant-garde experimentations of German proto-industrial pioneers Einstürzende Neubaten. Its closest cousin would probably be Tobe Hooper and Wayne Bell's clanging, discordant score for *The Texas Chain Saw Massacre* (1974), but for the most part Kawai's work stands in a class of its own.

Ably assisted by the score, Nakata winds up the tension by carefully hinting at the horrors to come. Some of these omens are relatively straightforward- the multiple shots of television sets, for example, or the many ringing telephones- while others only become significant later on, like the sight of Tomoko silently running upstairs and the disembodied sound of Tomoko and Yôichi playing together. By providing the date before Reiko has actually seen the tape (a trick also used in *The Amityville Horror*), Nakata warns the audience that something will be happening soon, so we're one step ahead of the heroine. When Reiko spots the video tape in the resort reception room, he cuts to a fuzzy close-up shot that resembles the images on the tape itself. Those images turn out to be similarly prophetic: the brief shot of a figure in white foreshadows the glimpse of Sadako that Reiko sees reflected in the surface of the television, while echoes of the page of jumbled characters- including the word 'eruption'- can be seen in the newspaper articles that she and Ryûji search through. Most significant of course is the 'pointing figure' that alerts Reiko to the danger her son is facing and to the eventual solution to the curse. In these portent-heavy surroundings, even the 'cigarette burns' on the film itself seem to resemble the view from the bottom of the well, the very first image on the tape. It wouldn't be the first time the cigarette burns have been included as an aspect of the film itself (cf. Shûsuke Kaneko's *My Soul Is Slashed*, 1991).

After Yôichi has watched the tape, Reiko and Ryûji's quest assumes a greater urgency and the film steps up a few gears. Together they visit Oshima, the birthplace of the woman seen on the tape. By tracking down the last of her relatives, they are able to uncover the tragic story that lies behind the curse. After accurately predicting the eruption of a local volcano, Shizuko Yamamura became a media celebrity, thanks in part to avaricious relatives who sought to profit from her abilities. Her unique gifts also attracted the attention of Dr. Ikuma, a professor from Tokyo, who (after beginning a somewhat scandalous affair with Shizuko) arranged a demonstration for a group of journalists with the intention of proving the validity of his research into psychic phenomena. But the demonstration did not go as planned; the assembled journalists were quick to label Shizuko a fraud and the professor a gullible fool. As if that were not bad enough, one of the sceptical reporters died during the demonstration, with the blame falling on Shizuko's daughter Sadako, who possessed similar powers to her mother. Ostracized by her family and hounded by the media, Shizuko threw herself into the volcano that had made her famous, leaving her daughter in the care of Dr. Ikuma. With his marriage and his career in tatters, the professor took his anger out on the girl by killing her and dumping the body down a well near his house. Years later, Dr. Ikuma's land became a holiday resort, and a cabin was built over the well where the child's remains were entombed. The video tape is the physical manifestation of Sadako's post-mortem fury.

With the answer finally within their grasp, Reiko and Ryûji rush back to the mainland and head for the holiday resort. Curiously, this is also where the problems start. Having uncovered the origins of the tape and proposed a solution, Ring threatens to become something a lot less interesting: yet another well made but derivative ghost story. Much of the final third is tense and exciting, but it's not noticeably different to similar scenes in many other films, the most obvious being one being Peter Medak's *The Changeling* (1980). Reiko and Ryûji manage to find the well and uncover Sadako's remains, with just a few minutes left. But it seems to work; Reiko's deadline comes and goes, and all would seem to be well. There's even a suggestion that the pair might have some kind of future together. Mercifully, it doesn't end there, and Nakata has a final devastating trick up his sleeve. For an audience weaned on Hollywood heroes who never put a foot wrong, it's unthinkable that the plucky heroine and her intellectual partner could have misjudged so much, from the required course of action to the depth of Sadako's rage. But they have.

The most significant change Nakata and Takahashi make to the traditional kaidan-Japanese ghost story- concerns the temperament of the ghost itself. Like the antagonists of *Stir of Echoes* (1999) and the awful *What Lies Beneath* (2000), Japanese ghosts were usually hurt and bitter rather than malevolent, and basically reasonable: once justice is satisfied and the religious obligations (proper burial and so forth) taken care of, the unquiet spirit is laid to rest. Sadako Yamamura is not so easily pacified, however. Unlike the majority of her predecessors, she is not entirely the innocent we are lead to believe she is, having already used her powers to kill. By painting Sadako and her mother as the victims of fickle media types, money-grabbing relatives and superstitious islanders, Nakata is able to provoke sympathy for the child, neatly distracting us from the uncomfortable truth behind the suspicions and the wholly indiscriminate nature of her revenge. It helps of course that many recent Hollywood hauntings had been built around personable spirits like Patrick Swayze (*Ghost*, 1990) or Richard Dreyfuss (*Always*, 1989) - decent men taken before their time but ultimately pragmatic about their new situation. In a time when ghosts, like witches, are simply 'misunderstood', it comes as something of a welcome surprise to encounter a creature that wasn't particularly pleasant in life and is still thirsting for vengeance (not justice) thirty years down the line.

In short, Sadako is not at all concerned about the fate of her mortal remains, or about bringing those responsible to justice. She has only one aim: everyone is to be made to suffer, using the video tape as the instrument of her vengeance. There is a way to escape the curse, but it's a lot less pleasant than digging up a few bones. The only solution is to make a copy within seven days and show it to someone else, who then has a week to do the same- ad infinitum. Reiko has survived, not because she found Sadako's remains, but

because she showed Ryûji the tape and thus shifted her fate onto him. Just as the television became the tool to find her victims, it becomes the means to take them too. Back at his apartment, Ryûji is finishing his work- he has another, less momentous deadline to meet- when the TV switches on. The picture it shows is the final image from the tape, the broken well. But this time, something is crawling out: a female figure clad in a white dress with her long, wet hair hanging down over her face. Her movements are jerky and sinister, more like the artificial movements of a bunraku puppet than a human being. When she reaches the screen, she leans through it as though it were no more solid than water and places her hands on the floor of the room, pulling herself through with broken and bloody fingernails. Ryûji recoils in terror, and realizing that they have failed to stop the curse, reaches for the telephone to call Reiko. He doesn't make it, but the phone rings on its own, as

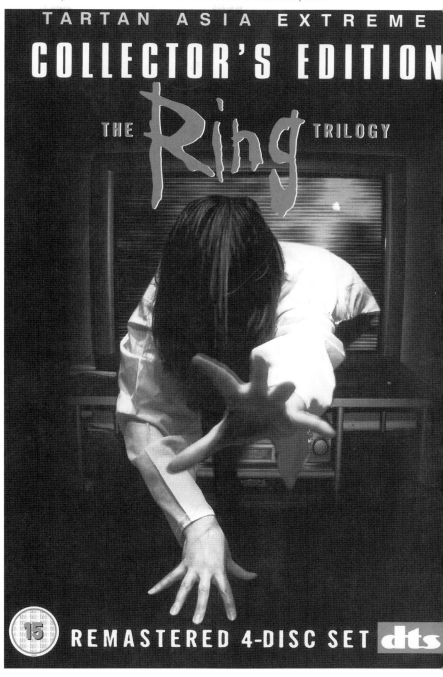

Reiko tries to reach her ex-husband and confirm that everything is all right. Desperately trying to crawl away from the lank-haired finger, Ryûji glances back just long enough to meet the gaze of the single grotesque eyeball visible beneath the long black hair. A freeze-frame and a sudden shift into negative black and white, and it's all over.

But not quite- Nakata has a final twitch for the audience. Reiko is still in the same predicament- how can she save Yôichi? She knows the solution, but who would risk their life for that of her son? With Ryûji gone, she has but one choice. The final shot of the film sees Reiko and her son driving off under a gathering storm, after phoning to ask for her father's help.

On paper *Ring* would seem to be little different from countless other Japanese horror films. For about a decade Japanese filmmakers had been reworking and updating the traditional kaidan for modern audiences, and combining it with elements drawn from the latest western horror films. Suzuki's novel had been a steady seller since its publication in 1991 (a sequel, *Spiral*, had been published in 1994) and had already been adapted into a popular made-for-TV version (1995's *Ringu: Kanzenban*), so it seems likely that Japanese audiences would be familiar with its central concepts. Urban legends had been a significant factor in horror movies since the success of the *Haunted School* (*Gakkô no Kaidan*) franchise and the many 'Hanako-san' movies in the early 90s. *Ring*'s blending of science and technology with the supernatural was not entirely new either. Many of the numerous direct-to-video horror anthologies released in the 90s featured technological items as conduits for the supernatural; Nakata himself had filmed a segment of *Gakkô no Kaidan F* based around a ghostly video a year before *Ring* was released. Obvious literary forebears include Hideaki Sena's *Parasite Eve* (also published by Kadokawa) which bears a number of similarities to Suzuki's follow-up Spiral and was later adapted into a feature film itself. Another possible influence is Seikô Ito's novel No Life King, the story of a mysterious computer game that kills those who die within the game. Like Ring's videotape, the game is being passed around by students who copying it for their friends. Only a special rare version carries the curse- but of course that is the version everybody wants, even after rumours about the dangers of playing the game. *No Life King* was filmed in 1989 by Jun Ichikawa, although it has not yet seen a western release.

Like John Carpenter's *Halloween* (1978), *Ring* does not attempt to carve out new territory or push the boundaries of the genre (although it did end up doing so, ironically). Its aims are much humbler: it seeks only to scare. Nakata establishes a thoroughly ordinary setting- a world characterised by suburban homes, holiday resorts, baseball games and VCRs- and allows his irrational supernatural terrors to subvert these trappings of a comfortable existence and use them against their owners. Unlike the irony-laden, slyly self-referential horror films that followed in the wake of Wes Craven's *Scream* (1996), *Ring* does not use humour to offset the darkness of the story or remove the sharper edges, thus allowing the audience to experience the full grim horror of the final act. Those final scenes, among the most effective seen in any genre film of the 90s, ensure that *Ring* will stick firmly in the memory of the viewer, especially after it seemed likely that the film would take the same path as so many other ghost stories. Rather than simply providing an easy opportunity for a sequel, the conclusion raises the possibility that there is no escape from the curse, whether you manage to evade death or not. Like a self-sustaining virus that seeks not to kill but to thrive and multiply through contagion, Sadako's curse has developed a near-perfect survival mechanism that relies on the endless curiosity of human beings. The concept is strong enough to survive even a lesser treatment, but

# Hideo Nakata and the Ring Cycle

Nakata's careful direction and steady pacing, coupled with solid performances and Kenji Kawai's innovative score, ensure that the material reaches its full potential.

Perhaps the most significant difference between *Ring* and the films that preceded it is the presence of a memorable, identifiable villain. Although she's only on screen for a few minutes, Sadako's emergence from the television is so unexpected and genuinely creepy that it quickly becomes the film's strongest scene. This is not entirely unprecedented; Pinhead from Clive Barker's *Hellraiser* (1986) has only a few moments' screen time (and is never named), but his appearance is so distinctive that audiences quickly made him the focus of their attention. In Sadako Japanese audiences were finally given their first true horror icon (*Godzilla* doesn't count), a character with the appearance of a traditional yûrei (ghost) but with the wordless, alien invincibility of a Michael Myers. Although she was based on the character from Suzuki's novel, Sadako's appearance (as well as her unique method of entrance) was created by Nakata and Takahashi. In *Ringu: Kanzenban* Sadako manifests herself as an entirely human (not to mention naked) woman. One of the many reasons that *Ring*'s first sequel *Spiral* (*Rasen*, 1998) proved unpopular was because it removed the grotesque figure of Nakata's film in favour of yet another disappointingly human figure, this time played by genre favourite Hinako Saeki (*Misa the Dark Angel*). While the other two have been largely forgotten, Nakata's version has become a media icon, resulting in a wealth of tie-in products (including Sadako dolls), not to mention the seemingly endless stream of imitations. In the years following two more icons have emerged, each different but both owing a certain amount to Sadako Yamamura: the eternally youthful and endlessly reborn Tomie, created by manga artist Junji Itô and living on through eight features (so far); and Kayako, whose twisted and bloody form has reached audiences across the globe through Takashi Shimizu's lucrative *Juon/The Grudge* franchise.

Like many directors of his generation, Hideo Nakata found early employment with Nikkatsu, working as an assistant director on pinku eiga, Although Nikkatsu's days were numbered and their output dwindling, by the mid-eighties they were still one of the few places where young would-be directors could gain some experience. Nakata ended up working closely with Masaru Konuma, one of Nikkatsu's most important figures throughout much of the 70s and early 80s, and director of the pinku classics *Hana to Hebi* and *Ikenie Fujin* (both 1974). He stayed with the company until the their collapse in 1993, and would later recall his experiences in the documentary *Sadistic And Masochistic* (2001), a tribute to Konuma, Interestingly, as well as Hideo Nakata, Konuma's other associates from the period included Kazuo Komizu (a.k.a. Gaira) and Toshiharu Ikeda, two of the most significant figures of the Japanese 'splatter scene' of the 1980s. Nakata's relationship with the pink film industry did not end with Nikkatsu's closure, and he later directed *Jokyôshi Nikki: Kinjirareta Sei* ('*female teacher's diary: forbidden sex*') for Toei in 1995, and *(Ura) Tôsatsu Nama Dô* ('*behind the scenes: hidden camera pick-up trick*') for the revived Nikkatsu a year later. The young director's first brush with the horror genre came in 1992, when he made his debut with three episodes of the TV series *Hontô ni Atta Kawai Hanashi* ('*true fear stories*'). The first, *Shiryô no Taki* ('*waterfall of the evil dead*'), pits a widower against an evil water spirit; *Norowareta Ningyô* ('*cursed doll*'), features

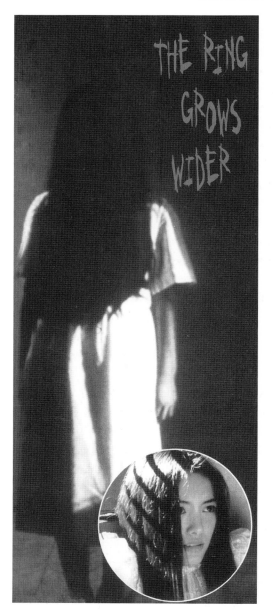

**Ring O**

a young girl who must stop a malevolent doll from harming her family; the third and best story, *Yûrei no Sumu Ryokan* ('*the inn where the ghost lives*'), involves three teenage girls who spend the night at a haunted hotel. Each one is a little over twenty minutes long.

Unsurprisingly these three episodes resurfaced after the success of *Ring*[1], with all the requisite hyperbole (the Hong Kong editions describe the director as a 'god'), but it's unlikely any of Nakata's new fans would find these bland made-for-TV horrors particularly impressive. There are a handful of stylistic and thematic touches that are reminiscent of his later work, most significantly the white-clad female ghosts that appear in the first and third stories, but for the most part they're typical Japanese TV horrors of the period: toothless, cheap and derivative. Nakata handles the job with the necessary professionalism, but he is hampered by the second-hand material and minimal budget. By far the most interesting aspect is the fact that two of the three episodes (the first and third) were written by Hiroshi Takahashi, who would later provide the script for Nakata's breakthrough film *Ring*, turning both director and writer into major figures in the Japanese horror boom. The second episode was written by Akihito Shiota, who would later direct a number of acclaimed films, including *Moonlight Whispers* (*Gekkô no Sasayaki*, 1999) and *Gips* (2000).

Aside from his pinku eiga work, Nakata's first feature film was 1996's *Ghost Actress* (*Joyûrei*). Also scripted by Hiroshi Takahashi, *Ghost Actress* was released through Takenori Sentô's J-Movie Wars project. With only a limited budget, Nakata decided to base the story around a film shoot, allowing him to cut costs by shooting within the studio buildings. The story centres on Murai (Yûrei Yanagi), a young director trying to finish his debut feature, a psychological drama set in the closing days of World War II. As well as dealing with a number of cast-related issues- one of his leads is having problems with her agent, while the other is a young and inexperienced actress- Murai must also contend with the unusual events that are plaguing his shoot. While he's reviewing the day's work, he comes across some old footage mixed in with his. Murai recognizes it as an extract from a film he saw in his childhood, but according to studio records the movie was never broadcast. Work was stopped when the star committed suicide on set- the same set that Murai is using- and the film was never finished. With the footage he's shot now useless, Murai's film is behind schedule. However, worse is to come, and production grinds to a halt when the young lead falls to her death from the rigging above the set. The police assume it was an accident, but Murai is sure he saw someone else up there: a figure in white with long dark hair.

The similarities between *Ghost Actress* and Nakata's later works are immediately apparent. Both films feature the same ghostly figure with long black hair and white robes (in *Ghost Actress* she has the black teeth of the 'Yuki Onna' from *Kwaidan*); at first she is obscured by shadows or reflective surfaces, only appearing fully in the final act. Like *Ring*, *Ghost Actress* has a sequence of mysterious 'found footage' at its core, and in both cases the images seem to have been created by the will of the ghost, who can also use the broadcast channels to intervene. Murai saw the film as a child, but no station showed it, and like the girl who catches a glimpse of Sadako, he was left petrified of the television. Murai's eventual death scene prefigures the climax of *Ring*, with the terrified director desperately trying to crawl away from the apparition before him. Both films end on the same pessimistic note, with no easy resolution in sight.

For a debut feature, *Ghost Actress* is a remarkably accomplished achievement. The careful pacing and atmospherics that characterized the later film are all present, enhanced by the sinister nature of the film Murai is shooting: it's the story of a woman who murders a friend and raises the victim's daughter as her own sister, eventually killing her lover when he threatens to overturn their comfortable existence. Nakata's efforts are supported by the solid performances of his cast, which includes cult favourite Ren Ôsugi and Hiroyuki Tanaka (*World Apartment Horror*), better known as Sabu. His role as the assistant director in *Ghost Actress* would be one of his last before stepping behind the camera to direct his own debut feature, *Dangan Runner* (1996).

Despite the quality of the film, *Ghost Actress* was not a success, eventually being relegated to a brief series of midnight showings. Having taken the job in order to raise funds for a documentary he was trying to finish, Nakata may have been disappointed with the film's profits, but it would prove beneficial in a number of other ways. As well as bringing him into contact with Takenori Sentô- later one of *Ring*'s producers- it also caught the attention of novelist Kôji Suzuki, who was favourably impressed with the director's abilities and put his name forward as a potential candidate for the feature film version of his novel *Ring*, which was then being developed by Asmik Ace, a subsidiary of Kadokawa Shoten. Of course, Nakata got the job, which saw him collaborating with Hiroshi Takahashi again, with Sentô, Takashige Ichise (the *Juon* series) and Shinya Kawai (*Another Heaven*) producing. After the success of *Ring*, *Ghost Actress* was re-released on DVD and optioned for an American remake, along with *Ring*, *Chaos* (2000) and *Dark Water* (*Honogurai Mizu no Soko kara*, 2002).

The popularity of Suzuki's novel had already been confirmed by the warm reception given to *Ringu: Kanzenban*, a made-for-TV version that was broadcast in 1995. Directed

# Flowers From Hell

by Chisui Takigawa, *Ringu: Kanzenban* takes a fairly literal but noticeably sensationalist approach to the source material. Instead of simply claiming to be a serial rapist (as he does in the novel), Ryûji Takayama is suspected of murdering his girlfriend. Despite being made for television, the story now boasts a sizeable amount of nudity; for example, before Tomoko dies she manages to crawl beneath the shower, allowing the water to make her t-shirt slowly transparent, while the two victims who die in the car are obviously a lot closer to 'getting down to it' than they are in Nakata's film. Viewers expecting something like the grotesque and unsettling phantasm of *Ring* are likely to be more than a little surprised at the sight of Takigawa's Sadako, who appears entirely naked, as portrayed by busty pin-up girl Ayane Miura. Perhaps the most alarming addition is an incestuous relationship between Sadako and her father, something that has no relevance to the plot and seems to have been included simply to provide Ms. Miura with yet another opportunity to strip off. In contrast to *Ring*'s restraint, the made-for-TV version is frequently flashy and over-the-top. The video itself is a riot of headache-inducing psychedelic colours and swooping camera acrobatics, while the rest of the film is a mess of pointless zooms and shaky handheld camerawork. Despite the presence of reliable performers like Yoshio Harada (*Azumi; Another Heaven*) and Tomorowo Taguchi (*Tetsuo*), *Ringu: Kanzenban* ranks as one of the weakest films in the '*Ring* cycle' and has little to interest anyone outside of *Ring* completists. In a curious coincidence, one of the many commercials that punctuated the film's original broadcast (sponsored by Nestlé) featured Miki Nakatani, who played Ryûji's girlfriend in *Ring* and *Ring 2* (1999).

In a curious move, Asmik Ace decided to release *Ring* as part of a double bill, something that had not been a common practice since the early 80s. Even more unusual was the decision to pair it up with an adaptation of Spiral, the second novel in the series, effectively releasing the original and its sequel at the same time. Designed to follow on from the end of Nakata's film, *Spiral* (*Rasen*, 1998) was written and directed by Jôji Iida, the co-writer of *Ringu: Kanzenban*. Miki Nakatani and Hiroyuki Sanada (appearing mainly in flashbacks and hallucinations) were brought over from the original, as well as a couple of lesser characters, although not Nanako Matsushima, who is only seen in a brief clip from *Ring*. The central character this time is Ando (played by Kôichi Satô, from Takashi Ishii's *Gonin*), a pathologist who becomes involved when he is asked to perform an autopsy on his old college friend Ryûji Takayama. Ando hears about the mysterious tape from Ryûji's girlfriend Mai Takano, but doesn't believe the story until one of Reiko's co-workers- after trying to track down the missing journalist- presents him with a copy. After viewing the tape, Ando becomes convinced that Ryûji wanted him to destroy all the videos and stop the curse, even if it means ending his own life.

Bizarrely, *Spiral* actually suffers from being too faithful to its source material. The scientific and medical elements of the novel that Nakata and Takahashi removed- the fact that the 'curse' is a virus made up of Sadako's DNA and smallpox, for instance- have been reinstated, even if they conflict with the first film. With the curse redefined as a virus, it can now be transmitted through physical objects, such as Reiko's diary, and also through sexual intercourse. Perhaps the most significant difference concerns Sadako's ambitions; whereas in Ring she is simply interested in spreading misery, here she is trying to engineer her physical rebirth by 'hijacking' a female victim's womb, in this case, that of Mai Takano. When Sadako does re-emerge, she takes on the appearance of her surrogate mother, after leaving her to die. The 'real' Sadako has even less screen time than she does in Ring, and she is now required to be sexually alluring rather than grotesque. Hinako Saeki (from *Misa the Dark Angel* and *Uzumaki*) certainly fits the bill, but stripped of her power to unsettle and reduced to three brief appearances, the Sadako of *Spiral* is largely superfluous. Sadako is not the only character to suffer a radical reworking. Ryûji Takayama has also been altered from the sympathetic character he was in Nakata's film, bringing him more in line with the ambiguous, unlikeable figure he is in Suzuki's novels.

With most of the supernatural elements removed in favour of cold scientific facts, *Spiral* becomes a very different film to its running mate. One of *Ring*'s greatest assets is its simplicity; its plot can be summed up in a few words, leaving Nakata free to concentrate on character, atmosphere and pacing, unburdened by the lengthy exposition that sometimes made the novels slow and difficult. *Spiral* on the other hand is saddled with too much information; in attempting to explain everything in detail it loses much of the mystery that made *Ring* so compelling. It doesn't help that Iida pads the story out with flashbacks and hallucination sequences that do little to advance the plot but inject an unwelcome (and unnecessary) note of maudlin sentimentality into the proceedings. The end result is a film that gives you plenty of information about the curse and its victims, but fails to generate any interest.

Given Iida's stated desire to make a complex science-fiction thriller rather a horror film, it's perhaps surprising that Asmik Ace would sanction the production of a sequel that conflicts so heavily with its predecessor both in style and in content. Predictably, audiences did not respond well to *Spiral*, but the widespread acclaim that greeted *Ring* and the sizeable financial rewards it reaped convinced them that it was worth trying a second time. After a nationwide competition failed to produce a suitable script, Asmik Ace turned once again to Nakata and Takahashi. This time the film would be a direct sequel to *Ring*, with little or no connection to Kôji Suzuki's work. *Ring 2* was released on 27th July 1999, on a double bill with *Shikoku*, Shunichi Nagasaki's rural ghost story. By then the virus had also spread to the small screen, courtesy of Fuji Television. The first attempt, *Ringu: Saishûshô* ('ring: the final chapter'), altered the basic premise considerably (certain female characters are now male, the cursed clip is hidden in a music video, the deadline is thirteen days, etc) and ran for twelve episodes. Despite moderate viewing figures, *Ringu: Saishûshô* was not greeted favourably by the critics, perhaps because of the similarity to popular US TV series such as The X-Files. A second series, entitled *Rasen*, fared little better, even with a new premise and several new characters. Without significant reworking, the *Ring* mythos is not complex enough to support a lengthy television series, especially when audiences will be already familiar with the main story.

Beginning a week after the end of the first film, *Ring 2* focuses on Ryûji's girlfriend Mai Takano (Miki Nakatani) who, having discovered her lover's body, is determined to find out exactly what happened to him. She tries to contact his ex-wife, but finds out that Reiko Asakawa has been missing since the day after Ryûji's death. Mai is not the only one looking for her; Okazaki (Yûrei Yanagi), a co-worker, is trying to follow up the

# Flowers From Hell

last story Reiko was working on before her disappearance, while the police are eager to speak to her about the growing number of mysterious deaths, including that of her own father. Okazaki suggests that they try to speak to Masami Kuruhashi, the only witness to the death of Reiko's niece, who has been held in a mental hospital ever since that night. Their visit produces unexpected results, however; when Masami approaches a television, the picture flickers and distorts until one image is clearly visible: the well seen at the end of the video tape. Even though the girl did not watch the tape herself, she has become a conduit for Sadako's power.

A chance meeting with Reiko and Yôichi causes Mai to suspect that the boy may also be falling under Sadako's influence, and her suspicions are confirmed when he begins to manifest the same destructive powers. Masami's psychiatrist is convinced that there may be a scientific way to drain this supernatural energy from the girl, leaving her free from the malign influence. When Reiko dies in a traffic accident, leaving Yôichi in Mai's care, she must decide whether to subject the boy to the doctor's experiments or to risk him becoming, like Sadako, a creature of immense destructive power. This combination of the scientific and the supernatural makes *Ring 2* a conceptual descendant of films like *The Entity* (1981), *Poltergeist* and *The Exorcist II: The Heretic* (1977)- an acknowledged influence on the movie- where teams of scientists are employed to find a solution to supernatural problems. Typically, the scientists find themselves out of their depth and their methods entirely useless, but *Ring 2* takes it a step further. Here the psychiatrist's experiments not only fail to solve problem but also threaten to release even more of Sadako's power into the world. However, like many of the earlier films, *Ring 2* works best when dealing with the mystifying and inexplicable; the scientific elements are frequently interesting but rarely terrifying.

Despite the seemingly endless nature of Sadako's curse, *Ring* itself was a largely self-contained film, providing both the problem and the solution. Rather than taking the *Friday the 13th* route- replaying the events of the first film with new characters in a new setting- Nakata and Takahashi chose to develop the existing characters further, detailing their lives after the conclusion of the first film. While this approach is infinitely preferable to simply creating a carbon copy of *Ring*, the finished film is not without its problems. The story is too complex and poorly defined to generate the same tension as its predecessor, and lacks the sense of urgency that made *Ring* so compelling. Nakata still has a fine sense of the macabre, and creates some genuinely unsettling moments. When Masami approaches the television in the mental hospital and the images from the tape appear, the other patients begin to panic and scream as if they instinctively sense the malevolent power at work. Such scenes help to maintain an atmosphere of otherworldly gloom, but few of them have any real significance to the story. Surprisingly, Sadako herself is curiously absent, even though her influence hangs over the film like a black cloud. Yôichi and Masami are both becoming vessels for her power, but aside from a flashback to the night of Tomoko's death, she is barely seen. A brief epilogue, reminiscent of the end of *Candyman* (1992), suggests that Sadako's victims are becoming 'vengeful spirits' themselves, as Okazaki is visited by the ghost of a teenager he bought the tape from; despite his promise to the girl, he didn't watch it, and now she is back for revenge.

# Hideo Nakata and the Ring Cycle

*Ring 2* is not a bad film, but it does highlight the difficulties of expanding such a simple premise into a franchise. After three feature films, two television series and one made-for-TV special, the material was clearly beginning to wear thin. However, Asmik Ace and Kadokawa were not convinced, so a further sequel- actually a prequel, based on a Kôji Suzuki short story- was commissioned. Wisely, Hideo Nakata declined the opportunity to direct, although once again the script would be written by Hiroshi Takahashi. With Norio Tsuruta filling the director's chair, *Ring 0: Birthday* was released on 22nd January 2000, on a double bill with Toshiyuki Mizutani's *Isola* (*Isola: Tajû Jinkaku Shôjo*).

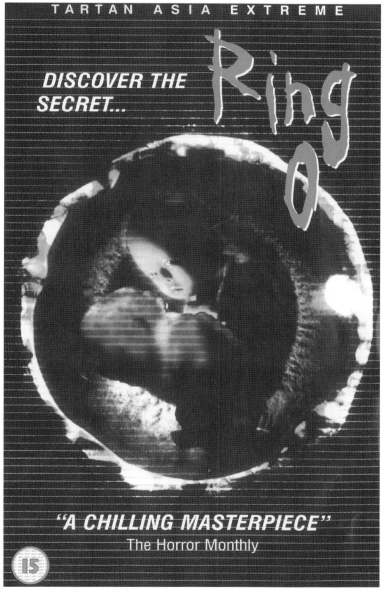

TARTAN ASIA EXTREME

DISCOVER THE SECRET...

*Ring 0*

"A CHILLING MASTERPIECE"
The Horror Monthly

15

Covering the events leading to her murder, *Ring 0* begins with Sadako (well played by Yukie Nakama) attempting to lead a normal life. She has joined an acting troupe, but her introverted nature does not endear her to the other actors. The situation does not improve when the troupe's leading actress is found dead during a rehearsal and Sadako, despite her inexperience, is given the lead role. Her only friend is Toyama (Seiichi Tanabe, from Takashi Miike's *Blues Harp*), the troupe's sound technician, but even this causes problems; on of the costume girls, played by Kumiko Asô (*Pulse*), is also in love with Toyama and sees Sadako as unwelcome competition. The jealousy of her co-workers is bad enough, but there are bigger problems on the horizon. For a start, the troupe's egomaniacal director has found out exactly who Sadako is, and intends to use the information to blackmail her into providing him with her services, both as an actress and a woman. More of her past resurfaces when a female journalist- the wife of the man who died during Shizuko's fateful demonstration- tracks Sadako down, determined to take revenge for her husband's death.

Although the main story is interesting enough, *Ring 0* is hampered by the need to present Sadako as a both a sympathetic figure and the monster she is in the earlier films. In order to accommodate this, Takahashi creates two versions of her, one good and the other evil. While the good Sadako is trying to lead a normal life, her evil twin is kept drugged and imprisoned by her father, Dr Heihachiro Ikuma. Even so, she still manages to escape periodically to dispose of anyone who stands in her better half's way- the troupe's lead actress, for example. This potentially interesting duality is treated rather simplistically- evil Sadako can kill; good Sadako can heal the sick and the wounded. When the two halves are untied, she supposedly becomes much more dangerous, but since evil Sadako could kill on her own anyway, this revelation isn't quite as effective as it could be. The film's final act contains some surprisingly creepy moments, but on the whole Tsuruta fails to find a decent balance between sympathy and terror.

Saddled with an over-complicated plot and too much sentimentality, *Ring 0* is definitely the weakest of the three films. It is debatable however whether anyone could have made a successful film out of the increasingly tired material, and it is still better than *Ringu: Kanzenban* and *Spiral*. Thanks to the poor box offices returns, Asmik Ace and Kadokawa wisely decided to bring the franchise to a well-deserved end. A symbolic funeral was held for Sadako on August 11th 2002, clearing the way for Samara, her American incarnation. Just a few weeks later, Dreamworks released *The Ring*, their Gore Verbinski-directed remake.

After branching out with the teen romance of *The Sleeping Bride* (*Garasu no Nô*, 2000) and the complex kidnap thriller *Chaos*, Nakata returned to the genre that had made him famous with 2002's *Dark Water*, his second best film. In practical terms, *Dark Water* has much in common with *Ring*: it's also based on a Kôji Suzuki story and produced by Takashige Ichise, while both films feature the same cinematographer (Junichirô Hayashi) and editor (Nobuyuki Takahashi). However, *Dark Water* is not simply a recycled version of its predecessor. Although both are ghost stories with a strong western influence, *Dark Water* is a character-driven piece that drops the 'high-concept' components (the curse, the urban legends and the technophobic paranoia) in favour of dramatic and emotional elements. Although ultimately it is a less successful film than *Ring*, in many respects these changes make it a more interesting and mature piece of work.

The central figure is Yoshimi Matsubara (Hitomi Kuroki), a single mother trying to find a new home for her and her five-year-old daughter Ikuko (Rio Kanno), while fighting an acrimonious custody battle with her unpleasant ex-husband. More out of desperation than desire, she moves into a gloomy-looking old-fashioned apartment building. The apartment itself is damp and miserable, but Yoshimi needs to show the courts that she can provide Ikuko with a stable home, so they move in. Despite their problems, things are going fairly well for the family: Ikuko is attending a good kindergarten, and Yoshimi finds herself a job working as a proof-reader at a local publisher.

# Hideo Nakata and the Ring Cycle

It's not long before the cracks begin to show, however. The patch of damp on the ceiling has become a steady drip, and neither the aged building manager (Isao Yuda, from *Ring 2* and *Juon: The Grudge*) nor the letting agent are particularly interested in doing anything about it. It's an old building, they say, and old buildings sometimes leak. Poor plumbing is not the only problem. The water might be coming from the apartment upstairs, but no one is ever home. No one's home, but the sound of footsteps- a child's footsteps- can clearly be heard coming through the ceiling below. There are no other children living in the building, but there's a child's bag on the roof; Ikuko wants to keep it, but her hygiene-conscious mother throws it away. A few days later, it's back on the roof. And if there are no other children in the building, then who is the short, yellow-coated figure that Yoshimi has seen, once again on the roof?

Yoshimi is not the only one who has seen the figure; her daughter has seen her several times, often at the kindergarten. After the second of these incidents, Ikuko faints, and Yoshimi is called to the school. In conversation with the principle, she discovers who the yellow-coated figure is: Mitsuko Kawai, a local girl who disappeared on her way home from the kindergarten two years earlier. Her home, as Yoshimi soon realises, was the apartment above theirs, where all the water is coming from, Growing ever more frantic, Yoshimi begins to pack once again, convinced that Mitsuko has returned to the building and intends to take Ikuko away. Worried that her increasingly irrational behaviour is threatening her chances of retaining custody, Yoshimi's sympathetic solicitor manages to convince her that there is a rational explanation for these events; if the apartment above hers has been unlocked since Mitsuko's father left over a year ago, anybody could have gained entry, with the taps left running until they flooded the apartment and soaked through to the rooms below. Reassured, Yoshimi resolves to keep her emotions and her imagination in check, and to focus on fighting the custody battle. For a moment it looks as if everything might be okay after all; but then the bag appears again, this time in their apartment. As the tensions reach breaking point, Yoshimi is forced to confront Mitsuko and uncover the truth about her death and her designs on Ikuko.

While the basic plot- family moves into a new home that also has a few supernatural residents- has been a staple of the horror genre for many years, *Dark Water* belongs to a more select group that is epitomized by Jack Clayton's Henry James adaptation *The Innocents* (1961), Robert Wise's 1963 classic *The Haunting*, and most recently, Alejandro Amenábar's *The Others* (2001). All of these films are built around unstable female characters whose supernatural experiences may or may not be a product of their own fragile psychological state. Often these characters are single mothers- or mother-figures, as in *The Innocents*- struggling to cope with the pressures of life and motherhood with little or no support from anyone else. In interviews Nakata has acknowledged the influence of *The Innocents* and *The Haunting* upon his work, including one scene in *Dark Water*- in which Yoshimi sees her daughter running out of the elevator and wonders exactly whose hand she is holding- that is highly reminiscent of the latter film. In keeping with the director's love of British cinema, there are also nods to *Don't Look Now* (1973)- the small, rain-coated figure, often glimpsed but rarely fully visible- and Stanley Kubrick's *The Shining* (1980), with the deluge of water that appears when the elevator doors open. It's also tempting

to draw parallels between *Dark Water* and Roman Polanski's *Repulsion* (1965), as the physical decay of Yoshimi's apartment- specifically, the ever-spreading patch of damp and mould- comes to symbolise her own mental decline. However, Nakata is smart enough to pay tribute to his favourite films without appropriating them wholesale, and the credit for *Dark Water*'s most effective moments is rightfully his. Even so, it's interesting to note that little of the story had to be altered in order to prepare it for western audiences, with Walter Salles' 2004 remake remaining largely faithful to the Japanese original.

*Dark Water* represents Nakata's most in-depth examination of one of his most prominent themes, the breakdown of the family unit. Although it was only part of the background in *Ghost Actress* (as seen in the film that Murai is directing), the theme achieved a greater significance in *Ring*. Both *Ring* and *Dark Water* focus on single mothers, while dysfunctional family relations are the catalyst for the supernatural chain of events: Sadako's mother abandoned her by committing suicide, leaving her to be slain by her father, while the failure of Mitsuko's parents to properly take care of their child leads to her tragic accidental death. This is not only the case with Nakata's horror films: infidelity lies at the heart of the web of murder and deceit that runs through *Chaos*, while even the handyman's background features yet another broken marriage. Much of *Dark*

# Hideo Nakata and the Ring Cycle

*Water*'s emotional resonance comes from the similarity between Yoshimi's childhood and Mitsuko's, since both were raised by mothers who had little time for them and eventually abandoned them altogether. The pattern is repeating itself with Ikuko and her father: he is only interested in using the child as a means to attack his ex-wife, caring little about her personal welfare. But these things are never black and white; ironically, by the end of *Dark Water* Yoshimi is forced to accept that the best thing she can do for Ikuko is to leave her with her father and become Mitsuko's surrogate mother.

To his credit, for the most part Nakata manages to strike a careful balance between the drama and the horror, making sure that one does not overpower the other. Although the film's climax- when Yoshimi tells Ikuko to stay away from her- is undeniably melodramatic, it's preceded by the genuinely unsettling sight of the decomposed, water-bloated Mitsuko throwing herself at Yoshimi with an ear-piercing shriek. Once again Nakata's efforts are supported by a memorable score from Kenji Kawai. His work on *Dark Water* is less alien and discordant than *Ring*'s score, but it's also entirely appropriate, often evoking the muted clanging of water pipes. Less memorable are the melodic strings that Kawai adds to the film's more melodramatic moments, however. *Dark Water*'s main flaw is the unnecessary epilogue, where the now-teenaged Ikuko (played by Asami Mizukawa, later in 2004's *Shibuya Kaidan*) returns to their apartment to find her mother still there, still caring for Mitsuko. It adds little to the story except another dose of sentimentality. Although on the whole the original is the superior film, the American remake found a more satisfactory way of ending the story, with the daughter meeting her mother in the elevator for a final, brief farewell.

Nakata's attempts to move away from the horror genre have proved problematic. After *Ring 2* he began work on *Sleeping Bride*, an adaptation of an Osamu Tezuka manga about a 17-year-old girl (played by Risa Gotô) who wakes up after being in a coma since her birth. Based on a script by Chiaki Konaka, the writer of *Evil Dead Trap 2: Hideki* (1992) and *Marebito* (2005), *Sleeping Bride* is a contemporary fairy tale, shot in sun-drenched colours and infused with gentle nostalgia. Although a solid respectable effort, it's also little more than a pleasant diversion, and neither critics nor audiences responded favourably. Nakata returned to melodrama with 2003's *Last Scene*, a character-driven piece about the relationship between an ageing, faded movie star and a young prop girl. Having played at a few foreign film festivals, *Last Scene* was denied a Japanese theatrical release when the production company who backed the film went bankrupt, leaving the work in a legal limbo. A few months later it slipped quietly onto home video, with little fanfare or public interest.

The director's best non-horror effort is the convoluted kidnap thriller *Chaos*, based on a novel by Shôgo Utani and scripted by Hisashi Saitô. The opening scenes set up a deceptively straightforward plot, as wealthy businessman Komiyama

**Dark Water**

# Flowers From Hell

(Ken Mitsuishi) discovers that his attractive young wife Saori (Miki Nakatani) has been kidnapped. Although he pays the ransom- 30 million yen, about £150,000- Saori is not released and police begin to suspect the worst might have happened. In the first of many flashbacks we are then shown what actually happened- Saori has faked her own kidnapping with the assistance of a divorced handyman played by Masato Hagiwara, the blank-faced psychopath from Kiyoshi Kurosawa's *Cure* (1997). From there Nakata fills in the story little by little, adding twist upon twist until every expectation and assumption has been repeatedly overturned. The most densely plotted of all the director's films, *Chaos* benefits greatly from Nakata's even-handed restraint. His low-key approach to pacing, camerawork and editing makes an ideal 'poker face', comfortably hiding the tortuous plot that lies behind it. Like *Ring*, *Chaos* changes the central character of the drama from male to female, the focus of the novel having been Komiyama rather than Saori. After appearing as the grieving, withdrawn Mai Takano in *Ring* and *Ring 2*, Miki Nakatani's sensuous, attractive performance here comes as something of a revelation, making it easy to understand why the film's male characters are willing to risk so much for her sake.

Despite his misgivings about making his American debut with a horror film- rumour has it he turned down remakes of both *The Entity* (1981) and *The Eye* (2002)- and his refusal to helm *Ring 0: Birthday*, Nakata eventually agreed to direct *The Ring Two* (2005), the sequel to Gore Verbinski's remake. Like Nakata's earlier *Ring 2*, the film attempts to evolve the central story rather than simply presenting a re-run of its predecessor. Supported by a strong cast- including Simon Baker (*Land of the Dead*, 2005) and Sissy Spacek (*Carrie*, 1976)- Nakata handles the material with his customary skill, providing a handful of effective scares and a tangible sense of dread throughout much of the film. Unfortunately his efforts are frequently undermined by a lacklustre script that needlessly recycles a number of the key moments from *The Ring*. Even more perplexing is the decision to lift half of the material from Nakata's own *Dark Water*, a situation not helped by DreamWorks' decision to release *The Ring Two* just a few weeks before Walter Salles' *Dark Water* remake. Rather than simply attempting to spread her vengeance across the world, Samara now wants Rachel (Naomi Watts) to be her mother, possessing Aidan (David Dorfman) in order to achieve this. Since the only way to force Samara to leave Aidan's body is to make her think that he is about to die, we're forced to watch slightly uncomfortable scenes of Rachel trying to drown her own son, an act that child welfare officials- and at least one critic, who claimed the film was actually about the self-serving delusions of an abusive parent- interpret as a sign of maternal instability. It doesn't help that the story is cluttered up with excess details about Samara's childhood, added to support her new ambitions and generate some misguided sympathy. Not only was she murdered by her foster-mother, but her real mother (played by Sissy Spacek) also attempted to drown her child shortly after its birth- hence her desire to finally find the mother she never had. The appearance of Samara's new *Village of the Damned*-style powers is also problematical- since she can force a child welfare official to kill herself, why can she not stop Rachel from trying to drown Aidan? In short, *The Ring Two* is a mess, and one that even a director of Hideo Nakata's talents is unable to salvage.

After the creative and commercial disappointment of *The Ring Two* Nakata

130

# Hideo Nakata and the Ring Cycle

**The Ring Two**

returned to Japan. His next project- *Kaidan* (2007), another version of the oft-filmed Shinkei Kasane-ga-fuchi story- could easily be interpreted as a step backwards for the director. Although by all accounts not a bad film, many critics questioned the validity of releasing a traditional period kaidan at a time when the best (and most popular) domestic horror films are entirely modern in origin and execution: Shûsuke Kaneko's *Death Note* manga adaptations, Yukihiko Tsutsumi's *Forbidden Siren* (based on Konami's popular video games) and Shinya Tsukamoto's excellent and unusual *Nightmare Detective*. Unsurprisingly, *Kaidan* did not perform particularly well at the box office, leading Nakata to turn his hand to a more commercially promising movie, the forthcoming *Death Note* spin-off *L*. If *L* manages to achieve the same degree of success as Kaneko's films, it could well return Nakata to his position as one of the most important directors of Japanese horror films.

*(Footnotes)*

*1 They were issued as three separate VCDs in Hong Kong and Macau: Dead Lake, House and Special Motel. The UK Region 2 release was called Cursed, Death and Spirit and included on the UK release of Nakata's kidnap thriller Chaos (2000).*

# CHAPTER SIX
## Vengeful Spirits, Part Two

According to the movie, a new copy of the *Ring* video has to be made every seven days. The timing might be slightly different, but ever since 1998 the Japanese film industry has been operating on roughly the same basis. Like John Carpenter's *Halloween* (1978) and Wes Craven's *Scream* (1996), *Ring* (1998) soon became the inspiration for a succession of similar movies that to a greater or lesser extent relied upon the template laid down by Nakata's film. Certain aspects emerged as dominant factors, recurring time and again in the films that followed. The most prominent was the presence of an intelligent heroine, opposed by a malevolent female figure with a tragic or violent past, and the use of technological items as conduits for supernatural vengeance. Not all of the post-*Ring* ghost stories featured these elements, although they were by far the most common. *Ring*'s prior existence as a best-selling novel was also perceived as a significant factor, leading to a high number of literary adaptations in the years following[1]. Initially, this placed Masato Hara and Asmik Ace in a good position to dominate the market, thanks to their status as a subsidiary of Kadokawa Shoten, Japan's largest publishing house. Each of the *Ring* films was therefore released on a double bill with another literary adaptation from the Kadokawa stable: *Ring* itself with Jôji Iida's *Spiral* (*Rasen*), *Ring 2* (1999) with Shunichi Nagasaki's *Shikoku*, and *Ring 0: Birthday* (2000) with Toshiyuki Mizutani's *Isola* (*Isola: Tajû Jinkaku Shôjo*). Away from the *Ring* franchise, Asmik Ace also released Masato Harada's *Inugami* (2001) alongside Ten Shimoyama's *St. John's Wort* (*Otogirisô*).

Based on a story by Masako Bandô and co-written by *Ring* producer Takenori Sentô, *Shikoku* is a rural ghost story set on the eponymous island, the smallest of Japan's four main islands. When Hinako (Yui Natsukawa, from Takeshi Kitano's *Zatoichi*) returns to her childhood home to put her deceased father's affairs in order, she re-establishes contact with Fumiya (Michitaka Tsutsui), a boy she had been close to when they were much younger. Their reunion is a pleasant one, but before long the darker shadow of the past begins to exert itself. She is shocked to learn that Sayori, another of their friends, died in a drowning accident several years before. Her short life had not been a pleasant one; although Sayori dreamt of escaping from the island and making a new life in the big city, her family's traditions insisted that she become the next priestess of the clan, effectively tying herself to the family and the island forever. Since her death (which may not have been accidental), Fumiya believes that Sayori has been a constant presence in his life, always observing him, always making sure he doesn't get too close to any other women. But the recent arrival of his old friend on the island has made this situation even more difficult. As Hinako and Fumiya 's friendship slowly develops into love, mysterious incidents begin to plague the area. At first they are symbolic but fairly harmless- family jizo statues are beheaded, and so forth- but before long, Sayori (played by Chiaki Kuriyama, just before her career-boosting appearance in *Battle Royale*) is manifesting herself physically, and the locals are beginning to blame Hinako for reawakening old spirits. Meanwhile,

# Vengeful Spirits, Part Two

Sayori's mother (Toshie Negishi, from Audition) has been on a pilgrimage for many years, visiting each of Shikoku's eighty-eight shrines and temples. When visited in order, these eighty-eight temples reinforce the island's status as a 'holy precinct', a place where the dead come before moving on to their eventual fate. But Sayori's mother is visiting them backwards, as if she seeks not to confirm the sacred boundary but instead to remove the barrier that separates the living and the dead.

In contrast to *Ring*'s urbanized, techno-informed terrors, *Shikoku* focuses on rural life and long-standing traditions. Nagasaki presents the island of Shikoku as a sun-drenched bucolic haven where life has not altered greatly since pre-industrial times. Traditional religion is still a significant part of life and the ancient rituals are still observed, but these rites sometimes become distinctly sinister; for example, Sayori's role as the family priestess includes allowing her body to be used as a vessel for the spirits of the dead. The combination of Nagasaki's shaky handheld camera and the smoky gloom makes these scenes genuinely eerie, especially when it becomes apparent that the girl is not entirely a willing participant. This contrast between benign religious traditions- as embodied by the village's colourful festivals- and its darker, more unpleasant counterpart is a central theme of the film. The pilgrims who travel around the island's eighty-eight holy sites are upholding an ancient tradition that signifies respect for the souls of the departed, but by following the route backwards, Sayori's mother threatens to subject those souls to a tormented, earthbound existence, purely for her own selfish ends.

Despite the disturbing implications of the story, Nagasaki is noticeably more interested in the blossoming romance between Hinako and Fumiya and the pastoral paradise that is Shikoku itself. Although the hazy, sun-drenched look of these scenes is undeniably attractive, it's clear that the film's more overtly supernatural moments have not received the same attention. Sayori's ghostly manifestations seem to be lacklustre echoes of similar moments from *Ring*, added simply to justify the film's presence on a horror double bill rather than out of any genuine necessity. Nagasaki also fails to make much use of his talented cast, with Ren Ôsugi reduced to a brief throwaway role. Tarô Suwa and Toshie Negishi fare a little better, but even they struggle to make the material come to life. Any impact the film might have salvaged is swept aside by diluting the potentially powerful climax with an unwelcome streak of sentimentality. Compared to the malevolence and power that Sadako Yamamura brought to *Ring*, it's something of a disappointment to discover that Sayori is just another angst-ridden teenager, petulantly lashing out at her former friend for having the life she wanted. Unable to decide whether it should be a nostalgic romance or a horror film, Shikoku fails to do justice to either one.

Worse still is *Isola*, *Ring 0*'s running mate. Based on the award-winning novel by Yôsuke Kishi, *Isola* is set in the aftermath of the great earthquake that hit Kobe city on January 17th 1995, causing millions of dollars worth of damages and leaving 300,000 people homeless. Yoshina Kimura stars as Yukari, a young girl troubled by telepathic powers that she keeps under control with the help of antipsychotic drugs. Signing on as a volunteer during the earthquake crisis, she befriends a psychologist with a particularly puzzling case: that of Chihiro (played by Yu Kurosawa, granddaughter of Akira), a teenage

天海祐希【迷霧】

渡部篤郎【天國情書】

狗神
INUGAMI

*Japanese sleeve art for* **Inugami**

girl with multiple personality disorder. When the area is struck by a series of violent and inexplicable deaths, Yukari's psychic abilities lead her to suspect that Chihiro may be responsible. As she begins to investigate, she realises that there may be more than psychological disorders at work.

For the most part *Isola* is a sloppy and derivative film. Like *Ring*'s Ryûji Takayama, Yukari uncovers vital information using her psychic powers, but by repeating this device over and over again the film is robbed of much of its suspense, since there's no real need for any investigation. Despite the gruesome deaths she's causing, Chihiro herself is a bland character who does little more than sulk and pout throughout the movie. Her alternate personalities are indicated primarily by different hairstyles, with little or no attempt made at characterisation. When it does manifest itself, her malevolent thirteenth 'personality'- unsurprisingly, it's actually a ghost- appears in heavy gothic makeup and a bizarre S&M-style costume. It's certainly a change from the standard woman in white with long black hair, but it's not necessarily an improvement. A handful of scenes do generate some interest, but even the most memorable one- the sight of Susumu Terajima stabbing himself in the neck with a handful of meat skewers- is considerably less effective than it could be. Takashi Miike, director of *Audition* (2000) and *Ichi the Killer* (*Koroshiya 1*,2001), shows up in a blink-and-you'll-miss-it cameo, but as with Eli Roth's *Hostel*, it's not easy to see why he'd want to appear in this.

Like *Shikoku*, *Inugami* is based on a story by Masako Bandô and set on the island of Shikoku, where the sprawling Bonomiya clan live under the tyranny of their drunken patriarch. Although he has personally run up vast gambling debts on the Internet, the patriarch vigorously opposes the use of modern technology by the rest of the family- they have only recently been allowed to have electric lighting, for example. His spinster sister Miki (Yuki Amami) lives away from the main family buildings, where she continues to make paper in the traditional way, selling her product to the island's stationers. She leads a quiet life, remaining outside the family power games and largely ignored by her squabbling relatives. Miki's quiet existence is disrupted by the arrival of a handsome young schoolteacher who recites poetry and follows her on her walks through the woods. The teacher's amorous advances awaken Miki's long-dormant sense of femininity and sexuality, an event that has a marked effect upon both her life and her appearance, making her seem younger and filled with vitality. While this change does not go unnoticed by the rest of the family, for the moment it is overshadowed by other, more sinister events. All of the women in the family have been having unpleasant dreams that hint at buried secrets and imminent tragedy, while the region has been plagued by a number of apparently random murders. The superstitious elders claim that the Inugami ('dog gods'), the guardian spirits of the Bonomiya clan, have been released to wreak havoc throughout the land. As the intended inheritor of the Bonomiya traditions, Miki has a psychic link to the Inugami, and the locals are not slow to suspect that there might be a connection between the spinster's sexual reawakening and the wave of portents and mysterious deaths.

Not only does *Inugami* share a setting with *Shikoku*, it also shares the same basic strengths and weaknesses. Writer-director Masato Harada is more than adept at capturing the breathtaking natural beauty of Shikoku, and *Inugami* is certainly one of the best-looking Japanese films released in recent years. But like *Shikoku*, it also has difficulties fitting into the horror genre. Harada's main interest lies in examining the Japanese royal family through the antagonistic power-games and dark secrets of the Bonomiya clan, with the supernatural elements added almost as an afterthought; the Inugami themselves have little direct impact on the plot, for example. As a horror movie *Inugami* barely even qualifies, and it's unlikely that typical teenage audiences looking for *Ring*-style chills would have much patience with a lengthy, slow-burning critique of the emperor system. Even when approached as a non-horror movie, it's not a particularly successful film, unfolding at a somnambulistic pace that ruins any attempt at suspense. When it does eventually build up to the climax- the moment when the patriarch finally goes berserk and slaughters most of his family- Harada loses his nerve and shifts the scene into black-and-white, lessening the impact considerably and wasting an opportunity to at least provide a memorable ending. It's a sadly limp conclusion to a potentially interesting film.

*Inugami*'s problems did not end when the credits roll, however. In a miracle of poor planning, Harada's art house melodrama was released on a double bill with *St. John's Wort*, a teen-oriented adaptation of a popular novel and computer game, thereby ensuring that few people would be interested in seeing both films. Harada has since claimed that by misrepresenting his film as a typical teen horror flick Kadokawa (and distributor Toho) effectively killed off its chances of scoring with the critics or the box office, and he's probably right; but even so, it's unlikely that *Inugami* would have found much favour with mature audiences either, thanks to the film's would-be controversial subject matter and general lack of vitality. It doesn't help that *St. John's Wort* isn't a terribly good film either, although it's certainly better than rubbish like *Isola*. Co-written, like *Shikoku*, by Takenori Sentô, *St. John's Wort* is a fairly ambitious attempt to recreate a computer game on film. The story itself- a girl (Megumi Okina from *Juon: The Grudge*) explores her long-deceased father's home, turning up some unpleasant family secrets- is straightforward enough, combining the age-old 'Old Dark House' conventions with a few plot devices lifted from Shirô Toyoda's *Portrait of Hell* (*Jigokuhen*, 1969) and Italian cult classic *The House With the Laughing Windows* (1976). More interesting is the execution: in an effort to create a deliberately artificial world Shimoyama employs almost every cinematic trick in the book- shooting on film and video, handheld cameras, colour filters, digital manipulation and many more- as well as a number of computer game techniques, including onscreen dialogue boxes and stationary backgrounds. Unfortunately, he also adheres too closely to the repetitive search-every-room structure that many games have. It's not a problem when you're playing it yourself, but in a film, without the interactive elements, it just becomes as tedious as watching someone else playing the game. Without a solid story to support them, Shimoyama's flashy visual tricks quickly become tedious.

Eventually Kadokawa and Toho realized that the double bills weren't particularly successful, even when backed up with superior films like *Ring*. The obvious reason is quality; most of the films released under this scheme simply aren't very good. With typical accountant's logic, Kadokawa had attempted to repeat their success by adapting other literary works for the screen, without stopping to consider whether *Ring*'s success was actually due to its original status as a novel. In the process of creating their film, Hideo Nakata and Hiroshi Takahashi had revised Suzuki's work extensively and included elements drawn from other films and novels, as well as contemporary urban legends and traditional mythology. Many of *Ring*'s most memorable scenes- including Sadako's emergence from the television- were created by Nakata and Takahashi alone. The same 'fuzzy logic' can be seen in the choice of directors too: neither Jôji Iida nor Masato Harada were particularly interested in the horror genre, with Iida even stating in advance that *Spiral* wouldn't be a horror film. However, both of them had a good track record: Iida had scored well on the small screen with his sci-fi series *Night Head* (as well as the hit movie that followed it), while Harada had found success at the box office with *Bounce KoGals* (2000). Similarly, Shunichi Nagasaki had never made a horror film, but like Iida and Harada he'd had some recent success, mostly with the drama *Romance* (1996). From a purely financial viewpoint all three looked like reasonably safe bets. In retrospect however it's not hard to see why Kadokawa failed to produce another *Ring*-size hit.

Not all of the post-*Ring* literary adaptations fared so badly. Away from the Kadokawa stable, Daiei released Shûsuke Kaneko's *Crossfire* (2000), a superior special effects-driven thriller based on the novel by Miyuki Miyabe. Kaneko had already established his credentials as a skilled handler of complex special effects with his recent *Gamera* films, and although *Crossfire* relies more on computer-generated images than men in rubber suits, his work here is no less impressive. Akiko Yada stars as Aoki Junko, a young woman with the power to start fires at will. Since her powers manifest themselves when she becomes angry or excited, Junko leads a quiet, solitary existence, haunted by her guilt over the death of one of her schoolmates. When a male co-workers invites her to a company party, she decides to accept, but her elation at making a new friend turns to anger when his sister is murdered by a gang of thrill-seeking young punks on the way home from the party. The ringleader of the gang escapes punishment thanks to his age and his wealthy father's connections, but Junko decides to use her abilities to make sure that justice is done. With a little persuasion from another psychic, Junko's personal vendetta soon escalates into a moral crusade, but before long she starts to question both her own status as a vigilante and her new ally's motives.

Although influenced by the works of Stephen King- most obviously *Firestarter*, but also *Carrie* and *The Dead Zone*- *Crossfire* is not entirely unrelated to the traditional Japanese horror films. This time the Vengeful Spirit is not an external being, but Junko's righteous fury. Even so, by the end of the film she has joined Sadako in pursuing vengeance from beyond the grave; like Johnny Smith, the hero of *The Dead Zone*, she is able to save the day but only at the expense of her own life. Junko is a more sympathetic figure than Sadako Yamamura, but they are cut from the same cloth. Like the Sadako of *Ring 0*, Junko is a lonely character whose incredible powers have set her apart from society, leaving her unable to form meaningful human relationships. In childhood both used their powers to kill, Sadako to protect her mother, Junko to protect herself. Kaneko himself channels a fair amount of righteous fury into *Crossfire*, most notably on matters of law and order. The police are shackled by laws that protect the guilty, and young offenders in particular, while wealth and influence affords criminals immunity; at worst senior police officials are actually complicit in the murders themselves. This negative social commentary, together with Junko's ever-present personal guilt and the downbeat ending- not to mention the sizeable mountain of flambéed humans- often make *Crossfire* a decidedly grim viewing experience. Mercifully the pessimism is somewhat offset by Kaneko's energetic handling of the action scenes, although the pace does lag at times. The major attraction here is the excellent special effects, which are similar in quality (and content) to those in *Hellboy* (2004), but accomplished on a fraction of the budget. Using the same technicians he worked with on the resurrected *Gamera* franchise, Kaneko has created some of the finest computer-generated effects to be found in any Japanese film of recent years. After directing *Godzilla, Mothra, King Ghidorah: Giant Monsters All-Out Attack* (2001) and *Azumi 2: Death or Love* (2005) Kaneko returned to the themes explored in *Crossfire* with *Death Note* and *Death Note 2: Last Name* (2006), before moving on to the forthcoming Kazuo Umezu adaptation, *The Right Hand of God, the Left Hand of the Devil*.

**One Missed Call**

One of the more unusual literary-based horror films of the period- and certainly one of the most genuinely unsettling- is Kiyoshi Kurosawa's made-for-TV *Séance* (*Kôrei*, 2000), based on the novel *Séance on a Wet Afternoon* by Mark McShane. The story of a fake medium and her hen-pecked husband who decide to stage a fake kidnapping, McShane's novel had already been filmed in 1964 by Bryan Forbes, starring Richard Attenborough and Kim Stanley, who was Oscar-nominated for her performance. Kurosawa keeps the bare bones of the story, but alters two crucial details. In his version a middle-aged sound technician and his wife- played by Kôji Yakusho and Jun Fubuki, both from *Charisma* (1999) and *Pulse* (*Kairo*, 2001)- become involved in the kidnapping purely by coincidence; more importantly, the wife's psychic powers are real. Unlike Kim Stanley's character, she is not a charlatan trying to engineer her own fame, but a woman whose abilities have brought her nothing but pain and distress. When a young girl escapes from her kidnapper and hides in one of Yakusho's boxes, the couple realise that they can turn the situation to their advantage by offering to 'find' the girl for the police. It's hard not to sympathise with their plight at first: as Fubuki sees limbless phantoms hovering over customers at the restaurant where she works, it becomes obvious that her powers make her life very difficult. However, their desperation clouds their judgement, and eventually leaves the couple in a far worse situation than before. Ironically, when the girl accidentally dies, Fubuki's abilities become far more of a curse than they were before, as she is haunted by the spectre of their victim.

For the most part Japanese TV horror is dominated by gimmicky shows like *Kaidan Shinmimibukuro*. Released in the west as *Tales of Terror from Tokyo*, the series recruits first-time/music video directors and the usual big names- Norio Tsuruta and Takashi Shimizu primarily- and gives them five minutes to tell their story. The format doesn't allow for anything experimental or in-depth but occasionally something interesting shows up, like 'The Visitor', in which Keisuke Toyoshima manages to wring a surprising amount of tension from a simple story about a young girl who finds something sinister knocking at the door. Even more effective is Akio Yoshida's 'Examination Room #3', a two-part story in which a young couple break into an abandoned hospital to get intimate, only for the girl to become possessed by the spirit of a dead nymphomaniac. Most of the episodes range from the silly to the predictable, drawing on *Twilight Zone*-style weirdness (the elevator to hell in Shimizu's 'Elevator') or popular urban legends, like the haunted toilet cubicle in 'The School Excursion'.

*Ring*'s combination of the supernatural with the technological obviously struck a chord with audiences, and it quickly became one of the most heavily copied aspects of the film, much like *Halloween*'s use of point-of-view camerawork or *Scream*'s self-referential irony. It was not an entirely new concept, having already manifested itself a number of times, from the deadly computer game of Seikô Ito's novel *No Life King* to the demon-possessed kotatsu heater in Jôji Iida's horror spoof *Battle Heater* (*Battle Heater: Kotatsu*, 1989). Unsurprisingly many of the later efforts featured the same noroi no bideo ('cursed video') as Nakata's film. By that time rumours had begun to circulate that *Ring* was based upon real events, an assertion supported by a slew of zero-budget V-cinema releases, all carrying the same spurious claims of authenticity ('Dare you watch the real cursed video?') and containing snippets of grainy, out-of-focus home video footage. The more professional efforts feature staged or digitally-added 'ghosts', although most just settle for zooming in on a tiny blur in the corner that could easily be mistaken for the cameraman's thumb, were it not for the narration or text intertitles provided to help you out.

Occasionally a worthwhile item turns up in the pseudo-documentary arena.

# Vengeful Spirits, Part Two

The best of them is *The Curse* (*Noroi*, 2006), a Takashige Ichise-produced effort that turned up several years after the boom in *Ring*-inspired 'true stories' had passed but has enough interesting ideas to lift it above the majority of such films. Director Kôji Shiraishi is best known for the *Jurei* franchise- a series of cheap and entirely suspense-free *Juon* knock-offs- but *The Curse* actually manages to provide a number of genuinely unsettling moments, hinged around the search for a mysterious and bloody cult that supposedly died out decades ago. There are a few attempts at establishing authenticity, most notably the presence of actress Mariko Matsumoto- playing herself, but effectively reprising her role in Takashi Shimizu's *Reincarnation* (2005)- and a number of realistic extracts from TV shows about the supernatural. Although the film passes right through *Blair Witch Project* territory- the documentary maker has since disappeared, with his footage turning up a few months later- Shiraishi takes the time to establish an actual plot, rather than relying solely upon the viewer's imagination. Even so, he does not provide a narrator to steer the audience towards the expected conclusion, allowing them to interpret the footage themselves. The end result may not be particularly convincing, but it's arguably more satisfying as a horror film than its more famous predecessor.

Occupying the other end of the spectrum is Kiyoshi Kurosawa's *Pulse* (*Kairo*, 2001), the best of the post-*Ring* technophobic horrors. Like *Cure* (1997), Kurosawa's breakthrough film, *Pulse* operates in a genre-based framework, but also explores deeper themes, in this case the isolation and loneliness that exist within modern technology-oriented society. It's a testament to the director's skill that he manages to balance both his philosophical concerns and the 'surface' considerations of genre- that is, the necessity of making a movie that is scary or disturbing- without sacrificing either one. As well as providing a cerebral and thought-provoking discourse on urban life, Kurosawa also manages to create some of the scariest moments seen in modern Japanese horror cinema. Although frequently described as being *Ring* with computers rather than videotapes, *Pulse* owes as much to apocalyptic science-fiction films like Geoff Murphy's *The Quiet Earth* (1985) as it does to contemporary domestic horror.

Unlike the carefully paced, patiently unfolding *Ring*, *Pulse* seems initially to be a jumble of meaningless and apparently unconnected supernatural incidents. The first indication that something is drastically wrong is the sharp increase in suicides and disappearances; even more disturbing is the revelation that many of the dead and missing individuals continue to exist as amorphous black phantoms, trapped in the places they died. Some exist only through the mass media networks, murmuring plaintive cries for help through cell phones or repeating the same few seconds of activity on computer screens. Others fade away entirely, leaving behind nothing more than black stains to mark their passing. As the process continues, the streets of Tokyo- one of the world's largest urban centres- become quiet and empty, haunted by the formless black spirits. This is the nightmare into which Kurosawa thrusts his central characters, a plant store worker called Michi (played by Kumiko Asô from *Ring 0: Birthday*) and Kawashima, a bored economics student played by Haruhiko Katô (*Loft*). Michi becomes involved when she witnesses one of her friends committing suicide; during his first attempt at exploring the Internet, Kawashima discovers the grainy black-and-white footage of 'ghosts', pallid figures alone

**One Missed Call**

in darkened rooms. The pair to do not meet up until the film is almost over, but through them Kurosawa explores different aspects of his 'quiet apocalypse'.

Much of *Pulse*'s impact stems from the persistent atmosphere of gloom and the nerve-rattling shocks that occasionally puncture it, often backed up by Takefumi Haketa's discordant, jarring score. After a television picture freeze-frames on a newsreader with the top of his head severed by a line of static, a glass bottle crashes down on a metal sink. It's nothing more than a simple misdirect followed by a loud noise, but it's effective nonetheless. The film's most memorable moment is equally straightforward: while Michi stands in the foreground, a figure in the distance- a woman in a brown coat- climbs to the top of an industrial silo and throws herself off, hitting the pavement with a muted thud. All of this is done in one single, unbroken take.

Unlike the protagonists of *Ring*, Michi and Kawashima have no power to affect the events taking place. Sadako's curse might have implications for the wider world, but to all intents and purposes Reiko and Ryûji are dealing with a personal crisis rather than a global one. In contrast, the heroes of *Pulse* have little chance of even understanding the situation, let alone finding a solution. They're ordinary people caught up in events well beyond their control, and Kurosawa is more interested in exploring the reactions of the individual than in explaining or resolving the events themselves. One character puts forward a hypothesis- essentially a variation on George Romero's 'When there's no more room in Hell, the dead will walk the earth' tagline that singularly fails to explain the suicides and the disappearances- but it's immediately rejected and never mentioned again. While possibly contentious, *Pulse* actually benefits from Kurosawa's refusal to provide a rational explanation. Many horror films become progressively less terrifying as the mystery is explained- *Ring*'s weakest point is when the heroes have discovered who and where Sadako is, for example- but *Pulse* remains inscrutably compelling until the end.

Predictably, *Pulse* proved to be too downbeat, ambiguous and cerebral to score at the box office, but it did influence a handful of films, including Toshikazu Nagae's entirely awful *Ghost System* (2002). Originally an internet-released amateur short, then dumped to video (by Pony Canyon) with extra footage added, *Ghost System* brings in a mad scientist to create the gateway between the world of the living and the world of the dead. In keeping with its origins the film is ludicrously cheap- the 'ghost system' turns out to be an industrial fan, for example- and so tedious that it even manages to outstay its welcome in just seventy minutes. Bizarrely enough, the publicized multimedia franchise never materialised. More competent but equally derivative is Yôichirô Hayama's *Dead Waves* (*Shiryôha*, 2005), also from Pony Canyon. Like *Pulse*, *Dead Waves* follows two storylines, but Hayama never gets around to linking them together, eventually dropping the more interesting one- a TV program appears to be causing mass suicides- in favour of clichéd tripe about ghosts punishing their killer. Pony Canyon finally managed to produce a half-decent techno-horror movie with 2005's *Booth*, directed by Yoshihiro Nakamura, co-writer of *Dark Water* (2002). Although *Booth* treads no new ground, it is at least entertaining to watch arrogant DJ Ryuta Satô get his comeuppance, as his past misdeeds- and some recent ones- are dredged up and scrutinized by the ghost of a suicide victim lurking in Booth No. 6.

The post-*Ring* wave of technophobia hit its commercial peak with Takashi Miike's *One Missed Call* (*Chakushin Ari*, 2004), the first mainstream horror film from one of Japan's most controversial directors. Despite conceptual similarities with the South Korean hit *Phone* (2002), it's actually a more or less straightforward reworking of *Ring* in which the curse spreads through cell phones instead of videos. With singer-actress-whatever Kô Shibasaki starring- and providing the all-important theme song- *One Missed Call* is a slick exercise in franchise-building aimed squarely at the teen demographic: watch the film, see the TV series, download the ringtone. Given Miike's reputation as a purveyor of such delights as extreme sadism (*Audition*, 2000), twisted sexuality (*Visitor Q*, 2001) and flat-out surrealism (*Gozu*, 2003), his decision to release an accessible and overtly commercial film was greeted with a fair degree of head-scratching from fans and critics alike. His more ardent supporters have suggested that *One Missed Call* is in fact a clever parody, Miike's attempt to subvert the conventions of mainstream horror from the inside out. Given the director's willingness to work within the commercial mainstream- the kiddie-friendly nostalgic fantasy *The Great Yokai War* (*Yôkai Daisensô*, 2005), for example- this seems somewhat unlikely. There is one scene- a psychology lecturer describes the way that violence gives rise to a repetitive cycle of abuse- that could easily be read as a sideswipe at both the derivative nature of the film industry and the core elements of the post-*Ring* horror films (victims of violence return to commit violence, and so on), but for the most part *One Missed Call* is content to play it straight.

Obviously competing for the title of World's Most Unpleasant Nuisance Call, the curse begins with the victim receiving a phone message dated two or three days into the future; unknown to the recipient, it's a recording of the last few moments of their life. When the appointed time comes, the victim is seized by unseen hands and dragged to their death- in front of a train, down an elevator shaft, or simply torn apart. The next target is selected from the victim's phone book, and the cycle begins again. Thankfully Miike was able to demonstrate his flair for grotesque brutality, and these death scenes are the most effective moments in the film- witness the first victim's severed arm, still gripping the cell phone, slowly dialling the number of the next unfortunate soul. *One Missed Call* hits a high point with the third victim, whose head is ripped off during the televised exorcism that was supposed to save her life, while the terrified audience stampedes out the door. This streak of inventive cruelty is the film's most obvious point of similarity with the director's earlier works, although perhaps unsurprisingly it does not reach quite the same heights as *Audition* and *Ichi the Killer* (*Koroshiya Ichi*, 2001).

Unfortunately *One Missed Call* would also have benefited from the energy and creativity that characterise many of Miike's less conventional works. Like *Ring*, the bulk of the film consists of the heroine- Yumi, a psychology student, played lethargically by Shibasaki- trying to track down the origins of the curse, spurred on by the revelation that she is to be the next victim. Once again it involves the murder of a child by a parent, an act of familial violence that gives rise to justifiable post-mortem fury; but there's also a twist waiting in the wings that suggests any preconceived notions about the victim might be very wrong indeed (again). On top of the plot similarities *One Missed Call* also resembles *Ring* visually, probably thanks to Hideo Yamamoto, director of photography on both Nakata's *Ring 2* (1999) and *The Grudge* (2005). It's even possible to see shades of *The Ring*'s Samara Morgan in Miike's rotting, semi-decomposed phantom. There are times when his approach to the material becomes just as heavy-handed as Gore Verbinski's- witness the opening montage of cell phone users, apparently intended to remind the audience that such items are really quite popular. Like the repeated shots of television aerials in *The Ring* and the internet-based montage in Jim Sonzero's US version of *Pulse* (2006), it serves absolutely no purpose, except to provide a patronizing comment on the perceived intelligence of the average moviegoer.

When it does slouch out from beneath the shadow of other films *One Missed Call* manages to be both more surprising and more effective than many of its contemporaries, but too much of it is cut-and-paste moviemaking. However, this did not prove to be much of a hindrance at the box office, where it quickly became the most successful Japanese horror film of 2004, holding its own respectably against Hollywood horrors like *Underworld* (2003). The production line worked with alarming speed, and a sequel was in theatres less than twelve months later, under the obvious but somewhat clumsy title of *One Missed Call 2* (*Chakushin Ari 2*). With Miike departing for fresh pastures, the directorial chores were handed to relative newcomer Renpei Tsukamoto (no relation to Shinya Tsukamoto, director of the *Tetsuo* films), best known at the time for his 2004 supernatural comedy *Ghost Shout*.

As a sequel, *One Missed Call 2* hovers somewhere between building on the first film and re-inventing the material from scratch. Thanks to the televised decapitation the cell phone curse has become a well-known phenomenon, so when a waiter in a Chinese

# Vengeful Spirits, Part Two

restaurant is found with his head in a pot of boiling water after receiving a mysterious phone call, his friends immediately assume that he's the latest victim. Viruses mutate to become more contagious, and the curse now attacks whoever answers the phone, killing them even quicker than before. As it starts to spread through the waiter's friends, schoolteacher Kyoko (played by TV actress Mimura) and her boyfriend dig into history of the case, hoping to stop the curse before it takes them too. With the help of apathetic cop Renji Ishibashii- reprising his role from the first film- they trace the story back even further, to a tragedy that took place in Taiwan many years before. From there it's business as usual, with the couple racing to appease the vengeful spirit before their deadline runs out.

To his credit, Tsukamoto seems to appreciate that the standout moments of *One Missed Call* were the inventive death scenes, and devotes a certain amount of creativity and effort to getting them right. The best manages to rival Miike's offerings, with a female victim reduced to a grotesque human pretzel of twisted, broken limbs and crammed into a shower cubicle. However, like Miike he faces an uphill struggle to make the rest of the film seem as interesting, especially when hampered by the pointless compulsion to adhere to the *Ring* template. This attitude is most evident in the botched ending, which tries to copy Nakata's twist but succeeds only in rendering the entire film redundant. It's certainly surprising, but only because few professional scriptwriters would be daft enough to use it. Tsukamoto even recycles that irritating cell phone montage, although at least it's used here to reinforce the heroine's sense of despair about the task that lies ahead of them. A few interesting touches can't hide the fact that *One Missed Call 2* is even more creatively challenged than its predecessor.

Nevertheless, *One Missed Call 2* fared reasonably well at the box office- although not as well as the first film- so few people can have been honestly surprised when the

**One Missed Call**

optimistically titled *One Missed Call: Final* (2006) was announced, with the obligatory short-lived TV series in tow. Manabu Asô, director of the limp *Hypnosis* (*Saimin*, 1999) follow-up *Senrigan* (2000), was put in charge of both. By the time the film went into production a new horror phenomenon had burst on to the scene: *Death Note*. Directed by Shûsuke Kaneko and starring *Battle Royale* heartthrob Tatsuya Fujiwara, *Death Note* is about a teenager who acquires a book that allows

him to kill simply by writing the intended victim's name within it; needless to say, although the boy's motives are initially loosely altruistic, he soon begins to use it for purely selfish and increasingly megalomaniacal motives. *Death Note*'s commercial success did not go unnoticed, and one of the first films to throw itself upon the bandwagon was *One Missed Call: Final*, which now featured a frustrated and victimized teenager with the ability to send the curse out to each of the classmates that have made her life such a misery. Having received it from the ghost of another girl driven to commit suicide by their mutual enemies, class victim Asuka (Maki Horikita, from *Shibuya Kaidan* and *Premonition*) uses the cell phone curse to take revenge upon her tormentors while they're enjoying their last high school trip.

Like its predecessor, *One Missed Call: Final* changes the details a little- obviously influenced by the *Ring* curse, it can now be forwarded on, but only once- and stages most of the action in another Asian country, this time opting for South Korea (the film is a

# Vengeful Spirits, Part Two

Japanese-Korean co-production) instead of Taiwan. Unwisely, it also repeats the 'surprise' ending from *One Missed Call 2*. In a change from the formula, Asô steers clear of the kind of graphic and grotesque murders that characterized the earlier films, settling for sound effects and shots of the onlookers recoiling in horror from something we never see. Equally damaging are the characters. As usual the targets are typically irritating kids, but unlike the majority of Japanese movie teens they're also exceptionally unpleasant- when they discover that the curse can be avoided, they lose no time in consigning their friends to death by sending it to them. One boy is locked inside a closet so he can't forward the message to anyone else. Needless to say, he dies moments later. This approach serves only to undermine the film, since the victims so obviously deserve their fate that it's hard to root for Emily (Meisa Kuroki), the girl trying to stop the curse. Emily herself is the polar opposite of her friends, a considerate, intelligent girl who's dating a Korean deaf-mute she met on an international sign-language exchange trip. Although there's a certain amount of pleasure to be gained by watching this vile bunch get picked off one by one, by keeping the killings off-screen Asô fails to supply even the minor thrills that *One Missed Call 2* provided.

By the time the *One Missed Call* franchise ground to a halt, the wave of techno-oriented horrors had largely dried up. In Suzuki's novels Sadako eventually discards the technology that allowed her power to spread in favour of the benefits of physical existence, and subsequent vengeful spirits like Kayako are able to manipulate technology for their own ends without shackling themselves to *Ring*-style plots. While later ghost stories are far more likely to ape *Juon*'s haunted house and fractured chronology, the occasional cursed item still shows up. If nothing else, Takeshi Furusawa's *Ghost Train* (*Otoshimono*, 2006) demonstrates how little mileage is left in the concept. This time the item in question is a rail pass that mysteriously appears on the platform where its owner committed suicide; anyone public-spirited enough to pick it up and hand it in at the lost and found falls prey to the curse. Adults are simply thrown in front of a train, but if a child picks it up, the ghost steals their identity and attempts to murder their parents. Even Furusawa- a former classmate of Takashi Shimizu and assistant director on Kiyoshi Kurosawa's *Bright Future* (*Akarui Mirai*, 2003)- seems to recognize the inherent silliness of the plot, and drops it midway through in favour of a bizarre story about a 'supernatural hotspot' near the railway station. Apparently something lives in an underground cavern by the railway line, although precisely what is never actually explained. The only clue is a large statue of a vaguely Lovecraftian horned demon the heroes find in the cavern. Even more curious is the revelation that the teenage heroine plans to go abroad and study at Miskatonic University, the former home of the Reanimator himself, Dr. Herbert West. While *Ghost Train* is a resounding failure as a film, it has to be the first attempt to crossbreed *Ring* with *Quatermass and the Pit* (1967).

*(Footnotes)*

*1 It is worth noting that Japanese horror films have always relied more heavily on novels and manga as source material than their western counterparts, although this practice became even more popular after the success of Ring.*

# CHAPTER SEVEN
## Love and Mutation
## The Works of Junji Itô on Film and TV

The importance of manga in the development of modern Japanese horror cannot be underestimated. A sizeable number of the films described in this book are manga adaptations, from Shinya Tsukamoto's *Hiruko the Goblin* (1991) and Shimako Satô's *Wizard of Darkness* (1995), to Shusûke Kaneko's *Death Note* films, while many others-including the *Ring* series, *Battle Royale* (2000) and Katsuhiro Ôtomo's *World Apartment Horror* (1991)- have been adapted into manga themselves (*World Apartment Horror* was adapted by *Perfect Blue* director Satoshi Kon). Few manga artists have profited from the post-*Ring* Japanese horror boom as much as Junji Itô, creator of the acclaimed *Uzumaki* and *Tomie* mangas. Over the past decade, his work has been adapted into nearly a dozen features (both theatrical and V-cinema) and a clutch of made-for-TV specials, with the *Tomie* series alone reaching eight instalments. J-horror luminaries such as Takashi Shimizu and Norio Tsuruta have directed Itô adaptations, as well as genre regulars like Ataru Oikawa and Higuchinsky.

The most successful Itô-inspired effort - both as a film and an adaptation- is undoubtedly Higuchinsky's *Uzumaki* (2000). Thanks to the unusual theme and the parade of grotesquery that the Ukrainian-born director creates, it's also perhaps the strangest horror film released anywhere in recent years. The plot itself is simple but decidedly weird, told through the experiences of giggling schoolgirl Kirie (Eriko Hatsune) and her nerdy boyfriend Shuichi (Fhi Fan). For reasons that are never fully explained, the people of the town of Kurouzu are becoming obsessed with spirals. One of the first casualties is Shuichi's father (Ren Ôsugi), who has begun collecting anything that features a spiral pattern, from snail shells and vases all the way up to pilfered shop signs. His mounting obsession has taken over his life, forcing other considerations like family and work to take a distant back seat. But he is not the only victim; one schoolboy throws himself down a spiral staircase, dying immediately, while a girl begins to sculpt her hair into ever more elaborate spiral patterns. Other symptoms are even less explicable, such as the student who only comes to school when it rains and seems to be growing increasingly slimy, or the mysterious spirals of black smoke emerging from the crematorium.

Higuchinsky is in no hurry to provide an explanation for the events that are taking place. Instead he concentrates on presenting a series of vignettes that escalate from the slightly odd, right up to full-blown lunacy, such as the scene when Shuichi's father is found twisted into a spiral shape and stuffed in the spin-dryer. Shot in sickly shades of green, *Uzumaki* becomes a showcase for Higuchinsky's technical brilliance, as he employs almost every cinematic artifice imaginable, including abstract camera angles, flashy editing, extreme close-ups, colour filters, and a host of computer-generated images and digital manipulations. Most of these are deliberately eye-catching, but some are surprisingly subtle, such as the lengthy slow fade that almost imperceptibly shifts the camera's point of view from looking out of a car to looking in. Dotted throughout the film are a number of digitally-added spirals that appear briefly in the corners of the frame, lasting for a few seconds before fading away. All this is underpinned by Keiichi Suzuki and Tetsurô Kashibuchi's eccentric score, which combines cartoonish melodies, loopy guitar riffs and dark electronica into an unusual but entirely appropriate mixture.

Equally important is the cast, with Higuchinsky setting reliable, physically distinctive supporting players like Ren Ôsugi, Tarô Suwa and Denden opposite young, attractive genre favourites like Asumi Miwa and Hinako Saeki. Most of the actors give broad performances that verge on the grotesque but suit the mood of the film perfectly. Curiously, South Korean celebrity Shin Eun Kyung- star of the hit *My Wife Is A Gangster* series- also appears, playing a reporter covering the unusual events. The emotional centre of the film is Eriko Hatsune, who comes across as a genuinely innocent and sweet girl, adrift in the increasingly bizarre brand of madness that has overtaken the town. She also provides *Uzumaki*'s occasional sentimental moments, riding on the back of Shuichi's bike- in slow

*Japanese sleeve art for* **Uzumaki**

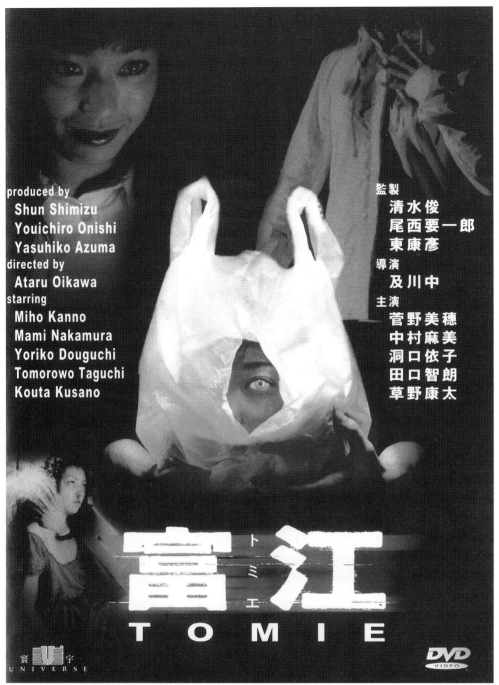

*Sleeve art for* **Tomie**

motion, of course, with the obligatory plaintive melody in the background- or cooing over pictures of the pair of them as children. Most of this is done with tongue firmly in cheek, although their final scene together, as a spiral begins to take over Shuichi's body, manages to be both genuinely affecting and rather silly at the same time.

The film's often-criticized episodic feel and lack of overall coherency are usually blamed upon the director's background in commercials and music videos, suggesting

# Love and Mutation

he is capable of five minute bursts of style-over-substance flashiness but unable to hold it together for an entire feature. Such accusations tend to ignore the fact that *Uzumaki's* structure is entirely inherited from the source material, which is distinctly episodic and stylized itself. In adhering to the spirit of Junji Itô's manga Higuchinsky has certainly created a film that values style over substance, but in a work as deliriously offbeat and inventive as *Uzumaki*, it's not necessarily a drawback.

Unsurprisingly, Higuchinsky has had difficulty following up such a distinctive film. In 2000 he also directed *Long Dream* (*Nagai Yume*), a made-for-TV adaptation of another Junji Itô manga, starring both Eriko Hatsune and Masami Horiuchi from *Uzumaki*. The story concerns a young man who complains of exceptionally long dreams- first days, then months and finally years. Although he wakes up in the hospital the following morning, to him it has been years since he was there, and decades since he last saw his visiting fiancé. When his dreams start to last far longer than the normal human lifespan, the patient begins to change physically, as if his unnatural lifespan is causing him to evolve into something else entirely. Working on an even smaller budget than *Uzumaki*, Higuchinsky is unable to reproduce that film's elaborate grotesquery and settles for a defiantly tongue-in-cheek tone that suits the cheap and silly special effects perfectly. Despite the technical shortcomings, *Long Dream* is rarely less than entertaining and makes an interesting companion to Higuchinsky's masterpiece. His only other release has been *Tokyo 10+01* (2002), an entertaining *Battle Royale* pastiche directed, produced, written, edited and shot by Higuchinsky himself.

*Uzumaki* represents one of Itô's two favourite themes: physical mutation and transformation. The *Tomie* series also deals with the second: love than distorts into obsession and finally murderous violence. Of the modern Vengeful Spirits, Tomie Kawakami is without a doubt the most persistent. So far she has appeared in four theatrical features and three V-cinema films, including one anthology piece. In most of these Tomie has been killed off at least once- in Takashi Shimizu's *Tomie: Rebirth* (2001) she's murdered three times- and subsequently resurrected to take revenge upon her killers. She made her first appearance in 1998's *Tomie*, written and directed by Ataru Oikawa, who also helmed *Tokyo Psycho* (2005). Mami Nakamura (*Tokyo Trash Baby*) stars as Tsukiko, a college student troubled by dreams of blood and violence. She's also suffering from amnesia, having lost three months of her memories. Her mother tells her the amnesia dates back to a car accident, but the persistent bad dreams and insomnia lead Tsukiko to seek the help of a psychiatrist. Through hypnosis Tsukiko hopes that she can recover her lost memories and put a stop to the nightmares. Tsukiko isn't the only person trying to find out what happened in those three months, however. Oddball detective Tomorowo Taguchi is investigating the killing of a teenage girl several months earlier; since then a number of the girl's classmates have committed suicide and even more have gone insane. Of course, the incident that Tsukiko is struggling to remember is the murder of her classmate, and the victim's name was Tomie Kawakami. Jealous of Tomie's increasing control over her boyfriend, Tsukiko took an axe to her former friend and buried the dismembered body parts before repressing all memory of her actions. Naturally, Tomie (played by Miho Kanno, a favourite genre villain since *Wizard of Darkness*) has little intention of remaining dead for long.

# Flowers From Hell

Oikawa's *Tomie* highlights many of the problems that the rest of the series would face. Told predominantly in short stories, the *Tomie* mangas do not lend themselves easily to full-length treatments. Itô's sometimes leaden pacing and simplistic (or occasionally non-existent) plotting are counterbalanced by his exceptional imagination and his flair for the unsettling- a trick that Higuchinsky wisely repeated in *Uzumaki*- but Oikawa relies too heavily on a plot that is effectively just another contemporary update of the standard Vengeful Spirit story. Hiroshi Futami's avant-garde score is hypnotic and atmospheric, and there are a few moments of typical Itô weirdness- the single orange eye peering out from a split in a bloody carrier bag- but for the most part *Tomie* limps along at a soporific pace before arriving at its entirely predictable conclusion.

Although still saddled with a sparse and predictable plot, Fujirô Mitsuishi's *Tomie: Replay* (2000) manages to be far more memorable and interesting than Oikawa's *Tomie*. The film opens with a young girl lying on an operating table, her stomach greatly swollen and distended. As the chief surgeon makes the first incision, he is greeted by the same single orange eyeball blinking up at him. When the head is removed and placed in a tank, Tomie (Mai Hôshô) begins to grow, stalks sprouting from her neck and developing into arms and legs. Meanwhile all the surgeons and nurses involved in the operation are disappearing, committing suicide or going insane. The chief surgeon's daughter Yumi (Sayaka Yamaguchi, from Naomi Kawase's *Suzaku*) is determined to find her missing father, assisted by the friend of a boy who has fallen under Tomie's spell. Mitsuishi is unable to overcome all the deficiencies of Satoru Tamaki's script- the two teenagers are simply not very interesting, and the climax is protracted and dull- but the inclusion of a number of horrifying images and sequences, combined with Hideo Yamamoto's excellent cinematography, helps to lift *Tomie: Replay* above the tedium of the first film.

The best film in the series is *Tomie: Rebirth*, the theatrical debut of Takashi Shimizu, director of the *Juon* films. Shimizu takes a noticeably less serious approach to the material than his predecessors, wringing plenty of black humour out of the repeated attempts to get rid of Tomie (Miki Sakai) once and for all. The victims this time are a group of students who assist one of their friends in disposing of the body of his troublesome girlfriend (Tomie of course), only to find her resurrected and eager for revenge. Much of the humour derives from the power struggle between Tomie and her new boyfriend's possessive mother, who is determined to separate her beloved son from his girlfriend, whatever the cost. Tomie proves more than a match for her however, exploiting any situation to make it appear that the mother is physically abusing her. Eventually the son decides it's time to get rid of Tomie, and mother is all too happy to help dispose of the body. In the film's most memorable scene, mother and son relive fond moments from his childhood, all the time elbow deep in the dismembered remains of his girlfriend. As well as *Tomie: Rebirth* Shimizu also directed the second- and best- episode of the *Itô Junji Kyôfu Collection* ('*Junji Itô fear collection*'), a three-part anthology film, with the other episodes directed by Ryûta Miyake and Issei Oda.

*Tomie Final Chapter: Forbidden Fruit* (*Tomie Saishûshô Kindan no Kajitsu*), the last theatrical entry in the series, appeared in 2002, directed by Shun Nakahara. Jun Kunimura (*Audition*) stars as a middle-aged widower who lives alone with this shy and withdrawn

# Love and Mutation

daughter Tomie (Aoi Miyazaki), who he named after a girl he knew many years ago- a girl who was later murdered by her jealous boyfriend. When a new student (Nozomi Andô, from *Suicide Manual* and *Gamera 3*) shows up at school, Tomie is drawn to her because she's attractive, confident and- most importantly- she has the same unusual name. Unfortunately her father is also interested in the new Tomie- he was obsessed with her years ago and his attentions provoked her boyfriend's murderous rage. But her affections do not come for free, and Tomie's price is the death of her suitor's daughter. Although it boasts a more interesting story, *Tomie Final Chapter* is another lacklustre and disappointing entry in the series. There is little here that hasn't already been explored in the earlier films, and a pair of talented leads cannot rescue yet another failed attempt to stretch the threadbare plot even further. After Nakahara's film *Tomie* retired to the world of direct-to-video releases,

the elephant's graveyard of horror movie franchises. Before that came the made-for-TV *Tomie: Another Face* (*Tomie: Kyôfu no Bishôjo*, 1999), a mediocre three-part anthology starring Runa Nagai in the title role. Ataru Oikawa returned to the series in 2005, writing and directing two back-to-back sequels, *Tomie: Beginning* and *Tomie: Revenge*, with little of interest in either of them. The eighth film in the series was 2007's *Tomie vs. Tomie*, directed by Tomohiro Kubo. In quantity the *Tomie* franchise has outstripped both the *Ring* and the *Juon* series, but in terms of quality has yet to produce a film that rivals even the weakest entries in either of those.

FROM THE MIND OF **JUNJI ITO** CREATOR OF **UZUMAKI** AND **TOMI**

*Love Ghost*

In much the same way that *Deliverance* (1972) and *The Texas Chainsaw Massacre* (1974) reflect urban America's distrust of its rural equivalent, films like *Shikoku* (1999),

# Flowers From Hell

*Inugami* (2001) and *The Curse* (*Noroi*, 2005) suggest that the city-dwelling Japanese are equally suspicious of their rural cousins; once you get away from the urban sprawl of civilisation you're in a different world, where ancient magic still holds sway and sinister rituals are still observed. It might seem like a stretch to connect the horrors of Leatherface with quiet, restrained films like *Shikoku*, but the only major difference between Tobe Hooper's family of cannibals and *The Curse*'s grotesque, baby-eating rituals is simply one of approach: *The Texas Chainsaw Massacre* shows you the full extent of the brutality, while *The Curse* leaves it to the viewer's imagination. With British cult classic *The Wicker Man* (1973) as its template, Norio Tsuruta's *Kakashi* (2001) sees another unwary traveller straying off the path. When Kaoru (Maho Nonami) arrives in the village of Kozukata looking for her brother, the reception is predictably frosty: he's not here, and you can't stay either. Undeterred, Kaoru discovers

**Love Ghost**

that her brother came to the village at the request of old school friend Izumi (Kô Shibasaki), who is nowhere to be found. Meanwhile, the villagers are gathering up a large number of kakashi ('scarecrows') in preparation for the festival of the year. The roots of this ritual are to be found in the distant past and reflect the Shinto belief that all objects have souls. For centuries the villagers have called upon benevolent spirits to possess the kakashi and look after their fields, but in recent years they have taken to summoning their deceased loved ones, giving them a second lease of life in the straw bodies they construct. Unfortunately not all of these new spirits are benevolent and kind, and now the villagers cannot control them. Izumi herself died years before- probably at her own hands- and her mother intends to bring her back at the next festival.

Alternating between sullen stares and open hostility, Tsuruta's villagers are a typically morose lot that wouldn't look out of place in The Slaughtered Lamb. Very few of them speak, and many wear white gloves that help to hide the village's Dark Secret. In this respect they're similar to the townspeople in Gary Sherman's underrated *Dead and Buried* (1981); like the good folk of Potter's Bluff, the inhabitants of Kozukata have found a way of securing eternal life. In *Dead and Buried* they're turned into zombies after their natural

# Love and Mutation

life ends, while in Tsuruta's film their souls are transferred to the kakashi themselves, and the white gloves cover up the fact that they are literally men of straw. The scarecrows are also one of the most interesting variations on *Ring*'s Vengeful Spirits seen in recent years. Although Tsuruta still feels compelled to include the more typical ghostly manifestation, his kakashi are far more effective and provide the film's most memorable and atmospheric moments. They are just as deadly as their more commonplace incarnations, however: when the resurrected Izumi does appear, she is obviously not interested in playing the dutiful daughter any more, and her first action is to snap her mother's neck like a twig. Another moment of *Night of the Living Dead*-inspired parricide occurs when a little girl comes back to life as a kakashi and kills her abusive father. When compared with her bland performance in *One Missed Call* (2004), *Kakashi* provides further evidence that Kô Shibasaki is better suited to playing monsters- whether human (as in *Battle Royale*) or non-human- than heroines.

Like Tsuruta's earlier *Ring 0: Birthday* (2000) and the later *Premonition* (2005), *Kakashi* suffers from the director's inability to inject the material with the kind of urgency and pace it deserves. Kaoru and the other escapees might well be running for their lives, but the film itself is struggling to catch up. What little tension has been generated is entirely lost when the ludicrous conclusion arrives and Kaoru decides she'd rather stay with her recently resurrected brother, even though she knows the kakashi are thoroughly evil and has barely survived their repeated attempts to kill her. Like Stephen King's *Pet Sematary* and the Italian cult horror film *Zeder* (1983), *Kakashi* asks us to believe that the heroine would be willing to overlook these difficulties in order to have her loved one back, but the idea is not particularly convincing, and the film suffers because of it. Similar problems afflict Zenboku Satô's *Oshikiri* (2000), which doesn't even have an interesting monster, although Eriko Hatsune does appear briefly (again).

Perhaps the most underrated Itô adaptation is Kazuyuki Shibuya's *Shibito no Koiwazaru*, released in the US under the faintly silly title of *Love Ghost* (2000). Like *Tomie*, *Love Ghost* is a tale of murderous and obsessive love, but rather than stretch a single short story out to feature length, Kazuyuki Shibuya and co-scriptwriter Naoyuki Tomomatsu (himself the director of the 2001 zombie spoof *Stacy*) combine two Itô works into one consistently interesting and often surprising film. Midori (Risa Gotô, from Hideo Nakata's *The Sleeping Bride*) is a high school student returning to the town where she was born after several years' absence. Ever since she arrived, Midori has been having a recurring dream about a roadside shrine, and a handsome black-clad boy who appears in a cloud of mist. On her way to her new school she sees the same shrine, and realizes that the dream may not entirely be a product of her imagination. However, it's her first day at a new school, and she has other things to worry about. Very soon Midori has met her old friend Ryusuke (Ryûhei Matsuda), made a new one (Asumi Miwa) and attracted the attention of Tejima, a handsome basketball player. Unfortunately, Tejima has other admirers, and before long Midori has acquired an enemy too. In order to see if her crush will work out, the girl decides to perform tsujiura, an ancient method of fortune-telling that involves standing in front of a roadside shrine, covering your eyes and asking the first passer-by to tell your fortune. When she does this, the mists gather and the handsome black-clad boy from Midori's dream appears, but his prediction is not a happy one: not only will her current crush remain unrequited, but she will never be loved at all. Distraught, the girl takes a craft-knife and slashes her throat. But the problems do not end with the girl's suicide; Midori's new friend is also obsessed with Tejima, and resolves to seek advice by performing tsujiura.

As with many post-*Ring* horror films, the root of the problem lies in a tragic and unresolved incident that took place some years before. However, Shibuya and Tomomatsu wisely avoid recycling most of the *Ring* and *Juon* cliches and scare tactics. Instead they have created a carefully plotted, atmospheric film that is equal parts supernatural thriller and sentimental drama. In appearance *Love Ghost* resembles the latter, being set in a small rural town and shot in naturalistic shades of green and yellow (occasionally interrupted by sprays of bright red arterial blood). The casting of Risa Gotô in the lead is no doubt intended to echo the romantic fantasy of Nakata's *Sleeping Bride*, while Kumiko Akiyoshi, the actress who plays Midori's mother, appeared in a similar role in Nobuhiko Obayashi's nostalgic fantasy-horror *Ijintachi Tono Natsu* (1987). Equally significant is the decision to cast both Asumi Miwa and her sister Hitomi. The pair have appeared in a number of films together (including the first V-cinema *Juon* and Toshiharu Ikeda's *Shadow of the Wraith*), but in *Love Ghost* they play parallel roles, distant in time but conceptually linked: each sister plays a woman with an unrequited obsession who eventually kills herself in a final bid to gain her love's attention. The bloody conflict to come is hinted at several times in the surprisingly clever script: a teacher jokingly describes his pupils as 'warriors' who must compete for Midori's hand, while a biology lesson focusing on the alarmingly brutal mating practices of the sparrow prefigures the devastating revelations about Midori's past. The frequent references to fortune-telling and superstition littered throughout the film- from tsujiura to tarot cards, horoscopes and even a four-leaf clover- are also connected to an incident in the her childhood, although many of these symbols and portents only become apparent on a second viewing.

A bizarre footnote to the main Itô adaptations is Hideyuki Kobayashi's *Marronnier* (2003). Presented by Itô himself, *Marronnier* is a curious low-budget horror film about an insane dollmaker who is turning human corpses into popular and highly sought-after 'Marronnier' dolls. Itô's actual creative input was limited to designing the dolls themselves, which are suitably creepy and occasionally reference the author's own works, including *Uzumaki*. As well as Itô, a few other manga artists were involved with the production too- acting roles were also played by Misao Inagaki, who drew the *Ring* manga, and popular horror veteran Ochazukenori (*Horror Mansion*). Although the production standards are even lower than *Long Dream*, *Marronnier* does manage to capture some of the feel of Itô's manga, and the artist's own involvement makes it something of an interesting curiosity.

# CHAPTER EIGHT
## Takashi Shimizu and the Juon Series

The most important of the post-*Ring* horror franchises is the *Juon* series. Having progressed from direct-to-video (*Juon* and *Juon 2*, both 2000) to theatrically released (2002's *Juon: The Grudge* and 2003's *Juon: The Grudge 2*) and on to US-funded remakes (*The Grudge*, 2004, and *The Grudge 2*, 2006), the *Juon* franchise has become a key factor in the continued popularity of Japanese horror, both domestically and internationally. Although he has now handed over the reins to an American director for the forthcoming *The Grudge 3*, series creator Takashi Shimizu has been in the unusual position of retaining control over the franchise from its inception, directing all six instalments released to date. This in turn has allowed him to divide his time between comparatively high-profile mainstream US releases like *The Grudge* and smaller, more experimental projects such as *Marebito* (2004), in much the same way that Guillermo del Toro alternates between multiplex fodder like *Blade II* (2002) and highly personal efforts like *The Devil's Backbone* (2001).

The seeds of his lucrative career were sown in 1997 when, at the suggestion of Kiyoshi Kurosawa, Shimizu was asked to direct a couple of short segments for *Haunted School G* (*Gakkô no Kaidan G*, 1998), part of Kansai TV's hit series. Kurosawa, one of Shimizu's film school lecturers, had been involved with the series since 1994 and put his student's name forward as a potential contributor. Not only did this provide Shimizu with his first professional assignment, but these two segments- '*4444444444*' and '*In A Corner*', each of them only three minutes long- also introduced Kayako and Toshio, the now-familiar stars of the *Juon* series. Two years later, thanks to the backing of *Ring* producer Takashige Ichise and a distribution deal with Toei Video, Shimizu was able to expand the two *Haunted School G* shorts into a pair of 70-minute V-cinema features, *Juon* and *Juon 2* (a.k.a. *Juon: The Curse* and *Juon: The Curse 2*), with *Ring* scriptwriter Hiroshi Takahashi on board as 'creative consultant'. Although shot at the same time the two films were released separately. *Juon 2* begins immediately after its predecessor, but recycles 30 minutes of footage from the first film before continuing the story. With little more than half-an-hour of new material, it seems likely that the decision to release a sequel was a financial rather than creative one.

Like the 'true story' anthologies of the mid-90s, Juon is broken up into 10-20 minute segments, each named after the central character. Rather than create stand-alone episodes, Shimizu follows several different story lines, distant in time but anchored to the same place, a house in Tokyo's Nerima ward. Like all haunted houses, it has an unpleasant history; after discovering that his wife Kayako (Takako Fuji) was obsessed with a schoolteacher, unhinged artist Takeo Saeki (Takashi Matsuyama) killed her and their son Toshio (Ryôta Koyama), before murdering the teacher's pregnant wife. Since then the ghosts of wife and son have remained in the house, preying upon anyone unfortunate enough to enter. Like Sadako, they're not particularly interested in revenge- although

# Flowers From Hell

Kayako's first victim was her insane husband- but simply in spreading fear and death, as the curse moves through each victim's family, friends and associates. The first of *Juon's* parallel plots follows the immediate aftermath of the murders, as Kobayashi- the unwitting focus of Kayako's obsession- goes to visit the house in order to find out why Toshio has been absent from school, unaware of the events that took place there the night before and the gruesome fate that awaits his wife. From there the story jumps backwards and forwards in time, following the curse from its inception through the ever-widening circle of victims, including Kobayashi and his wife, the next family to move into the house, the estate agent trying to sell the property two years later, and so on. Each of the films in the franchise follows the same pattern, using one character as the 'anchor' for the plot, while the curse moves further afield.

Despite the low budget *Juon* is surprisingly well cast, with several genre and cult favourites making appearances, although most of them have relatively little screen time. Yûrei Yanagi, a comedian and former member of the 'Kitano Army' who had already starred in Hideo Nakata's *Ghost Actress* (1996), plays the unfortunate schoolteacher Kobayashi. He is not the only comedian in the cast- stand-up comic Denden (*Uzumaki*) appears as a detective, partnered up with Tarô Suwa, probably the busiest man in Japanese horror. Scream queen sisters Hitomi and Asumi Miwa

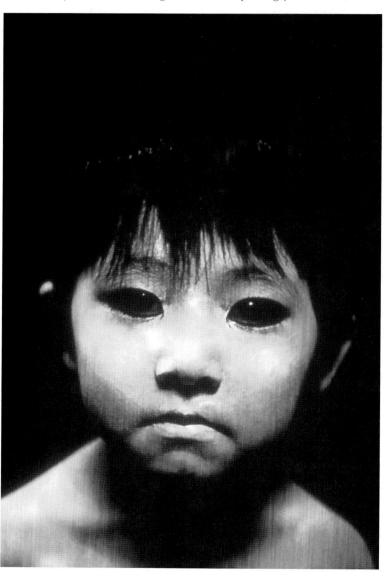

**Juon: The Grudge**

also star, in their first appearance together, as does a pre-*Battle Royale* Chiaki Kuriyama. Takako Fuji and Takashi Matsuyama would become series regulars, appearing in every instalment, including the US remakes, while Yûya

**Juon: The Grudge**

Ozeki replaced Ryôta Koyama in *Juon: The Grudge* (2001) and the films that followed.

Unsurprisingly, the *Juon* films take a fair amount of inspiration from *Ring*. With her twisted form and jerky movements, Kayako is obviously modelled on Sadako, and her appearances are sometimes reminiscent of the infamous crawling-out-of-the-TV scene from *Ring*, although more frequent and generally less unnerving. Shimizu has also learnt some valuable lessons from Nakata about the use of sound as an effective replacement for more expensive special effects-driven scares. In the *Juon* series each of the ghosts are given 'signature sounds' that precede their appearances- the clicking of the box-cutter that killed her for Kayako, and the pattering of a child's feet or the mewling of his dead cat for Toshio. The director pays close attention to the uniquely Japanese characteristics of the house- the tatami mats, the sliding doors, the family altar, and the closets in particular. By attaching these everyday objects to his supernatural themes, Shimizu underlines the connection between Japanese tradition and the darkness at the heart of the story.

Equally important is the influence of American horror of the 1980s- in particular the *Friday the 13th* and *A Nightmare on Elm Street* franchises- most visible in the shift of focus from the victim/hero to the villain. While Megumi Okina and Noriko Sakai make attractive, interesting heroines, their primary purpose is to provide the films with a coherency they might not otherwise have, allowing Shimizu to build to an appropriate climax. Rarely do his leading ladies survive the end of the movie; Sarah Michelle Gellar is an exception, but then she jumps off the top of the hospital in the first few minutes of *The Grudge 2* (2005). Like Jason Voorhees and Freddy Krueger, Kayako and Toshio are the real stars; the audience aren't there to root for the good guys, but to see what unpleasant fates Kayako and Toshio have in store for their unsuspecting victims. They're also the only recurring characters, aside from a group of schoolgirls that form the link between the V-cinema instalments and the theatrical ones. Shimizu is fond of throwing in references to his favourite slasher movies - the second segment in *Juon* ends in a montage depicting the empty rooms in the house, a sequence lifted from the final moments of John Carpenter's *Halloween* (1978). Appropriately enough, the star/victim of the segment is a young private tutor (Hitomi Miwa), a profession that could be justifiably described as the Japanese equivalent of the American babysitter. When Kayako croaks down the phone at her victims, it's hard not to think of similar moments in *A Nightmare on Elm Street* (1984). Like many of his contemporaries, Shimizu also draws upon urban legends for inspiration, from the cursed cell phone number ('*4444444444*') to the moment in *Juon: The Grudge* where Kayako emerges from the last cubicle in the public toilet, a favourite haunt of legendary ghosts.

Despite some of the conceptual similarities, Shimizu's approach to the material is often very different to that of contemporaries like Hideo Nakata and Kiyoshi Kurosawa, particularly in the early instalments. His theme is the cyclical nature of violence- always set within the family unit- and he punctuates the narrative with appropriately bloody and brutal sequences. Instead of *Ring*'s atmosphere of unseen menace, *Juon* gives us the sight of a blood-drenched schoolgirl with her jaw ripped off. Thanks to the low-budget special effects- both computer-generated and practical- this explicit approach isn't always entirely successful but at the very least the film leaves behind some very memorable images, several of which found their way into Shimizu's big-budget US remake, *The Grudge*. Perhaps unsurprisingly, *Juon*'s most shocking sequence- the one involving the body of Kobayashi's unborn child- was not repeated. As the series moved from V-cinema to multiplex, Shimizu has toned down the brutality, although it still appears in his work outside the franchise.

*Ring* is about the story, but in the *Juon* films the story is mainly a device to frame Shimizu's elaborate death scenes. The mystery has been almost entirely removed, replaced by simple visceral scares. Nakata uses the possibility of a solution as a red herring, and films like *Shikoku* and *Isola* are content to provide clichéd happy endings, but Shimizu wastes little time on either. Unlike Sadako's curse, exposure is enough to kill, and the majority of victims are dead before they know what's happening. Conveniently, few people survive an encounter with the house, so there's never anyone around to warn the new tenants. Occasionally Shimizu allows a character to uncover the nature of the mystery- an estate agent in *Juon*, or a cop in *Juon: The Grudge*- but by that point their own association with the house has sealed their fate. Unknown to the hapless estate agent, he's living in the same apartment as the pregnant housewife that Takeo Saeki murdered, and his son has already succumbed to the curse.

Like many ghosts, Shimizu's phantoms are obsessed with their own deaths, and frequently force the house's new guests to witness the events that took place that night, or to act out the murders in morbid role-playing games. In a nod to *The Amityville Horror* (1979), the unfortunate husband in *Juon: The Grudge* ends up looking more and more like the insane Takeo, chewing his fingernails and muttering paranoid gibberish before dragging his wife's body up to the attic where he meets the same fate as his predecessor. In an intentionally humorous moment, a housewife beats her irritating husband over the

# Takashi Shimizu and the Juon Series

head with a frying pan, but Shimizu doesn't say whether she is actually possessed by Kayako or has simply had enough of his constant whining. As her husband lies twitching on the kitchen floor, she sits down to finish her breakfast in peace. The scene is replayed in *The Grudge 2*, but without the ambiguity or the humour.

The best film in the series- and Shimizu's best film overall- is 2001's *Juon: The Grudge*, a bigger-budgeted theatrically released reworking of the formula. Produced by Takashige Ichise with support from Nikkatsu and Kadokawa- and the assistance of 'creative consultants' Hiroshi Takahashi and Kiyoshi Kurosawa- *Juon: The Grudge* doesn't deviate too much from the formula laid down by the earlier films, but it's a leaner, more technically polished effort. The presence of a central character gives it a structure that its predecessors lacked, allowing Shimizu to generate tension within each separate episode and throughout the film as a whole. In the process of smoothing down the rough edges some of the raw, energetic feel of *Juon* and *Juon 2* has been lost, and the more shocking aspects have been diluted in line with the demands of mainstream horror. Despite these alterations, *Juon: The Grudge* is not simply a watered down version of the V-cinema films, and Shimizu's growing experience and confidence in the material more than make up for anything that might have been lost in the move to the mainstream.

Shimizu's star victim this time is Rika (Megumi Okina, from *St. John's Wort*), a volunteer care worker who becomes embroiled in the curse when she goes to visit an old woman living in Nerima. Although the woman is supposed to live with her son and daughter-in-law, she is alone in the house- except for a young boy Rika finds taped into a closet with his cat. Even more disturbing is the sight of a white-faced phantom hovering over the petrified old woman. Despite her encounter with Kayako and Toshio,

**Juon: The Grudge 2**

### Juon: The Grudge 2

Rika is allowed to escape unscathed- albeit as a temporarily catatonic wreck with a nice twitch that resurfaces whenever she hears that familiar meow. After digressing with other characters, Shimizu returns intermittently to Rika's story, eventually revealing her fate: to end up as one of Kayako's proxy victims, wrapped in plastic and hidden in the attic. The house has claimed another victim but also, it is suggested, another resident. The film's final moments are typical of the director's mock-serious, tongue-in-cheek approach, as we are shown a solemn montage of the empty Nerima streets, windswept and deserted, strewn with 'Missing Person' leaflets.

No longer hampered by the financial and technical limitations of low-budget filmmaking, Shimizu takes full advantage of the facilities available to him. Even though they were generally competent and professional productions, on a purely technical level *Juon: The Grudge* is far superior to its predecessors. Composer Shirô Satô provides a dense, multi-layered soundtrack that veers from discordant guitar feedback through dark muted electronica to Herrmannesque screeching violins. The sound effects are equally interesting, featuring the 'signature sounds' of Kayako and company- increased in volume significantly- but also throwing in a great deal of simplistic but surprisingly eerie noises. Despite its comfortable suburban setting Shimizu fills the house with sounds more appropriate for crumbling English manor houses and Transylvanian castles, including

# Takashi Shimizu and the Juon Series

creaking stairs, the cobweb-strewn chandelier that squeaks as it swings back and forth, and the disembodied sound of footsteps upstairs. At certain key moments Shimizu relies entirely upon sound to create the atmosphere and tension- such as the indistinct dragging sound that accompanies one character as she walks down a deserted corridor- allowing him to keep the ghosts themselves off-screen until the last minute. *Juon: The Grudge* showcases Shimizu's non sequitur scares at their best, providing a wealth of unsettling moments. As one nervous victim (Misaki Itô) takes the elevator up to her apartment, Toshio appears on every floor, peering in unobserved; when she reaches her home, the picture on the television twists and distorts into a bizarre version of Munch's *The Scream*; when she hides in her bed, Kayako appears beneath the duvet with her. In a variation on *A Nightmare on Elm Street*'s bathtub scene, a pale white hand reaches out to touch Megumi Okina on the shoulder as she showers.

Although *Juon: The Grudge* adheres to the template laid down in the earlier films, Shimizu also explores ways of stepping outside the anthology format, literally and figuratively breaking down the barriers between the different segments. Here the chronological games are even more elaborate than usual: in the house a teenage girl meets her father who fell victim to the curse several years before, while a radio informs us in advance of another victim's as-yet-unseen demise. The connections between characters and segments have become increasingly complex, and the segments themselves follow a less strictly linear timeline. This process continued in *Juon: The Grudge 2* and reached its logical conclusion with *Reincarnation* (*Rinne*, 2005), a film that followed a similar narrative path to the *Juon* series, but dispensed with the format entirely.

Work began on the sequel while *Juon: The Grudge* was still in theatres, motivated by the film's strong box office performance and the favourable response from audiences. Although Yui Ichikawa returns as schoolgirl Chiharu, *Juon: The Grudge 2* introduces a new set of primary characters, most importantly Kyoko Harase (Noriko Sakai from *Premonition*), a pregnant actress known as 'the horror queen'. As the celebrity guest on a TV show, Kyoko visits a supposedly haunted house and soon finds herself the unwelcome focus of Kayako and Toshio's post-mortem fury. An accident on the way home from the shoot leaves Kyoko's boyfriend in a coma and causes her to miscarry, but a medical check-up weeks later shows her to be pregnant once again. As the curse spreads through the television crew, Kyoko begins to suspect that something malevolent may be growing inside her.

Television and film crews have been the focus of a number of Japanese horror films, including Kiyoshi Kurosawa's *Sweet Home* (1989), Hideo Nakata's *Ghost Actress* (1996), *St. John's Wort* (2001), *Dead Waves* (2005) and *The Curse* (2006). Unlike most of those films, Shimizu takes the opportunity to throw in a few satirical comments about the horror industry. Kyoko Harase is trying to make a name for herself as a serious actress, but her agent keeps pushing her as 'the horror queen', a title she does not appreciate. The quality of her roles also leaves something to be desired; few people are likely to take her seriously while she's appearing in films with memorably cheesy titles like The Cursed Sliding Door and pretending to be psychic on lousy TV documentaries about haunted houses. In one scene we see Kyoko filming a new movie, playing a typically challenging role that requires her to walk into a darkened room, scream, and then faint theatrically. These comments are not intended as genuine criticisms of the low-budget, mass-produced horror market; after all, Shimizu works perilously close to that arena himself and has often been accused of the same mercenary cynicism that produces films like The Cursed Sliding Door. There are a number of other humorous moments in *Juon: The Grudge 2* too. It's hard to know how seriously we're supposed to take the sight of a woman being menaced by a wig, but certainly the *It's Alive* - inspired climax in a hospital delivery room is so ludicrously over the top that it automatically raises a smile. Along with the humour, *Juon: The Grudge 2* also includes a number of Shimizu's well-timed scares and suspense scenes. The standout episode concerns a young TV presenter who hears a knocking sound on her wall late at night, even though she lives in the corner apartment and has no neighbours on that side. She only understands at the moment of her death, when Shimizu's fractured chronology reveals that the noises are the sound of her feet hitting the wall as Toshio swings her hanging corpse back and forth. Most of the scares hit their mark, and if the result is not quite as great as *Juon: The Grudge*, it's probably because the concepts are becoming repetitive, rather than any flaws in Shimizu's execution.

Scripted by Stephen Susco and produced by Sam Raimi and Robert Tapert's Ghost House Pictures, Shimizu's English-language debut *The Grudge* plays it safe by reworking the most effective moments from the previous Japanese instalments. The bulk of the film is drawn from *Juon* and *Juon: The Grudge*, with expatriate Americans replacing most of the characters: the central figure is still the home care volunteer, but this time played by Sarah Michelle Gellar. The end result is a film that holds no surprises for established fans of the series, but does a reasonable job of tailoring the basic ideas to mainstream international audiences. Some elements make the transition quite well. For example, Shimizu's preference for traditional Japanese housing and furniture- intended to seem commonplace and ordinary to domestic audiences- seems alien and unusual when presented alongside an American family, highlighting just how far from home they really are. The decision to set the film in Japan was a wise one, separating *The Grudge* from the flawed attempts to transplant *Ring* and *Pulse* (2001) into American locales. However, there's also very little here that hasn't been done before, and generally better, by the same director. A notable exception is a scene taken from the first *Juon* film and originally let down by the low-budget special effects. In *The Grudge* the scene is repeated, but with better and more realistic effects.

*The Grudge* justifies its existence as an attempt to bring Shimizu's work to a wider audience and relies on tried and tested elements from the earlier efforts. In contrast *The Grudge 2* is primarily composed of new material written for the sequel. Shimizu himself has stated that it was his intention to bring the series- or at least the American franchise-to a close with *The Grudge 2*, but was unable to decide on a suitable conclusion and ended up simply continuing the story. It's hardly surprising then that the resulting film is somewhat half-hearted. Like *Ring 0: Birthday* (2000), *The Grudge 2* tries to squeeze more mileage from the material by providing more information about the characters and their history. Unfortunately, it also falls into the trap of providing too much information and sacrificing the brevity of the original. Rather than simply being a woman murdered

# Takashi Shimizu and the Juon Series

*The Amercian remake of* **The Grudge**

by her jealous husband because of her obsession with another man, it now emerges that Kayako has been cursed since her own childhood, when her shaman mother forced her to become a vessel for the psychic evils she removed from her clients. Her murderous rage is not the result of her unjustified murder, but a side-effect of the evils she carried throughout her life. Not only does this sit uncomfortably with the previous explanations, but it also unnecessarily shifts some of the blame off Kayako's insane husband. Coupled with the clumsy attempts at making the curse spread across the Pacific, it makes *The Grudge 2* the weakest film in the series, and perhaps Shimizu's least enjoyable film overall.

Shimizu pushed the gore and the black humour to the forefront in his theatrical debut, which saw him handling yet another icon of modern Japanese horror, the eternally youthful *Tomie*. Although the series as a whole is somewhat mediocre- of the other films, only Fujirô Mitsuishi's *Tomie Replay* (2000) is worth seeing- *Tomie Rebirth* (2001) benefits greatly from Shimizu's tongue-in-cheek approach, resulting in a number of memorable moments, including a nicely subversive mother-and-son bonding session that takes place while they're dismembering his murdered girlfriend.  Misty-eyed childhood memories are underscored by the sound of hacksaws cutting through flesh. In *Juon* the jealous husband slaughtered his wife and son, but in *Tomie Rebirth* it's the mother and son's turn to indulge in a little murderous rage. As with all of Shimizu's films, it's the dysfunctional family unit

# Flowers From Hell

that provides both the killers and the victims.

In the weeks before beginning work on *The Grudge*, Shimizu filmed his second non-*Juon* feature. Shot mainly on digital, *Marebito* (a.k.a. *The Stranger From Afar*) follows unhinged cameraman Masuoka (Shinya Tsukamoto) as he uncovers a doorway into a mysterious world beneath the streets of Tokyo. As he explores this subterranean world, Masuoka finds a girl, naked and apparently half-dead, lying in the ruins of a strange city. Naming her simply 'F', the cameraman takes the girl back to his apartment. Mute and lethargic, F will not touch food or drink, even though she is growing weaker by the day and will probably die soon without nourishment. After accidentally cutting himself, Masuoka discovers why the girl will not eat or drink- her preferred diet is blood, preferably human. By opening his own veins he is able to restore her health, but realises that before long he will have to find another source of blood for the girl.

*Marebito* is easily Shimizu's most experimental and unusual film to date. Chiaki Konaka's eclectic script mixes together elements of Hollow Earth theory and HP Lovecraft, throwing in references to Madame Blavatsky, Werner Herzog's *The Enigma of Kaspar Hauser* (1974) and *Kolchak: The Night Stalker* along the way. Appropriately enough for a film that might be taking place entirely in one man's mind, Shimizu uses the confined spaces and handheld camerawork to establish a claustrophobic atmosphere, deliberately avoiding long shots wherever possible. *Tetsuo* director Shinya Tsukamoto plays Masuoka as a blank-faced, inscrutable figure whose apparent lack of emotion conceals the precise depths of his psychological instability. Unfortunately Marebito begins to falter about the halfway point, when Konaka's script becomes caught up in more traditional symptoms of Masuoka's insanity and eventual revelations that are a lot less interesting than the cameraman's fantasies. However, despite its flaws Shimizu cannot be accused of simply

# Takashi Shimizu and the Juon Series

recycling typical conventions or his previous work- there are no pallid, long haired ghosts or infectious curses here- and *Marebito* indicates a definite willingness to push the boundaries of his preferred genre,

In contrast to the low-budget, low-key *Marebito* is *Reincarnation*, Shimizu's contribution to Takashige Ichise's J-Horror Theatre series. Shot on a budget of around $4 million- a surprisingly large amount for a Japanese horror film- *Reincarnation* is perhaps the most complex manifestation of the themes the director explored in the *Juon* films. The film follows two main characters, the first a young actress and the second a college student. Despite being a relative unknown, Nagisa Sugiura (pop star Yûka) has managed to secure a prominent part in the latest movie from Ikuo Matsumara (Kippei Shiina, from Takashi Ishii's *Gonin*), a director with a reputation for grotesque and gory films. His next project is based on the real-life massacre of eleven people- including the killer's own wife and daughter- at a Tokyo hotel in 1970. As she prepares for the role of the killer's daughter (converted in the movie to a teenager), Nagisa begins to see visions of her real-life counterpart everywhere she goes. Eventually these visions become full-blown flashbacks, and the young actress starts to doubt her sanity. But she's not alone; a college student (Karina) has been seeing the same images since she was a child, and now she's trying to track the source.

Like the *Juon* films, the plot of *Reincarnation* is anchored to the site of several bloody murders- committed by a father- and ultimately driven by supernatural vengeance. While Shimizu doesn't stray far from established territory here, *Reincarnation* is a complex and consistently interesting take on the Vengeful Spirit tale. During the climax the film cuts between events in no less than three different versions of the hotel: the one in 1970, just before the murders; the derelict, ghost-ridden building of the present day; and the full-size replica sets made in the studio. Shimizu uses different colour palettes and film stock for each of the timelines- the events in 1970 are taken from a home movie, so they're shot on 8mm, for example. His stylish, technically fluent camerawork and the use of digital effects suggest that the director has learnt a few tricks from his experiences working on bugger-budgeted, US-backed movies like *The Grudge*, and *Reincarnation* is certainly one of Shimizu's most visually impressive films. He also includes a few references to his other works, with Tarô Suwa and Takako Fuji appearing in small roles. Kiyoshi Kurosawa also has a clever cameo appearance as a psychology lecturer attempting to debunk the core concept of the movie.

Unfortunately, *Reincarnation* failed to appeal to either critics or fans, suggesting that Shimizu might have visited that particular well too many times. Although more financially successful, *The Grudge 2* was equally slated by the critics, and few people can have been disappointed when the director announced that he would not be returning to the franchise for the third English-language *Grudge* film. With another Japanese instalment ready for release it remains to be seen if Shimizu can replicate the quality of the earlier films. Even if he cannot, it's only a matter of time before he turns his sizeable talents to another subject and demonstrates why he is considered one of Japan's most important horror directors.

# CHAPTER NINE
## The Post-Juon Horror film

Much like *Friday the 13th* (1979), the release of *Juon* and *Juon 2* in 2000 and the theatrical follow-ups was the catalyst for an almost immediate wave of similar low-budget horror films. Although *Ring* (1998) had been undeniably influential, it was the *Juon* series that really opened the floodgates. An adaptation of a bestselling novel, produced by a major studio and featuring a clutch of well-known TV and movie stars, *Ring* was not an easy act to follow, particularly for smaller production houses. The shot-on-video, direct-to-video *Juon* came from the opposite end of the spectrum, and provided ambitious but financially challenged filmmakers with a template they could copy without spending the kind of money that the major studios had to play with. Before long croaking, crawling Kayako-style ghosts had become commonplace, framed by Shimizu's episodic, fractured timelines and fleshed out with a cast of unknowns plus one or two minor league name actors with prior connections to the genre. However, the *Juon* formula was never wholeheartedly embraced by the major studios. Shimizu's own work aside- *Juon: The Grudge* (2002), *Juon: The Grudge 2* (2003) and *Reincarnation* (2005)- bigger-budgeted horror films were just as likely to pursue other directions - such as the *Death Note* (2006) series- or return to *Ring* for inspiration, like *One Missed Call* (2004).

Typical of these new V-cinema horrors is 2004's *Jurei: Gekijô ban: Kuro Jurei*, one of several in-name-only sequels produced by the prolific but notoriously cheap Broadway Films. Although director Kôji Shiraishi would later be responsible for the interesting faux-documentary *The Curse* (2005), *Jurei* is a poorly directed, slackly paced piece of derivative trash. Shiraishi is bold enough to steal the reverse-chronology from Christopher Nolan's *Memento* (2001) but since there's no mystery element to the story it makes no difference to the film. The story itself- after a teenager encounters a ghost at the cinema, a succession of her friends, family members and acquaintances die mysteriously- is so thin that Shiraishi is forced to pad the film out with lengthy pointless scenes just to reach the standard 70 minute V-cinema running time. As if to underline the *Juon* connection, Yûrei Yanagi is roped in for a single throwaway scene, once again playing a teacher. Despite its lack of redeeming features, Jurei received a US DVD release, under the title of *Jurei: The Uncanny*.

Slightly more deserving of their international DVD release are Kei Horie's *Shibuya Kaidan* and *Shibuya Kaidan 2* (2004), retitled *The Locker* for US audiences unfamiliar with the Shibuya district of Tokyo. In the first film, a group of fashionable young students-including Asami Mizukawa from *Dark Water* (2002)- begin to disappear after a date club party, presumably as a punishment for a practical joke that involved the destruction of a religious statue; in the second film ties the curse in with a an unpleasant real-life story about babies left in coin lockers. Since then, the spirit of the child has been killing anyone who uses the locker. Although the low budget is often apparent in the film's technical limitations, director Horie- who played one of the victims in *Juon: The Grudge 2* and appears as a cop here- shows enough talent to make it a genuine disappointment when he chooses to simply re-stage scenes from more famous films. Unlike many contemporary films, *Shibuya Kaidan* benefits from realistic characters and some imaginative scares but too often falls back on elements lifted from *Ring*, *Dark Water* and the *Juon* series.

As well as the newcomers, a handful of established filmmakers were drawn into the post-*Juon* explosion, such as Toshiharu Ikeda, director of *Evil Dead Trap* (1988), arguably the best Japanese horror film of the eighties. Based on a Nanaeko Sasaya manga, the two-part anthology *Shadow of the Wraith* (*Ikisudama*, 2004) found Ikeda collaborating with some of the *Evil Dead Trap* crew- cinematographer Norimichi Kasamatsu and composer Tomohiko Kira- and genre favourites Hitomi and Asumi Miwa. Unfortunately *Shadow of the Wraith* was also conceived as a vehicle for Kôji and Yûichi Matsuo- better known as pop duo 'Doggy Bag'- so periodically the film grinds to a halt while the handsome brothers show off their musical talents. Along with an irritating scene of the brothers performing a track from *Grease* (in Japanese), their presence also seems to have inspired the gimmicky casting of the Miwa sisters, allowing each of the film's two parts to feature one brother

*Sleeve art for* **The Booth**

and one sister. The first episode sees one brother being stalked by a female fan (Hitomi Miwa), who along with the usual psychosis seems to have supernatural powers and is determined to kill anyone who gets between her and her dream lover. The second part- in which the other brother suspects that his girlfriend Naoko (Asumi Miwa) may be living in a cursed apartment- is yet another retread of the Juon formula, with a few

*Sleeve art for* **Pray**

interesting touches and a reasonable performance from the female lead. Although the production values are solid, *Shadow of the Wraith* is strictly 'safe' horror, with none of the visceral terror of *Evil Dead Trap* and only a few watered-down echoes of the films that inspired it. A cursed apartment also appeared in Ataru Oikawa's dismal *Apartment 1303* (2007), a US-Japanese co-production starring Eriko Hatsune as the Vengeful Spirit causing a wave of suicides.

Most popular horror trends eventually devolve into parody, and the Vengeful Spirit theme was no different. Having helped spark off the entire movement by writing *Ring*, Hiroshi Takahashi also provided scripts for two over-the-top spoofs directed by Hirohisa Sasaki, *Crazy Lips* (*Hakkyôsuru Kuchibiru*, 2000) and *The Gore From Outer Space* (*Chi wo sû uchû*, 2001). In an apparent attempt to create the same anything-goes comedy as Takashi Miike's *The Happiness of the Katakuris* (*Katakurike no Kôfuku*, 2002), Sasaki and Takahashi blend together elements from half-a-dozen different genres, including ghost story, splatter movie, musical, pinku eiga and Hong Kong martial arts movies (a Hong Kong fight choreographer worked on the fight scenes). Hitomi Miwa, Hiroshi Abe, Ren Ôsugi and Kazuma Suzuki (*An Obsession; Tokyo Trash Baby*) do their best to navigate through this anarchic mixture, but almost everything here is poorly executed: the horror scenes are undercut by the humour, the comedy is too dark to be funny, and with no budget for special effects, the splatter consists entirely of computer-generated blood splashes on the screen. Worse still is the wide streak of nastiness and bad taste, from comedy noises during rape scenes to an unpleasant necrophilia routine that makes you wonder how Takahashi made a name for himself as a creator of subtle, psychological chills. Yoshihiro Hoshino's *Cursed* (*Chô Kowai Hanashi A: Yami no Karasu*, 2005) lacks the bad taste, although this collection of *Ring* and *Juon* spoofs isn't much more entertaining than *Crazy Lips*. Points go to Hoshino and co-scriptwriter Hirotoshi Kobayashi for setting their film in a convenience store built over an ancient burial ground, but the best joke here is the tills- whatever customers buy, the total comes to either 666 or 4444 yen (four is an unlucky number in Japan).

In 2005 Pony Canyon did their best to monopolise the V-cinema market by releasing two separate horror movie series. The first, the ironically titled '*New Generation Thriller*' series, is mainly comprised of fairly traditional takes on the Vengeful Spirit theme. At the bottom of the pile is Yôichirô Hayama's *Dead Waves* (*Shiryôha*, 2005), a clumsy compilation of elements lifted from *Ring* and *Pulse* (2001). Slightly better is Yoshihiro Nakamura's *Booth* (2005) in which a callous- and potentially murderous- DJ finds himself being held accountable for his past misdeeds by an unhappy spirit. The best of the series is Yûichi Satô's *Pray* (2005). Surly rock star type Tetsuji Tamayama and his pouting girlfriend Asami Mizukawa (*Dark Water; Shibuya Kaidan*) kidnap a child and hold her to ransom in order to raise money for a big drug deal, but find their plans unravelling when they contact the girl's parents only to be told that their daughter has been dead for a year. That's just the beginning, as Satô throws in enough twists to make your head spin and recycles moments from sources as disparate as *Dark Water* (2002) and *The Hidden* (1988). The end result is silly and rather unlikely, but *Pray* is at least entertaining, which is more than can be said for its running mate *Dead Waves*.

Pony Canyon's second series was the six-part Hideshi Hino Horror Theater, a collection of films adapted from the work of horror manga icon Hideshi Hino (director of the notorious fake snuff movie *Flowers of Flesh and Blood*) and co-produced with Shochiku. Ever since his career began in the 1970s Hino has been one of Japan's leading purveyors of grotesque and gruesome manga, with his output running into hundreds of volumes. Despite his popularity Hino's work has received little attention from filmmakers and producers, with the Hideshi Hino Horror Theater being the first serious attempt and bringing his stories to the screen. The six films, each just under an hour in length, were shot by first-time directors, usually with a background in music videos or television. The main exception was *The Ravaged House* (*Tadareta Ie*), helmed by Kazuyoshi Kumakiri, director of the spectacularly brutal cult favourite *Kichiku* (*Kichiku Dai Enkai*, 1997). Unsurprisingly, *The Ravaged House*- based on Hino's first published story- is also one of the best instalments in the series, and one of the few completely serious efforts. Satoshi Morishita stars as Zoroku, a young man who contracts a virulent and disgusting disease that is slowly causing him to mutate beyond all recognition. When the locals learn of his disease, Zoroku and his family are ostracized, and eventually his own parents begin to avoid him, leaving him to the care of his sister. But the paranoid, xenophobic villagers are still not happy, and they decide to do something about the matter. *The Ravaged House* is a grim, downbeat film, but it's also a rewarding one that steers clear of genre clichés and aims a little higher that many of its contemporaries.

In contrast, Mari Asato's *The Boy From Hell* (*Jigoku Kozô*) is a garish and gory affair full of warped humour and camp grotesquery. In a variation of the oft-filmed 'Monkey's Paw' tale, Mirai Yamamoto stars as a doctor whose beloved son is killed in an accident. Unable to bear his loss, she carries out the gruesome rites necessary to resurrect her son- which include sacrificing another child- but is horrified to discover that the thing crawling out of his grave has little in common with the boy she loved. Looking much like the *It's Alive* (1974) baby in school uniform, the creature goes on a rampage to satisfy it's craving for human flesh. Like any good mother, she can't bear to see her son go hungry and begins helping him to find victims. Asato gets plenty of mileage from the relationship between loopy mother and undead cannibalistic son, even if her attempts to generate sympathy for the beast do fall a little short of the mark. However, *The Boy From Hell* does come very close to capturing the tone and style of Hino's manga, with his preference for gross humour and twisted portrayals of family life, which feature in three of the six stories in this series. There are moments when the nastiness goes a little too far- the murder of the child is shown in silhouette with very unpleasant sound effects- but on occasions the film can also be very witty: a Renaissance painting of the Madonna and child flips over to reveal Goya's bloody depiction of Cronos devouring his children.

The rest of the films in the Hideshi Hino Horror Theater range from mediocre to awful. Yoshihiro Nakamura's *Lizard Baby* (*Watashi no Akachan*) takes an interesting premise- a scriptwriter pens a story about a half-human, half-lizard baby and then discovers that his pregnant wife is carrying such a creature in her womb- and drains the life from it with clichéd plot developments and a monster that looks like a sock puppet. In *Death Train* (*Kyôfu Ressha*) three teenage girls find themselves pursued by a growing army of zombies. Director Kayazuki Sakamoto handles the zombie attacks well and creates a couple of good scares, but wastes them on yet another reworking of *Carnival of Souls* (1962). Even so, it's better than Kiyoshi Yamamoto's *Occult Detective Club: The Doll Cemetery* (*Ocult Tanteidan: Shininyô no Hakaba*), a tedious mishmash of urban legends, the *Eko Eko Azarak* series and shabby CGI that leaves Hitomi Miwa with little to do except look embarrassed.

In 2006 Shochiku released another series devoted to one of Japan's manga masters, the Kazuo Umezu Horror Theater. Made with larger budgets than the Hideshi Hino series, the films were written by some of Japan's most prolific and popular scriptwriters, including Hiroshi Takahashi (*Ring*), Chiaki Konaka (*Hellsing; Evil Dead Trap 2: Hideki*) and Sadayuki

Murai (*Perfect Blue*), while Atsushi Shimizu (*Eko Eko Azarak: Me*) and genre mainstay Kiyoshi Kurosawa direct an episode each. It's not surprising then that the films are generally of higher quality than the earlier series, although they are just as inconsistent. Scripted by Sadayuki Murai, Kurosawa's *House of Bugs* (*Mushitachi no Ie*) is a bizarre tale about a husband who suspects his wife might be unfaithful, insane or mutating into a giant insect

# 死亡筆記

## 最後的名字

DEATH NOTE
the Last name

夜神月・L・彌海砂・流克・雷姆…

DEATH NOTE

NTV
NIPPON TELEVISION NETWORK

dts 5.1

(and possibly all three). Like *Perfect Blue* (1998) and *Millennium Actress* (2001) plays off fantasy against reality, shifting from one character's perspective to another and leaving the viewing entirely wrong-footed. Although the resolution isn't entirely satisfactory, *House of Bugs* is new territory for Kurosawa, and is arguably more interesting than his previous genre project, the confused and confusing *Loft* (2005).

Noboru Iguchi's *Snake Girl* (*Madara no Shôjo*) covers one of Umezu's oldest and most popular themes- transformation and mutation- but his story of a city girl who goes to the countryside only to find herself menaced by an enormous half-human, half-snake witch does not translate well to the present day, now seeming to be derivative of a number of other films. Atsushi Shimizu manages to create some moments of genuine creepiness in *The Wish* (*Negai*) as a lonely young boy (Orito Kasahara) is menaced by a wooden doll he made to keep him company. When the boy finally manages to make a real friend, the murderous doll refuses to be pushed aside. With a mouthful of nails and large staring eyeballs, the doll is an eerie sight, but a believable performance from Kasahara isn't quite enough to stop the film tipping over into silliness. Tadafumi Itô's *Diet* is the pleasingly twisted story of a depressive girl with an eating disorder who decides she will ensure that her ex-lover never strays again by eating him. An unnecessary final twist doesn't do the film any favours, but *Diet* is still one of the more original instalments in the series, which hits its nadir with the awful *Death Make*, directed by Taichi. Hitomi Miwa and Tomorowo Taguchi star as two contestants on a reality TV show in which a group of allegedly psychic individuals are challenged to spend 24 hours in a haunted office building. The film starts out reasonably well, as the bunch of oddballs are picked off one at a time by a giant mantis-like creature, but goes downhill rapidly from there. The story, along with any attempt at coherency, is quickly abandoned in favour of bizarre fantasy sequences that rely heavily on poor CGI and have little to do with anything that has gone before. A perfect companion piece to *Occult Detective Club: The Doll Cemetery*, *Death Make* eventually grinds to a halt after a number of pointless reality shifts, having long outstayed its welcome despite lasting for less than an hour.

At the opposite end of the spectrum is the series' high point, Yûdai Yamaguchi's blood-drenched and frequently hilarious *Present*, a curious film about a group of friends attacked by a psychopathic Santa Claus and his team of flesh-eating reindeer (yes, flesh-eating reindeer). Mai Takahashi (*Booth*; *Forbidden Siren*) and Takakumi Suga star as two would-be lovers who head off to a hotel on Christmas Eve, hoping to become better acquainted. Their amorous adventures are interrupted by the arrival of an enormous gaijin Santa Claus, who produces an assortment of sharp objects and begins hacking the friends to pieces. His living victims he takes down to a basement and dismembered, hanging their limbs on meathooks and feeding their brains to his wild-eyed carnivorous reindeer. As well as buckets of blood and gore, Present also has a sharp sense of humour. Like Nick Hamm's *The Hole* (2001), Yamaguchi presents different sides of Takahashi's character, first the good-hearted and naïve innocent she claims to be, then the cold-hearted schemer she is in reality. The film also turns out to have been a little girl's nightmare, caused (according to her parents) by watching too many horror movies. However, rather than being the victim, the little girl was dreaming about being Santa Claus, and is actually quite happy that she finally got to punish Takahashi's manipulative bitch.

After the success of the *Ring* and *Juon* franchises, Takashige Ichise continued to build on his reputation as the leading producer of Japanese horror films. His next project was suitably extravagant and high-profile: a collection of six horror films, each helmed by an established horror director, marketed as the J-Horror Theatre, with Japanese and international releases lined up. The line-up was to include Hideo Nakata, Takashi Shimizu and Kiyoshi Kurosawa, as well as Norio Tsuruta (*Ring 0*) and Masayuki Ochiai (*Parasite Eve*; *Hypnosis*), with *Ring* scriptwriter Hiroshi Takahashi making his directorial debut. Despite an auspicious start with a fair degree of international publicity, the first instalment of the series- Masayuki Ochiai's *Infection* (*Kansen*, 2004)- proved to be something of a disappointment. An unusual setting- a ramshackle hospital during the outbreak of a contagious and disgustingly virulent disease- and a dose of black humour are the film's

**Forbidden Siren**

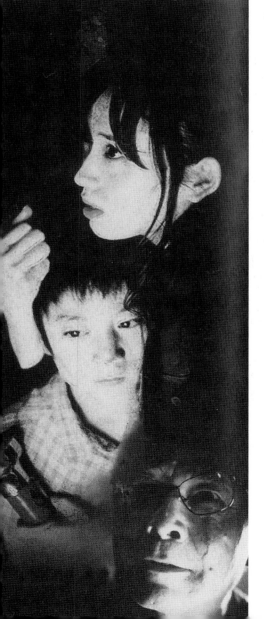

strong points, but the early promise is lost when the script runs out of ideas midway through. After a series of medically grotesque scenes- a nurse repeatedly practices injections on her own arm; a nervous doctor sits with a parcel of human skin, stitching it up over and over again; numerous messily decomposing corpses- *Infection* turns to a disappointing clichéd ending that throws the entire film into doubt. Thanks primarily to a host of nasty, incompetent and downright weird characters, Infection is occasionally compelling and rarely boring, but it's not enough to shake the feeling that Ochiai and co-scriptwriter Ryôichi Kimikuza had no idea how to bring the film to a satisfactory conclusion. Two years later Ochiai became the next Japanese director to head across the Pacific, to make his US debut in 2009 with a remake of the Thai horror film *Shutter*, starring an international cast that includes Megumi Okina from *Juon: The Grudge*.

More successful but also flawed is the second entry in the J-Horror Theatre series, Norio Tsuruta's *Premonition* (*Yogen*, 2004). For a series designed to showcase the cutting edge of Japanese horror, *Premonition* looks firmly to the past for inspiration by reworking a popular manga from the '70s, Jirô Tsunoda's *Kyôfu Shinbun* ('terror newspaper'). Filmed once before in 1989 by Teruyoshii Ishii, *Kyôfu Shinbun* now seems reminiscent of the US TV series *Early Edition*, since the basic concept is the same. Hiroshi Makami stars as a college professor who begins receiving advance warning of disasters, accidents and murders through the newspaper articles that appear in front of him. Rather than simply using the knowledge to prevent the incidents from occurring, Makami is given an unpleasant choice: ignore the warnings and risk insanity as they flood into his brain in ever greater numbers, or try to alter history and see more of the body fade away each time he does so. The plot isn't without interest, but Tsuruta and co-scriptwriter Noboru Takagi paint themselves into a corner- since both of Makami's options involve him dying unpleasantly, a third (and rather clichéd) possibility has to be conjured up. Like Masayuki Ochiai, Tsuruta made his US debut soon afterwards with 'Dream Cruise', an instalment of the Masters of Horror series based upon a Kôji Suzuki short story.

If *Infection* and *Premonition* are flawed but interesting attempts to break away from the standard Vengeful Spirit themes, then Takashi Shimizu's *Reincarnation* is the opposite: well-made but less original. Even so, it failed to provide Ichise's series with its first box office success, throwing the future of the J-Horror Theatre into doubt. Hideo Nakata's comeback picture, the period ghost story *Kaidan* (2007), performed badly too, and it is currently uncertain whether his proposed instalment of the series will ever materialize. With the leading lights of Japanese horror unable to produce films that matched their earlier efforts in either quality or success, many commentators began to question whether the post-*Ring* boom had finally ground to a halt.

Takashi Shimizu and Hideo Nakata were not the only established horror directors experiencing difficulties. *Loft*, Kiyoshi Kurosawa's first horror feature since *Pulse* (2001), was greeted with a mixture of polite silence and confusion when shown at foreign film festivals and after a brief theatrical run slipped onto DVD with little fanfare. Miki Nakatani stars as a writer who takes a house in the country to work on her new novel,

**Death Note**

but finds herself besieged by her unhinged editor, the ghost of a dead girl who haunts the building and the spirit of a centuries-old mummy that her anthropologist neighbour (Etsushi Toyokawa) has dug up. The ghostly manifestations vary from the usual- phantoms lurking in corners with their heads bowed- to the decidedly odd. Nakatani is coughing up large amounts of what appears to be greyish clay, the same substance the mummy swallowed five hundred years ago in the mistaken belief that it would preserve her beauty. That would be bizarre enough on its own, but she started doing if before she moved into the house and came into contact with the ancient corpse. Other elements are equally warped, making it very difficult to get a handle on precisely what is going on and why. *Loft* contains a number of effective scenes that work well as standalone vignettes but often become confusing when approached as part of the narrative. With enough individual plots for three movies, *Loft* is a curious mixture of horror movie and romance, suggesting the director is simultaneously attempting to live up to the hyperbolic title of 'Master of Horror' and leave it behind, but failing to do either particularly well.

Despite these setbacks, Japanese horror produced a number of commercial and creative successes during this period. *Crossfire* (2000) director Shûsuke Kaneko scored two big hits in 2006 with *Death Note* and *Death Note: The Last Name*, adaptations of the best-selling manga from Tsugumi Ôba and Takeshi Obata. Released three months apart, the films are two parts of the same story, rather than traditional movie and sequel. *Battle Royale* (2000) heartthrob Tatsuya Fujiwara stars as 17-year-old Light Yagami, a conscientious and clever student who hopes to become a lawyer in the future. As well as a pretty face and a genius level IQ Light also has a secret: he has recently come into possession of the 'Death Note', a notebook that the various shinigami ('gods of death') use to orchestrate the death of mortal beings. By writing a name in the Death Note, along with any details concerning the circumstances, the user can cause the death of anyone he or she chooses- all they need is the name of the victim and a mental picture of their face. Initially Light uses the book to 'execute' criminals who the state cannot or will not punish: those who avoid capture or escape punishment through plea-bargaining and exploiting loopholes in the law. By publicizing his acts on the Internet under the pseudonym 'Kira' ('killer'), Light has become something of a celebrity, hailed as a guardian of justice by some and a mass murderer by others. Before long his righteous morality has taken a back seat to his growing megalomania, and the killings are carried out simply to demonstrate his power. Aware that some kind of crime is being committed, the police task force- which is coincidentally lead by Light's own father- engage the services of a mysterious private detective known only as 'L', who speaks only through an intermediary and the internet, never revealing his face. Despite their suspicions about this unseen character, the task force agree to follow his orders when he manages to determine 'Kira's whereabouts in a very short space of time. The police now know that the killer lives in Tokyo and needs to see the faces of his victims, and Light realises he has found an opponent of equal intellect. By this point Light has lost any pretence at justice, and is prepared to kill anyone, including police officers, to ensure his freedom.

Like *Crossfire*, the *Death Note* films explore the dangers of exercising unchecked power, regardless of how altruistic the motives might be. In the earlier film Junko's distress at the failure of the legal system leads her to take the law into her own hands and punish the guilty using her pyrokinetic abilities. The same train of thought leads Light Yagami to use the Death Note, but whereas Junko eventually realises that her powers are open to abuse when wielded indiscriminately, Light quickly forgets any questions of morality and justice. Instead he is content to throw out hollow speeches about how the world is now a better place while casually disposing of anyone who stands in his way, criminal or not. Just as Junko's powers are being manipulated in *Crossfire*, in *Death Note* there is a definite suggestion that Light is also being manipulated by the bored and playful shinigami- named Ryuk- who dropped the book in front of him. Visible only to him, Ryuk is Light's constant companion and a bemused spectator to his battles with L and the police. The creature never intervenes in the events taking place, except when making his protégé an offer. For example, if Light sacrifices half of his remaining lifespan (however long that might be), he can receive the ability to look at a person and immediately know their name, something that would make his power over life and death almost absolute. Light refuses the offer, but the scene establishes Ryuk's character as a tempter, something that is underlined by his favourite food: shiny red apples, a well-known symbol of temptation from the Old Testament to Snow White.

Another Spine-Chilling Horror Masterpiece After <RESIDENT EVIL> and <SILENT HILL>
It All Began With A Mysterious Warning ...
When The Siren Sounds, Don't Go Out

サイレン
死魂曲
FORBIDDEN SIREN

Based on Sony's PS2 Cult-Classic Horror Game, <SIREN 2>

Japanese 日语
Chinese & English
Subtitles
中英文字幕

Directed by **Yukihiko Tsutsumi**
Starring **Yui Ichikawa  Reo Morimoto  Naoki Tanaka  Hiroshi Abe**

*Japanese sleeve art for* **Forbidden Siren**

Most of the film's tension is derived from the battle of wits between Light and the eccentric L, who is revealed to be another teenage genius much like his opponent- they could in fact be two sides of the same coin. Light is brilliant and handsome, a diligent student who always works hard, but the angelic face conceals the abyss within. L is equally brilliant, but with bad posture, a Robert Smith hairdo, eyes like a panda and an insatiable sugar craving. Beneath the sloppy exterior beats a good heart and a desire to see justice done, but most would quickly dismiss him as another lazy otaku underachiever. In contrast, Light possesses all the qualities most parents would love to have in a son,

### Nightmare Detective

but despite having the ideal Japanese background- stable family life, hardworking father, loving mother, comfortable financial situation- he's still a psychopath. L actually discovers Kira's identity quite quickly, and spends the rest of the film trying to assemble enough evidence to convince his co-workers, including Light's own father. The two characters become involved in a complex tale of plot and counter-plot that takes in some fascinating twists along the way, including the appearance of a second Death Note. This time a second book is given to Misa, a perky pop idol whose giggly public persona conceals a deeply unhinged mind. Ever since Kira bumped off the man who killed her family, she's been killing just for fun, doing anything in the hope of attracting the attention of her beloved Kira. The denouement features some exceptionally complicated manoeuvring, and Kaneko manages to bring the story to an appropriately impressive climax, throwing in a few more surprises about the extent of L's elaborate planning. Smart, suspenseful and consistently entertaining, the *Death Note* films rank among the best Japanese teen-horror movies of recent years. With the manga, anime and live-action efforts all extremely popular, a spin-off movie focussing on the earlier adventures of L has been announced, with Hideo Nakata directing.

Few movies based on computer games can be considered artistic or financial successes, and the general standard is represented by Uwe Boll's multiple and uniformly atrocious efforts; films so bad, in fact, that Paul W.S. Anderson's *Resident Evil* (2002) looks almost respectable in comparison. Christophe Gans' excellent *Silent Hill* (2006) bucked the trend by becoming not only the best computer game adaptation ever made but also one of the best horror films of 2006. *Silent Hill* was slightly preceded by Yukihiko Tsutsumi's *Forbidden Siren*, released by Toho in February 2006 to coincide with the release of the sequel to Konami's best-selling computer game. With an English-language adaptation also in production at Sam Raimi and Robert Tapert's Ghost House Pictures- producers of *The Grudge* (2004)- it's unlikely that the Japanese *Forbidden Siren* will see a western release before the English-language one arrives (if at all), but it will be interesting to compare Toho's modestly budgeted domestic effort with its bigger and bolder cousin.

The prologue introduces us to Yamijima Island in 1976. As rescue crews scour the island during a violent storm they are shocked to find half-smoked cigarettes in ashtrays and warm food on cookers, but not a soul around. The island is entirely deserted, except for one terrified, raving individual who repeats the same warning over and over again: "When you hear the siren, don't go out!" Thirty years later Yamijima has apparently recovered, and reporter Shinichi Amamoto (Reo Morimoto) takes up residence on the island with his teenage daughter Yuki (Yui Ichikawa from *Juon: The Grudge 2*) and asthmatic young son Hideo. The islanders are an odd bunch, apparently drawn from a number of different

Asian countries, and their shacks, built of wood and corrugated iron, are covered in signs and graffiti in a variety of different languages, including Japanese, English, Greek, Arabic and Latin. Although a lot of it appears to be gibberish, the words 'dog' and 'live' crop up frequently and are repeated in the nonsensical nursery rhyme about mirrors that they're often chanting. And then there's the siren, a relic of a post-war US radar station that has since become the focus of local legend. As one of the neighbours tells Yuki: "When you

# Flowers From Hell

hear the siren, don't go out." Soon afterwards the siren does indeed sound, during another violent storm. When her father disappears while photographing nocturnal animals, quickly followed by the family dog, Yuki realizes there is something drastically wrong with Yamijima- but can she get herself and Hideo off the island before the siren sounds a second time?

Like Norio Tsuruta's *Kakashi* (2001), *Forbidden Siren* can be loosely described as a Japanese version of *The Wicker Man* (1973), representing a vision of rural Japan as a place where suburban civilization has yet to make much of an impact- where cell phones don't work, the natives stare openly at the new people and the old men still gather to swap the same tales of mermaids and curses their forefathers did. Initially the set-up seems merely odd rather than threatening. As the family set about cleaning up their dusty traditional Japanese home, a neighbour comes and offers her assistance; she's definitely weird, but not so weird that alarm bells start to ring. As more and more information about the island and its past comes to light the tone shifts to one of menace and unease. Tsutsumi's handling of these scenes is capable and assured, and his pacing excellent. The film does not grind to a halt while the plot is explained, and unlike many other horror movie heroines, Yuki does not walk around with blinkers on, blithely unaware of the threat we know is present. There are a few concessions to *Forbidden Siren*'s origins- most notably several brief attempts at conveying the game's 'sightjacking', but these are mercifully less

*Japanese sleeve art for* **Death Note**

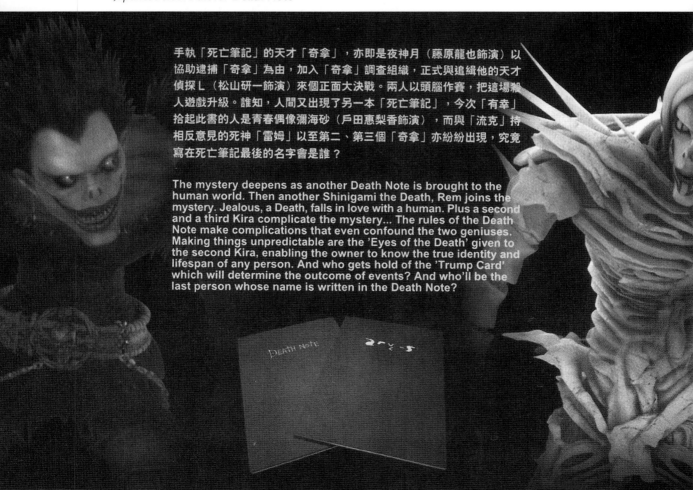

手執「死亡筆記」的天才「奇拿」，亦即是夜神月（藤原龍也飾演）以協助逮捕「奇拿」為由，加入「奇拿」調查組織，正式與追緝他的天才偵探L（松山研一飾演）來個正面大決戰。兩人以頭腦作賽，把這場殺人遊戲升級。誰知，人間又出現了另一本「死亡筆記」，今次「有幸」拾起此書的人是青春偶像彌海砂（戶田惠梨香飾演），而與「流克」持相反意見的死神「雷姆」以至第二、第三個「奇拿」亦紛紛出現，究竟寫在死亡筆記最後的名字會是誰？

The mystery deepens as another Death Note is brought to the human world. Then another Shinigami the Death, Rem joins the mystery. Jealous, a Death, falls in love with a human. Plus a second and a third Kira complicate the mystery... The rules of the Death Note make complications that even confound the two geniuses. Making things unpredictable are the 'Eyes of the Death' given to the second Kira, enabling the owner to know the true identity and lifespan of any person. And who gets hold of the 'Trump Card' which will determine the outcome of events? And who'll be the last person whose name is written in the Death Note?

intrusive than similar moments in *House of the Dead* (2003). The puzzle-solving elements common to many survival horror games are carried over, although the fact that several of these are presented in English means that English-speakers will probably figure them out relatively quickly.

Unfortunately *Forbidden Siren* stumbles heavily at the last hurdle. Having provided a number of tantalizing clues that hint at an interesting and rather unpleasant secret (involving mermaids in Japanese folklore), the film suddenly drops them all and heads of in a new- and wholly unoriginal- direction that completely rewrites everything we have already seen, from the events back in 1976, to the present day incidents, and even the actual characters (the dog's name is a clue). Simply put, the new explanation resolves nothing and leaves behind a mass of loose ends. Like Tsutsumi's earlier genre efforts- *Shinsei Toire no Hanako-san* (1998) and the hilariously violent *2LDK* (2003)- *Forbidden Siren* is a decent, well-made horror movie, and one that deserves a much better ending than the one it's saddled with. Even so, it performed well at the box office, no doubt benefiting from the extensive publicity campaign promoting both the film and the computer game, as well as a degree of controversy when the game's teaser trailer was withdrawn after a number of complaints.

The best Japanese horror film of recent years comes from an unlikely source. Having made some of the most distinctive and unusual films of the past twenty years, *Tetsuo* director Shinya Tsukamoto would seem to be the last person to release a mainstream horror film. And *Nightmare Detective* (2007) is certainly a mainstream effort, with a pop idol as the female lead, a poster-boy heartthrob as the male lead and a high-concept plot that at first glance seems to be equal parts *A Nightmare on Elm Street* (1984) and *Paprika* (2006). Even more surprising is the fact that *Nightmare Detective* is also very much a Shinya Tsukamoto film- co-produced, co-shot, co-edited, written and directed by the man himself, who also found time to take the role of the psychopathic Zero.

Pop idol Hitomi, making her debut appearance, stars as Keiko Kirishima, an attractive, career-minded policewoman who has made a name for herself dealing with high-profile fraud and corruption cases. Having transferred to the homicide squad, Keiko finds herself up against a number of obstacles- the fact that she has had little experience of corpses, for example. Not the least of her difficulties is her obnoxious superior (Ren Ôsugi), who thinks Keiko is a pampered princess more likely to cry over a broken high heel than to contribute to any serious police work. While investigating a pair of possible suicides Keiko and her young partner (*Battle Royale*'s Masanobu Andô) discover that both victims dialed the same phone number shortly before stabbing themselves to death, with the second one apparently asleep at the time. Following up the possibility that they died during a nightmare, Keiko comes across a reference to Kagenuma, a man known as the 'Nightmare Detective' (Ryûhei Matsuda, in one of his best performances), who claims to have the power to enter a sleeping individual's dreams and uncover the meaning behind them. Suspecting that the killer- known only to the police as 'Zero'- is using the same ability to murder his victims, she persuades the reluctant Kagenuma to help them stop him.

With the exception of the unjustly maligned *Hiruko the Goblin* (*Hiruko: Yôkai*

# Flowers From Hell

*Hantâ*, 1991), *Nightmare Detective* is Tsukamoto's most accessible film. No doubt this is partially due to the material, which in loose terms is little different to any number of the nightmare-themed horror films that followed Freddy Krueger's first appearance in 1984. Although the combination of high-concept horror film and police procedural serves as a useful 'entry point' for mainstream audiences, Tsukamoto has not abandoned or diluted either his intellectual interests or his technical and stylistic preferences. Most of the film takes place against a blue-tinged urban backdrop, like the sharply angular police headquarters and Keiko's cold, modernistic apartment. Since the characters' psychological state reflects their immediate environment, the dream settings are also predominantly urban, from an underground parking area to a deserted labyrinth of concrete roads. In many cases the victims are trapped by these environments, unable to escape from the subterranean chambers and endless mazes. The result is a surprisingly claustrophobic atmosphere that emphasises the alienation and sterility of urban existence, ably supported by another collage of industrial poundings and metallic riffs from Chû Ishikawa, Tsukamoto's regular composer.

Although he has frequently made use of genre conventions and themes, Tsukamoto hasn't directed a true horror film since *Hiruko the Goblin*, but *Nightmare Detective* demonstrates that he can also craft highly effective horror sequences. As in *A Nightmare on Elm Street*, the standout scenes are the victims' nightmares, but rather than trying to capture the pointed surrealism of a dream Tsukamoto places his nightmares in recognizable, prosaic settings that are not immediately distinguishable from reality. In each case the victims find themselves alone and pursued by some unseen force; as they are hacked to death by the creature, they're able to catch occasional glimpses of the bloody, mutated thing that is attacking them. At the same time the sleeping victims' wounds appear on their body. Tsukamoto films these scenes using his trademark handheld cameras with rapid zooms and tracking shots that reflect the victims' panic and the whirling ferocity of Zero's assaults. These murders- among the most violent moments in any of the director's films- possess an impact and immediacy that is missing from all but the first of the generally lacklustre *Elm Street* movies. With fine performances from the two charismatic leads- Hitomi acquits herself surprisingly well- and the solid supporting cast (which includes Yoshio Harada), a compelling story and Tsukamoto's kinetic pacing and camerawork, *Nightmare Detective* is one of the best Japanese horror films of the past decade, and convincing evidence that there is still plenty of life left in the genre.

# AFTERWORD
## The Future of Japanese Horror

Over the past few years it has become increasingly common to find journalists and commentators proclaiming the death of Japanese horror. The commercial and creative potential of the Japanese horror has been lost, we are told, amid a rising tide of financially unsuccessful and artistically redundant cash-ins, sequels and soulless remakes that ape the conventions of *Ring* (1998) but cannot reproduce its originality. The evidence can be seen in the box office apathy that has greeted films such as Takashi Shimizu's *Reincarnation* (2005). Despite boasting a comparatively high budget and a sizeable publicity campaign, Reincarnation failed to cause much of a stir, leading many to suggest that Shimizu would never repeat the success of the lucrative *Juon* franchise, which had itself dissolved into a series of increasingly moribund sequels and remakes. There is of course a certain amount of truth in this; *Reincarnation* and *The Grudge 2* (2006) were neither as interesting nor as successful as, for example, *Juon: The Grudge* (2002). Like Shimizu, *Ring* director Hideo Nakata has struggled to find audiences for both his horror films- such as 2007's *Kaidan*- and his non-genre efforts (*Last Scene*, 2003). However, any pronouncements about the demise of Japanese horror, both creatively and commercially, are at the very least premature. *Reincarnation* and *Kaidan* may have flopped, but *One Missed Call* (2004) and *Death Note* (2006) both did exceptionally well at the box office, while less high-profile films like Yukihiko Tsutsumi's *Forbidden Siren* (2006) and Shinya Tsukamoto's *Nightmare Detective* (2007) also fared respectably, indicating that the Japanese public has not yet tired of domestic horror films.

There are also plenty of indications that Japanese horror has been artistically and creatively vital over the past few years. Despite the apparent monopoly that white-clad ghosts with long black hair hold on the market, there has been an increasing tendency to move away from the template established by *Ring*, *Dark Water* (2002) and the *Juon* films. The *Death Note* series, *Nightmare Detective*, *Forbidden Siren*, Kiyoshi Kurosawa's *Retribution* (2007) and Kôji Shiraishi's *The Curse* (2006) are all consistently interesting, more-or-less successful departures from the Vengeful Spirit theme that steer clear of many of the genre's clichés and attempt to carve out new territory. In recent years there has been a revival of the ero-gro genre, a characteristically Japanese blend of the erotic and the horrific with roots reaching back more than a century. Although they're unlikely to secure the same kind of commercial success as more mainstream offerings, films like Sion Sono's *Strange Circus* (2005) and the Edogawa Rampo-inspired anthology *Rampo Noir* (*Rampo Jigoku*, 2005) provide another avenue for contemporary genre filmmakers to explore. Even interesting failures like Takashi Shimizu's *Marebito* (2004) suggest that neither the director nor the genre itself is only capable of churning out mass-produced commercial efforts.

The widespread misconception that Japanese horror is on its last legs is due, in part, to the films that get released in the west. Thanks to distributors eager to cash in on the interest in Asian horror, zero-budget, direct-to-video films that are barely known in their home country are being granted international releases, frequently marketed as the 'next Japanese horror phenomenon!' Naturally, any critic who has been unfortunate enough to sit through *Ju-rei: The Uncanny* (2004), *Cursed* (2005) and *The Locker* films is unlikely to be left with a terribly optimistic view of the current state of the genre. Equally important are the films that haven't yet been released in the west. At the time of writing, the rights have been purchased but no English-language release scheduled for *Death Note* or *Death Note: The Last Name* (2006). Likewise for *Nightmare Detective*, the rights have been purchased, but no details about a release have been forthcoming. *Forbidden Siren* is an adaptation of a popular computer game available in Europe and the USA; Sam Raimi's Ghost House Pictures is preparing an American version, but no release is planned for the Japanese one, despite the runaway success of 2006's other horror game adaptation, *Silent Hill*. As part of Takashige Ichise's J-Horror Theatre series, *Retribution* should have already secured an international distribution deal (Ichise planned to use the money earned from these deals to fund the films themselves), but as yet, there is no word. Unsurprisingly, money plays an important part: low-budget V-cinema works from minor production companies are a lot cheaper to purchase than the latest smash hit from an established director on his way to Hollywood. Others might have been already picked up by western distributors, but are still sitting on a shelf somewhere, ready for a DVD release as part of the remake's publicity drive; the US release of *Ring* is a good example. Some companies purchase a large number of foreign films each year, but only release a few, leaving the rest in limbo, sometimes for years.

Japanese horror is certainly changing. After several years of dominating the field, the *Ring*-influenced ghost story is in a steep decline, with serious consequences for directors whose careers are heavily linked with that particular genre. However, important films are still emerging and new trends are being set in motion. Significantly, many of the directors who have managed to find success with horror films over the past few years- most notably Takashi Miike, Shûsuke Kaneko, Yukihiko Tsutsumi and Shinya Tsukamoto- are equally well-known for their non-horror efforts: Miike with his many violent yakuza/juvenile delinquent films; Kaneko with his earlier comedies and the *Gamera* series; Tsutsumi with the TV spin-off *Keizoku- Unsolved Cases* (*Keizoku/Eiga*, 2000); Tsukamoto with his entirely unique filmography. Contrast this with the career of Hideo Nakata, whose efforts to move away from the genre have been fraught with difficulty. It seems likely that the future of mainstream Japanese horror will rest- at least in part- with these individuals.

Miike and Kaneko have already made their American debuts- with *Imprint* (2006) and *Necronomicon* (1993) respectively- and the favourable reception given to *Nightmare Detective* will almost certainly prompt US movie moguls to approach Shinya Tsukamoto with similar offers. Whether he will accept is another thing entirely, of course, but the accessibility and popularity of *Nightmare Detective* can have done little harm to his career.

With several new talents to watch, and sizeable audiences around the world, Japanese horror is looking fairly healthy. The next few years will be crucial in determining whether this latest wave of films is the final twitch of a dying genre, or the beginning of a sustained period of remission. The last low point for the genre was the late 1970s and early '80s, when production sank to an all-time low. At the moment the horror scene is considerably more active, both in terms of quality and quantity, than it was then, so there seems plenty of reasons for optimism. In five or ten years time we will be able to look back on the late 2000s and assess its proper position in the development of modern Japanese horror cinema, but until then we only have the films. If they are of similar quality to *Death Note* and *Nightmare Detective*, then I for one will be more than satisfied.

# Index of Japanese and Alternate Titles

# Index of Japanese and Alternate Titles

# INDEX

# Index

# Flowers From Hell

# Index